REPORT ON THE GERMANS

REPORT ON THE GERMANS

W. L. WHITE

NEW YORK

HARCOURT, BRACE AND COMPANY

MGE

COPYRIGHT, 1947, BY

W. L. WHITE

first edition

TABLE OF CONTENTS

Part I

THESE ARE THE GERMANS

Part II

WILSON'S PEACE AND OURS

Part 1

THESE ARE THE GERMANS

CHAPTER I

HITLER'S REICH

"WE ARE all guilty," said Schultz as we bumped along the bomb-ruined streets of Berlin in my jeep. "Some did terrible things. Others did nothing, but knew what was being done and approved. Still others of us perhaps knew little, but at least approved of some of it.

"Yet now all of us, regardless of how much we ourselves did or of how little we knew of what others did, today do not want to remember it. We would like to forget what we did or knew, and cannot believe that we ever approved. The amazing thing is that so many have forgotten so much, and so now can deny that they ever knew or approved.

"Take my cousin, Trude. She is now twenty-four and was once prominent in the *Bund Deutscher Mädel*, the Hitler organization for girls between the ages of twelve and eighteen, which is about the age of your Girl Scouts. Even after eighteen, Trude was still very fervent, and so became a BDM *Führer*, or scout mistress. She was very patriotic in the war. Once when her brother wrote her, asking her to have made for him some prints from a photograph negative she had, she answered saying that she had no time for trivial things, because all of her time and life were dedicated to the service of the Führer.

"Once during the war, wearing her BDM *Führer* uniform, she came to Sunday dinner at our house in Zehlendorf. But when we started to say the old Lutheran grace, asking Christ to join us in the meal and bless our food, Trude rose and said proudly:

" 'I cannot sit at a table where a Jew is asked for dinner.'

"Now that the fever and propaganda of war is past, Trude has again become a quiet, simple girl like any other. The hysterical mysticism has vanished. She cannot believe that she was ever other than she now is.

"Only last week I reminded her of what she had said that Sunday. She stared at me in wonder, insisting that she never could have said such a thing, or believed it. When I tried to make her remember the particular Sunday on which it happened, she flew into a furor, and said:

" 'You must be a spy for the Russians, or you would not invent such a terrible lie against your own cousin!'

"We are all like Trude, we Germans. We try so hard to forget what we once believed that now we honestly do not know what we believed. So now, when I try to tell you, year by year, what happened to me during the war, and what I and others were thinking and feeling, you must remember that I, like all Germans, can hardly believe I ever felt as I did. So it will not be easy."

Only before he gets into his story you should know something about my friend Albrecht Schultz, former Hitler Jugend, former German exchange student at one of our West Coast universities, still more recently an employee of Herr Doktor Goebbels' Propaganda Ministry, where he was working when I first met him in 1939 on my second visit to Germany, my first having been made at the time when the American Army was occupying a Rhine bridgehead just after the First World War.

I had found little that was attractive in the Germans in 1919, and found them even less so twenty years later. It may have been because it was winter and I was in Berlin, which at best is a forbidding northern city. The war had just started, and even technically neutral Anglo-Saxon visitors were regarded with well-justified suspicion.

But more to the point was the fact that anyone, on entering the country, could instantly feel the iron grip of totalitarianism on the city and the nation. It was not just the pink-cheeked SS boys who scowled out from under their helmets as they stood guard in the rain around Hitler's Chancellery. It was the all-pervading fear and suspicion under which we lived. There were, we knew, "good" Germans—democratic ones who mourned the old freedoms and hated Hitler. But which were these, and which the Gestapo spies who might talk this way in order to draw us out?

My German teacher, for instance—he came recommended highly by a previous correspondent. He was most bitter against the régime and when he talked his voice would drop to a frightened, angry whisper. He would stop, with upraised hand, at the slightest noise in the corridor outside the closed door of my hotel room.

He listened every night to the BBC. Desperately he hoped that his country would lose the war and so be rid of Hitler and his gang. Or so he said. But who could be sure? Maybe he was working for them, had fooled the correspondent who preceded me, and now hoped to draw me out. Even if he was honest it was highly indiscreet to talk such open treason with me in wartime on so brief an acquaintance. They might catch him and, in his fright, he might blab on me. So I said little and if he were not a police spy, he must have thought me a singularly dull and unresponsive American with small interest in politics.

There were a good many who talked as he did. Most of them must have meant it, but which ones? That you never knew. Even among the American correspondents there you were never quite sure, for it was sharply divided between the staunch anti-Nazis, led by Bill Shirer, and those who were something less than staunch and who basked smugly in the quiet favors of the régime. Even before I arrived I had greatly admired Bill's broadcasts, and after I came he took me under his wing and taught me much about the totalitarian techniques as they operated on our press.

A newly-arrived reporter in any foreign capital is expected to make certain official calls and is then granted cards admitting him to government press conferences. I dutifully followed the procedure which, in Berlin, was similar to that of Paris and London.

The man in charge of the American section of the Foreign Office was Doktor Zalut. He was slight, blond and in his late thirties, neatly dressed in gray flannels, handsome, gentle in manner, with dreamy blue eyes, and with the round button of the Nazi party in his lapel. With gentle, hesitant, yet deft, questions he asked about me, and when I told him I came from Kansas it turned out that Dr. Zalut knew it well—Hillsboro, Marion, Macpherson, he named over a dozen tiny towns and the hotels where he had stopped.

How did he know all this about my state? Well, in the 'twenties he had been circulation manager for a German-language paper in the Middle West. Before that, he had been an officer in the First World War, and at its close had enlisted in the *Frei Korps*—the strongly nationalist group which fought the Spartacists and Socialists in the streets, and which regarded the Weimar Republic as a pollution of Germany. But after the Republic had suppressed the *Frei Korps* he had come to America, fleeing from the sickening spectacle of a defeated and degraded Germany, and had devoted himself to the circulation of this little Midwestern foreign-language paper because in that way he could help "keep alive the German language and the old German spirit among our people in your country."

Here his soft, blue eyes, looking away from me, narrowed a little and gleamed with the blue fire of fanaticism. And I left with my stamped and signed press card, feeling that Dr. Zalut was as dangerous as he was gentle and earnest—as deadly as our polite, soft-spoken, blue-eyed American outlaw, Billy the Kid. Both of them could kill quickly, casually and quite without hate.

But there were many types. For instance, the radio commentator at the broadcasting station on Adolf Hitler Platz. I met him because Bill Shirer, on leaving for a short vacation to see his wife Tess in Switzerland, had honored me by asking me to handle part of his broadcasts. It meant going three times a week out to the short-wave studios, submitting my script for censorship to a former admiral in the Austrian Navy, and presently going down to await my time at one of the tiny, soundproof booths which lined a long corridor. Usually there were two or three others waiting to go on. It was a polyglot crowd because the German radio, like the BBC and the later OWI broadcasts, tried to reach all parts of the world in all languages.

Loitering in this corridor with Arabs, Hindus, Chinese, Japanese and Balkanese, I struck up a casual acquaintance with the plump man largely because he spoke perfect English. This started with my asking him for a light, and was limited largely to remarks about the weather outside and the difficulties of the blackout. These were seldom satisfactory to him but his main grievance was against the Propaganda Ministry, which wrote the text of his broadcasts. They were always quarreling about the wording, he complained, with the result that usually they were so late sending him the final text that he only had time to scan it once hastily before he had to go on the air.

"Then they complain if I fumble at the words," he said pettishly. "Anyone would fumble." We had introduced ourselves, and he had said his name was Joyce, which at that time meant nothing to me.

(Later, in England, I found that he was just becoming world-famous as Lord Haw-Haw, the despised traitor who broadcast German propaganda to the British Isles each night; he was an unsuccessful Irish actor who had been mixed up with Oswald Mosely and other crackpot British fascists. After the war he was taken to England and hanged with considerable pomp and judicial ceremony as a traitor to the British Crown. I was never able to take the affair of Joyce with the seriousness which it deserved because I remembered the plump and pompous little man from whom I occasionally borrowed a match in the corridor, and whose value to the Third Reich lay not in his superficial brains or in his addled politics, but in his well-modulated actor's voice. He was, I felt, only a pitiable ham strutting in a silly rôle, of a stripe far different from Dr. Zalut.)

My 1939 visit to Berlin coincided with the "sitzkrieg" phase of the war. What the Germans called the Polish campaign had just been concluded and the Wehrmacht faced the Red Army across the River Bug.

The German people were being told by their leaders that there actually was no war now, and probably would not be one. It had been necessary to rescue the German city of Danzig from the foolish Poles, encouraged in their folly by the warmongering British and French politicians. To save face, the Allied statesmen had felt it necessary to declare war, and to mobilize their armies and navies. But in the end there would be no real conflict; in the meantime the German government, which felt it could afford to be magnanimous in victory, was searching for a formula which would permit the French and British politicians to climb down off their high horse without losing too much face with their own people, sign a peace treaty and end this farcical pretense of war.

We were to discover much later that this propaganda line to the German people was one which most of the top Nazis actually believed themselves. Ribbentrop, a bad observer and therefore a most unskillful diplomat, had convinced Hitler that England and France would not really fight over Poland, and that one more Munich was possible.

But in spite of these protestations of their peaceful intentions for the immediate future, I was deeply impressed and badly frightened by what I saw of the Nazi party, which actually was not a party in our sense, but a gang. It was shrewd, arrogant, purposeful and on the march—maybe not tomorrow, but soon. There were probably cynics among them but there were also fanatics, like Dr. Zalut, who actually believed their own propaganda, and were not less dangerous for that. They had a frightening contempt for our democratic softnesses, our indecisions and our scruples—these firm-jawed, hard-eyed, beefy young men who swaggered through the lobby of the Kaiserhof and in and out of Hitler's Chancellery just across the square.

I was frightened, first, because beyond the Rhine (Neville Chamberlain was still Prime Minister of England) I could see no one who matched them in shrewdness or strength of purpose. Second, I was frightened by their army. The German people then were, by American standards, a little shabby and not too well fed. And we were then in a period of world opinion when, if one disapproved of Hitler's treatment of the Jews, it was fashionable to believe that the tanks which he had sent rolling into Prague and Vienna frequently broke down, and were made of painted cardboard.

But in Berlin I saw what was clearly the world's best army. Their uniforms were stout, their cheeks were pink, and all of their equipment, which ranged from helmets to command cars and tanks, was new and well-designed, and made of sound steel and springy rubber. I could see nothing beyond the Rhine which I thought would be able to stop this German army, and was even more badly frightened later when I emerged from Germany and listened to reporters fresh from London and Paris talking about Allied strategy.

These blithe boys and girls explained to me that the Nazis had pulled their last bluff, and now the Allies had Hitler just where they wanted him. The Wicked Hun was slowly being strangled between the Maginot Line and the British blockade; statistically speaking, he was slowly but bloodlessly being brought to his knees through relentless starvation. They had all the figures on pivotal raw materials, fats, manganese, tungsten, and nickel.

It would be slow, of course, but there was also a ray of hope, and this lay in the skilled psychology which was being em-

ployed in London and Paris. Because experts were sure that
the particular brain malady from which Hitler suffered was
one which could not brook frustration or long delay. There
was, therefore, some hope that he could be trapped into making the fatal error of attacking the Maginot Line. Allied intelligence agents were already at work laying this trap, but of
course I must breathe the secret to no one. If it succeeded,
German manpower would be blasted to atoms by the big guns
in the French pillboxes and the war would be over in a few
weeks.

Whereupon I made a mistake. I told them heatedly that
they were living in a fool's paradise, that the German army
looked alarmingly strong, that stories of its weakness were traps
to delude them, that it seemed short of nothing that it could
not easily get by conquest, that they were in for a dreadful
surprise.

And then I learned something about the human mind. It is
seldom possible for it to be loyal to an idea unless it can also
persuade itself that this idea will prevail. Some of these reporters, fresh from the Allied side, looked at me pityingly:
clearly I was the dupe of Nazi propaganda. Others were coldly
silent, being sure that I was an enemy agent, consciously spread-
ing defeatist propaganda. But this is to get far ahead of my
story.

My self-appointed mission to Germany in 1939 was to find
out something about the German mind, and what had happened
to it behind the propaganda curtain. I started a one-man Gallup
poll by asking both the Germans and those Americans who knew
them best what the German people thought of Hitler.

Here I got another surprise. I knew that in the last free
election, seven years before, the Nazis had received only 32 per
cent of the votes. I expected a sharp division of opinion—a
cleavage between arrogant Nazis and terrified anti-Nazis. That
was the way it was in the books.

I found such groups, of course, but I was bewildered to find that in between them was the great mass of the German people, who could not be so glibly pigeonholed. When I propounded my question about Hitler, the average German would calmly reply, "Well, some things which he has done I like, and others I don't." It was very baffling, because it was strangely like the reply of an Englishman or an American, if you asked him whether or not he liked Churchill or Roosevelt.

I found I had to ask them exactly which things they liked and which ones they did not, and then I began to find out some most interesting things about the Germans. About 90 per cent of them said they approved his domestic policies. "He has put all Germans to work. Today there are no unemployed, and this is a very good thing." I could not quarrel violently with this: an American might have said something similar in praise of Roosevelt.

When it came to foreign policy there was more division. I quickly found that Germans were 100 per cent opposed to the Treaty of Versailles, which had been Hitler's principal issue. They argued (and on this point it was hard to argue back) that the 1919 Treaty had disarmed Germany but had promised that this was only a prelude to general world disarmament. This promise had been broken; therefore, if Germany was to have equality in the world, she must have an army, like other sovereign states.

All of them approved of Germany's new army, but there was the further question of what they thought of the way Hitler was now using it. I was delighted to find that at least 40 per cent of them staunchly opposed his foreign policy.

"We always said this fool would get us into a war," they said triumphantly. "Now, you see, it has happened."

The other 60 per cent were following the propaganda line.

"You will see!" they said. "Our Führer is very clever, and there will be no war. With the army's power behind us, they will now give us the things Germany should have, but there will be no war." They were all sure of this. "Already he has gotten much. Austria wanted union with us, and so did the Sudetenland. So with Danzig; it is a purely German city. True, the French and British have mobilized, but there will be no war. You will see!"

They were wrong, but the only heartening thing about this survey was that it proved that the overwhelming majority of the German people did not want war, and were divided only as to whether or not there would be one.

Probably no people has ever wanted war. They only want those things which they cannot have without war. The American North wanted only to preserve the Union in 1861, the South only its independence. Countless opinion polls have proved that even in 1941 the American people did not want war, although many feared it would come. They wanted only to save England so that Hitler would not dominate Europe, and to curb Japan by cutting off her oil, rubber and credits, all of which, incidentally, I favored.

Certainly the Nazi party leadership believed that an eventual war to establish German overlordship in Europe was not only inevitable but desirable. But they were careful to conceal this from their people, instead presenting the Fuehrer as a patient man who would endure all but the most insufferable indignities to maintain peace. Certainly a majority of these leaders did not yet believe, even in November of 1939, that their inevitable and desirable war was already on them. Stalin had already been paid off and was contented, and they hoped to squeeze one more Munich compromise out of England and France.

Because this story has a sequel I must again jump ahead of my narrative to Stockholm at the end of February in 1940 when, after the Russo-Finnish War, I was vainly hoping for another visa to enter Germany, which I felt was the most unpleasant and yet the most interesting country in Europe. While I waited, I encountered an American reporter whom I had known in Berlin and who was out for a brief vacation to eat Danish bacon and eggs.

"What's the news in Berlin?" I asked him. "What are they talking about now?"

He considered. "Mostly just what they were when you left, except that the top boys now realize there really will be a war, and are preparing the people for it. The inside dope is that they'll start it themselves. Probably go down through Holland and Belgium. In about May."

"How do the people like the idea?"

"They don't. But some of them have changed their talk a little bit."

"Which ones?"

"Remember the ones who didn't like Hitler and would tell you so?"

"Sure."

"Well, most of these are now saying, 'We never did like the son-of-a-bitch, and always said he'd get us into a war, but now that he's done it, we must make sure we win it. To avoid defeat is the main thing. We don't want to see 1918 again.

" 'We still don't like him, but we don't see anyone else in sight who would have a chance of winning it for us. Anyway, if we started opposition now, we might lose the war during the commotion. Better get in behind him until victory, and settle scores with him when the fighting is over.' That's what they now say. Not quite like when you were there."

I didn't like this. It seemed to me that these former German anti-Nazis were putting nationalism, or patriotism, ahead of principle. But having watched America in the war, I wonder now if I was fair to them. In our country, as in Germany, there were many people who bitterly hated our leadership and who felt it was deliberately involving us in an unnecessary European war. But when this war came, most of these people then said, "We still don't like Roosevelt, but we don't want to see our country lose, so we will support it to the utmost." Willingly they sent their sons to die in a hundred far-flung battles.

And if the tide of war had gone against us, if our country were now ruled by an Axis Military Government, what would be the fate of these people? The conquerors might well say to them, "You now pretend you were always against Roosevelt, but during the war your factories fattened on war contracts. Now you whine that if you had not taken these orders, the government might have confiscated your plants. Do you expect us to believe that? If Roosevelt had won his war, you would have been greedy for the fruits of victory and anxious to have people forget that you were ever against it. Get out of this office!"

A sad fate indeed, and another reason why I am glad we won, having seen what happens to people when wars are lost. For victors are seldom discriminating.

But back now to the rest of my 1939 Gallup poll. I wasn't surprised to find that about 80 per cent of the German people regretted their loss of freedom, but it was curious that these should include some who had supported Hitler and still did not regret having done so. They said that the Communists could be defeated only by their own methods. They felt that the curbs on free speech and opinion were necessary but temporary evils due to Germany's present situation. In this crisis, they argued, Germany had to have unity. When it was over they were sure that a kindly Führer would relax the stern Gestapo controls.

This was obviously not true, but I think it proves that all peoples, including Germans and Russians, normally crave freedom and can be persuaded to give it up only if they are convinced that their nation is beset by sinister enemies within or abroad. Once in the saddle, the dictator, to maintain his grip, must keep his people convinced of these perils. For if he announces an era of peace and plenty, the people will demand freedom as well.

Lastly, I was interested in what the German people thought of Hitler's policy toward the Jews, and the answer to this was in many ways the most surprising of all. That policy, while it shocked the world, was in 1939 far less brutal than it later became. The Nazi party had always been openly anti-Semitic, and this became the official policy of the government when it took over. Intermarriage was forbidden. Jews were debarred from most professions and were under countless other restrictions. Some had been sent to concentration camps, others had been beaten or killed in street brawls with storm troopers while the police looked on.

When the world protested, the Nazi reply was that they frankly wanted the Jews to leave Germany, and that any other government which desired them was welcome. Jews who planned to migrate had to dispose of their homes or businesses at forced sales for a fraction of their value, had to secure, usually with great difficulty, an exit permit, and then found they could take almost no money from the country. Their greatest difficulty, however, was in finding a foreign consulate which would give them visas. America, which could in this period have saved all the Jews of Germany, did little, for the majority opinion was that no nation had the right to declare some of its citizens "undesirable" and dump them as paupers on the world. Indeed, many Americans of Jewish origin did not protest against the American policy, privately fearing that an influx of penniless European Jews would result in the growth of anti-Semitism here.

What the result of our restricted immigration policy would be, most Americans did not care to foresee. I doubt, however, that history will hold that this deliberate lack of foresight absolves them from all blame for the tragedy which ensued.

In 1939, however, Germany's treatment of Jews was mild by comparison with what happened later. I had heard it excused on the grounds that the Nazis, being intelligent men, did not, of course, believe their own anti-Jewish propaganda, but found it a useful demagogue's tool with the German people. So I was naturally surprised to find that even this comparatively "mild" anti-Jewish policy was strongly disapproved by about 70 per cent of the people. This included a number who might be classed as mildly anti-Semitic. They said that while they might not personally care for Jews, it was nevertheless unfair to discriminate against them by law, to bar them from occupations and steal their money. If the German race was as superior to the Jews as Hitler said, why then did it need laws to protect it from their competition? As Germans, they were ashamed of the legal discrimination and held it to be medieval nonsense which was disgracing their country.

In other words, I discovered that Hitler was, in this respect, "sincere." He was not being a cynical demagogue capitalizing on an existing hate, but his twisted brain really believed the anti-Semitic propaganda which he was forcing on the country. National Socialism would have been more popular in Germany without it. And even of the 30 per cent who, after six years of propaganda, had come to approve this anti-Jewish policy, I doubt that 10 per cent would have approved it had they known that it would presently be extended to include gas chambers for "useless Jews." In this judgment I think the late Nazi hierarchy would agree, for they made every effort to conceal these murder camps from their own people as well as from the world.

In the course of my sojourn in this Germany of the "sitzkrieg," I came to know one German well. He was one of the younger attachés of Goebbels' Propaganda Ministry, assigned to its American section because he had lived in America and spoke good English. The Propaganda Ministry, I was presently to discover, was a very efficiently run institution, performing, in addition to more sinister functions, those of the British Ministry of Information or our own later OWI, which had similar bright young men with a gift for languages riding herd on neutral and foreign journalists, doing them minor services such as explaining how one got ration tickets, simplifying wartime red tape, enrolling them for propaganda tours, and of course always presenting their country in the best possible light.

Since the man I knew is still alive in Berlin, and since he will play an important part in this story and I wish to describe him with an accuracy which may at times be painful, I am not using his real name but shall call him Albrecht Schultz.

He was in 1939 a tall, blond, and yet rather frail-looking youth in his middle twenties, with blue eyes and a large head, and a face that was on the whole rather handsome in a pink-cheeked way, most sensitive and not particularly strong. His age put him exactly in the Hitler generation. He had been a small child during the First World War, with no memories of it except his family's tales of the food hardships under the postwar British blockade.

When Hitler was taking power Schultz was in his early teens. At the age of fourteen, like most of his generation, he joined the Hitler Jugend, largely, I would guess, in revolt, normal for that age group, against his father (who was dead when I met Schultz). The father had been a civil servant, principal of a Berlin high school, with leanings toward the Social Democrats, and had held the Nazis in low esteem. Since no one can take the political opinions of a teen-age boy seriously, I was not particularly disturbed by the fact that Schultz had been a member of the Hitler Youth, moving with the hysterical surge of that tragic generation. The curious thing was that as I came to know him better, I found that it disturbed him far more than it did me, for he was obviously in deep conflict.

There was one story which he told me half a dozen times in almost exactly the same words, forgetting each time that he had told it before.

"One afternoon"—so went his story—"our Hitler Jugend group had climbed upon the roof of a synagogue and we were fixing a swastika flag to its steeple—I and two others had the flag. But I happened to look down and there in the crowd below, which was watching us, I saw my father standing. My father was of course afraid to say anything, but he was looking at me and shaking his head, slowly and very sadly." Then he would stop.

"And what did you do?" I would always ask.

"We finished nailing the flag to the steeple. In those days we of the Hitler Jugend thought all the old were hopelessly reactionary. But my father was a very fine man, an old-fashioned Prussian. You would have liked my father."

So young Schultz kept on with the Hitler Jugend and after finishing two years at the University of Berlin, because of his high marks and his membership in the Hitler Jugend he was selected as a German exchange student to attend an American West Coast state university, where he spent the following two years studying journalism. The outcome, from the Nazi viewpoint, was not successful. Because Schultz acquired a tremendous enthusiasm for everything American—our food, our clothing, our free-and-easy customs and our viewpoint, as well as a keen understanding of us. I gathered that the Americans liked him quite as much as he liked them, for he was elected to a rather good Greek-letter fraternity.

He also acquired what was, from the Nazi viewpoint, a dangerous tolerance of our American tolerance. It was one of the things he liked, although he would then prudently add that of course the present situation in Germany was different, and she could not be judged by American standards. All this was further aggravated by several months which he had spent traveling in China, also on a government scholarship, during which he acquired a liking for the non-Aryan Chinese, their mellow old civilization, their keen sense of humor and their food.

To cap the climax, just before he finally returned to Germany he paused on the American West Coast to marry an American wife, who, I was amazed and amused to discover, was now not too discreetly anti-Nazi.

Shortly after I had arrived and on the first occasion that I met Schultz, he invited me to lunch, a week hence, at the Bristol. I knew that it was the perfunctory courtesy which he, as part of his official duties to visiting firemen, was obliged to discharge and add to his expense account. He made it clear, however, that it was more than that because, he said, his wife—being newly arrived in Germany—in many ways did not yet understand the country and its customs, and would be over-joyed to talk to another American.

Mrs. Schultz was in her early twenties, a pretty blonde and blue-eyed girl of Scandinavian descent, with firmly American opinions, although we did not get around to these at once because Schultz was bubbling with the news that the first copies of his first book were just off the press, and of course a young author needs considerable indulgence on his day of publication. It was on the subject of his Chinese trip, and I gathered that it was the familiar type of young man's travel book. Every author has deliriously high hopes of his first book, but Schultz was still shrewd enough to see that not much could come of his, because the war had drained from Germany what small interest its people ever had had in China.

He also had a grievance against the government censors, who had deleted a slighting reference he had made to one of Germany's consuls in China, on the grounds that a young man traveling on a government scholarship should not depict an officer of his government abroad as behaving in a manner un-worthy and, therefore, un-German.

Although he conceded it had not really damaged his book, he was greatly annoyed by the narrowness and the stupidity of the principle involved, under which all German officials must at all times be depicted as above reproach. He also added that he had many friends, left over from his University of Berlin days, among the younger generation of German intellectuals, and that he personally knew of three excellent books—novels of protest or of satire—which had been finished but their manuscripts were now tucked away in bureau drawers, waiting for publishers in a freer, happier day. Of these, he said, he had read two and they were excellent—just the kind which Americans would like to read, but their time in Germany was not yet.

At this point I asked Mrs. Schultz how she liked Berlin. There was a pause and then she said of course one had to get used to any new country, she realized that. And she tried not to be irritated by little things. But it really *was* very different.

And how?

Well, the people. Of course she didn't yet speak the language. When she knew them better that, of course, would make a difference. But they were so stern, so strict. And Berlin in winter seemed so gloomy. Of course, war made a difference in any city.

And then the newspapers. All of them saying exactly the same thing, and never any argument. And the way they were obsessed with their notions about Jews. It was all so strange to an American—maybe she'd get used to it.

And their ideas about women. This was the hardest to get used to. They always seemed surprised, even a little shocked, if you expressed an opinion of your own, even though they tried not to show it.

"You see," said Schultz proudly, "my wife is not a nice little German *Hausfrau* who always agrees with her husband; she is an American girl who says what she thinks!"

"Well, why shouldn't I?"

"But you should!" said Schultz again proudly. "Another thing which my family does not understand is that we always speak English together. They say she will never learn German."

"Well, I *am* learning German."

"But even when you do, there is no reason why we should not speak English," said Schultz severely.

"But it's embarrassing sometimes. Other people in the street car always stare so."

"Do they ever say anything to you?" I asked.

"Sometimes," said Schultz. "I explain that she is my wife and an American."

"There was that one woman who said still we should not speak English because it was an enemy language and Germany is at war with England," said the girl. "I'm learning German as fast as I can."

"We will always speak English," said Schultz sternly.

"Your sister says we mustn't after the baby comes."

"Pay no attention to her," said Schultz, and then, to me: "My sister is *echt Deutsch*, a typical German *Hausfrau* of the middle classes. She says that what we do now may be our own business but our child will be German and must have a thorough German upbringing."

"She thinks all Americans spoil their children," said the girl.

"I have told her it is no affair of hers," said Schultz.

The girl turned to me. "Do you think we'll get in it this time?"

"I don't know," I said.

"Nobody thought we would the last time," she said, a little sadly.

"I don't think there will be any war at all," said Schultz, "except what has already happened in Poland. My wife still keeps her American passport," he added, again proudly.

"That's another thing your family doesn't like," said the girl.

"What they like doesn't matter, because why shouldn't you be an American?"

"After all, that's what I am, and," she said seriously, "I'm going to keep that passport."

"I want you to." And here he smiled proudly at me. "A real American girl."

I wondered why, with all his strong admiration for things

American, Schultz had not stayed in the United States after their marriage, but did not yet want to ask this directly. It came out presently that he had tried to, and for some time had looked for a job, both on the West Coast and in New York. There seemed, however, to be no opening which paid enough to support a wife, for a young man with a strong German accent. The best offer he got was a job in the Berlin bureau of the United Press. In many ways it was ideal, for Schultz could use both his German background and his American journalistic education. It was, furthermore, only a stepping stone, because it could presently lead any place—perhaps back to America or to other foreign capitals.

For a few months they had been very happy in Berlin, and then the war, which was already changing so many lives, stepped into his. The German government notified him that he was to resign from the United Press and go to work at a smaller salary for the Propaganda Ministry, where his American background would be useful in contacting American journalists. He was a citizen of the Third Reich and also, as a Hitler Jugend, had been honored with an expensive foreign scholarship. It was an obligation which, now that his country was at war, he could not escape. The alternative was the uniform of a private in the Wehrmacht and duty on the Westwall. He chose the Propaganda Ministry. When Schultz had first told me of his early membership in the Hitler Jugend, I had assumed that sometime thereafter he had automatically been inducted into the ranks of the Party. When I came to know him better, it was clear that all its political nonsense had been knocked out of his head in his travels abroad. Once I was on the point of asking him when he had resigned. When I came to know Germany better, I realized that even now he must still be a member. For membership in any totalitarian party is a one-way road. You don't just cease paying your dues, or perhaps drop the secretary a polite note saying that your opinions have changed. Desertion is treason, and it would have meant at

least the certainty of concentration camp. He had, I am sure,
no taste for martyrdom and he also had an American wife to
support, with a baby on the way.

Here he was, a most intelligent and in many ways likable young
man, trapped by a decision he had made as a boy of fourteen.
I cannot see his rôle in this story as that of either a villain or
a hero, but only as an average member of the human race,
the product of a curiously mixed environment, following the
easiest path toward the best chance of survival.

But if he no longer believed in the Party's mythology,
which had stirred the imagination of a child, he remained a
German. They were his people and, for better or for worse,
their fate would be his. Because he liked America, he wanted
Americans to like his country. If they could not do this, he
wanted them at least to understand why his people were what
they were.

I have often wondered, then and since, what his tough-
minded superiors in the party and the Propaganda Ministry
thought of him. Probably they held him in mild contempt—a
promising lad, whose patriotism had been badly corrupted by
contact with the decadent democracies; a half-caste, a political
hybrid who was nevertheless still useful to Germany in that
he could talk the language, both in speech and in ideas, of
these foreign journalists, and so bridge a gap.

The Germans were at that time boasting that they exercised no censorship on foreign correspondents, except for radio
scripts to be broadcast to America; this was necessary, they
insisted, only to withhold from the British military information,
such as references to the weather, which would assist the Royal
Air Force, or any hints as to German troop movements behind
the Westwall. No correspondent could legitimately object to
such prohibitions but, in talking to the others, I soon found that
an indirect but powerful political censorship existed, although
no Nazi ever touched your copy with a blue pencil.

It was done, as in Russia, by the visa method,* and your first warning came when one of the alert young press attachés (like Schultz), either of the Foreign Office or of the Propaganda Ministry, frowningly explained to you that your writing had of late become dangerously "tendentious." This meant that, however cautious you had been in phrasing your criticism, you could not hope to stay unless you began to interlard it with a number of propaganda stories favorable to the régime—praising its achievements and depicting its people as happy, loyal and contented.

If you persisted in a sustained note of critical pessimism, you would presently find that when you went to Switzerland or to Denmark for a brief holiday, your visa would be canceled at the border, and you could not return.

For the agency men, this was (and is) a serious matter. American and British news agency heads frequently have words of high praise for the glories of the free press and courageous reporting. Actually, however, these are strictly for consumption outside the office. The men who work under them know (and all dictatorships understand even better) that a news agency is a highly competitive commercial enterprise which is, therefore, severely handicapped if it cannot cover Berlin, Moscow, or any other important world capital. An agency man expelled by a dictatorship may be momentarily a hero in the liberal press, but he quickly finds that he is somewhat less than that to his employer, who is now put to the trouble and expense of replacing him—if, indeed, a successor will be admitted at all.

"What's the matter, Joe, can't you get along with people? All you say may be true, but I notice our competitors there manage to stay out of trouble."

None of this touched me, for I was my own boss on a ramble through wartime Europe. The syndicate which handled my

---

* Of course Russia in addition applies to regular correspondents living there the world's most rigid censorship.—WLW.

HITLER'S REICH   25

daily airmail column did not want me to stay too long in any one country. I was unique among my colleagues then in that expulsion would not damage my career, and I was therefore free to write rather bluntly what I thought, disguised only slightly by irony.

When I returned eventually to America, I found that this had won me some small acclaim and a quite undeserved reputation for courage for "writing between the lines." But it was both flattering and bewildering to discover that the earliest and perhaps most enthusiastic admirer of my broad ironies was Schultz.

Early he had explained to me that the Propaganda Ministry was offering a new service to journalists for their airmail copy. If I simply dropped it in the post box, it would, of course, have to go through the routine military censorship of the army (there was, he assured me, no political censorship) and this would mean a delay, certainly of days and possibly of weeks. All mail was carefully examined because, he explained, "some of your Balkan colleagues" had the habit of trying to send out important military information written with invisible ink on the surface of what appeared to be an "innocent" political story.

The Propaganda Ministry was, therefore, making available a service under which I could, if I chose, turn in my dispatches to Schultz, who would deliver them to the ministry for re-typing on its own paper, thus avoiding the necessity even of military inspection. But I was not to jump to the conclusion that this was a censorship. It was only a service to save foreign journalists' time.

Somewhat suspiciously I complied, but what he said turned out in the main to be true. I soon found that he was reading my stories with an appreciation which could not but please any writer. Because of his years in America, none of my word shadings escaped him, and few writers are immune from the flattery of having their best sentences quoted back to them with a grin.

"After your story of yesterday was copied, I took it home to read to my wife," he would explain. "I hope you do not mind, she is homesick for the American viewpoint." Quite naturally, I didn't.

My stories were not, however, universally popular in the ministry. One day, in the typing room, I overheard an argument between Schultz and a colleague whom I had already come to dislike. He was Herr Bauser, a chunky, tough-looking man in his middle forties with heavy, somewhat apelike features, coal-black bristly hair, clipped so closely that the dead white of his scalp showed through, and who was never without his party button—a white celluloid disc, on which was imprinted a jet-black swastika bound with a rim of red. He was exactly the type of shrewd gangster gorilla who had muscled into power with Hitler. Since he had spoken only gruff German to me I had assumed that he knew no English. It turned out that he read it with great speed and he now held in his hand my dispatch of the previous day, talking angrily and accusingly to Schultz, and pointing to a particular paragraph.

Remembering the dispatch, I could guess which one it was. I had had a long talk with Louis Lochner, head of the AP bureau in Berlin, who had warned me that if I wanted to stay, I must watch my step. I had used this for my column—omitting, of course, his name. Louis had gone over the ticklish points in detail. "And aside from those," he had said, "they don't have any political censorship, except for one thing—be very careful what you say about The Boy himself. They are very sensitive about him."

The Nazi with the close-cropped hair was so indignant he was almost sputtering. Schultz, although he seemed frightened, was arguing, although weakly, something about American journalistic customs being different from those of Europe. They did not see me, so I walked quietly by.

I was due that evening for dinner at Schultz's apartment, a modest three-room one in a barrack-like stucco building in the Berlin suburbs. Before the other guests arrived, he brought up the subject of my article. Choosing his words carefully, he said he had, of course, enjoyed it. Then he said that the veteran American journalist I had interviewed must, of course, be Bill Shirer.

"No," I said, "it wasn't Bill Shirer." I don't think he believed me.

"There was one thing in it," he said, "I took the liberty of making one little change. I could not reach you to ask permission, but I was sure you would not mind."

"What was that?"

"You referred to Hitler as 'the boy himself.' Now I know that in America that would not be noticed. But, cabled back here in translation by our Embassy in Washington, it would read in German '*Knabe selbst.*' That is a very rude term. The very highest quarters might be offended." He looked away. "No," he said, "I could not take responsibility for passing '*Knabe selbst.*'"

He was noticeably short-tempered the rest of the evening. Some chasms are too wide to be bridged. Simultaneous membership in an American Greek-letter fraternity and the Hitler Jugend is not easy; it was hard in 1939 to bring a sympathetic tolerance to bear both on free peaceful America and Hitler's Germany at war.

Mrs. Schultz glanced at her wrist watch and, leaning forward, snapped on the handsome mahogany Telefunken radio.

"This is London calling," said a stately Oxonian voice, "in the overseas service of the BBC."

I started, and could not help glancing quickly at Schultz. He was staring straight ahead without expression. This was wartime Germany. We were listening to what the Goebbels ministry, for whom he worked, denounced as enemy propaganda for which the penalty was death, although no German was actually executed for this offense until the following year.

Mrs. Schultz had not changed the needle on the dial. Apparently she had been listening to the same station earlier in the afternoon. About halfway through the news broadcast the volume seemed to increase and, rising quietly, Schultz turned it down so that the voice was audible only in our room. I wondered how thick were the walls of this apartment. I wondered if he would ask me not to tell any other German that he allowed his American wife to listen to the BBC. It occurred to me that courage is always relative; that it was far more dangerous for a German to do this in Berlin than it was to be openly anti-Nazi in New York.

When the broadcast ended, Mrs. Schultz switched it off.

"Yesterday I heard over the BBC," Mrs. Schultz said, and then she paused. "Of course, maybe it isn't true, but anyway they said—"

"That," broke in Schultz, "is what I object to." His voice was stern, and yet he was grinning. "If you hear it over our German radio, you say, 'Of course it isn't true,' but if it is the BBC, then you say only, 'Maybe it isn't true.'"

We all laughed. And at this point some of the other guests arrived, a very pretty young American actress, blonde and vivacious, whose last New York rôle had been to play next to the lead in a fairly recent Broadway musical comedy, and who was now married to a handsome, neatly dressed German of thirty-five, by profession an electrical engineer. They had been invited, I gathered, largely so that his wife could talk English to Mrs. Schultz and to me. She was, of course, eager for any current news of Broadway. I had none, and the friends she spoke of were only names to me. But she prattled on gaily of New York as she remembered it. I gathered that she was too much in love with her quietly handsome young husband to be overwhelmingly homesick. She mentioned casually that they had asked her to do a few overseas broadcasts to America and she rather thought that she would keep on as it gave her something to do. (Remembering this later, I thought that she might have become the "Axis Sally" who broadcast to our troops from Berlin to North Africa in 1943. But in 1939 I only thought she should be good at radio to America because of her melodiously vivacious voice. She seemed too healthily and flexibly female to have any strong political opinions, although I dimly remember some passing, but not bitter, remark about the number of Jews in the New York theater.)

With her husband, however, it was different. At Schultz's prompting (he said it would amuse his wife) I was persuaded to tell an anti-Hitler joke which was then going the rounds in Berlin and which I had picked up only a few days before. It concerned the Jew who was being marched off to concentration camp in the middle of a column of SS troopers (they were presumably the loyal élite of the Nazi party) and who, deciding he would make one last desperate gesture of protest, called out, "To hell with Hitler!" The column only marched on in silence. Thinking they had not heard him, he repeated it, but still nothing happened. When, a third time, he shouted it out, the SS guard at his right turned and said: "My friend, we feel just as you do, but do not say that too loudly because the sergeant up at the head of the column might hear you, and he is still a Nazi."

When this was translated to the young engineer, he was clearly not amused. I guessed that had the group been purely German, he might have smiled. But we foreigners were going a little too far.

The talk now became general and I was surprised to hear Schultz speaking with the greatest contempt of Foreign Minister Ribbentrop. It developed that there was bitter and surprisingly open rivalry between the Foreign Office and Dr. Goebbels. Ribbentrop was, Schultz explained, a pompous fool who invariably gave the Fuehrer bad advice, who considered himself an expert on British psychology, and who was directly responsible for the present mess. It was he who had persuaded Hitler that England, in a showdown, would not really oppose German intervention in Poland, overruling the more prudent advice of cautious men like Dr. Goebbels.

With proper timing, it all could have been worked out, but as a result of Ribbentrop's fumbles, Germany had both sides mobilized along the Westwall although nobody really wanted war. Ribbentrop furthermore filled the Foreign Office with his own gang of intriguing sycophants who were constantly reaching out for more power—trying, for instance, to get control of supervision of the foreign press, a function which obviously should belong to the Propaganda Ministry.

I listened with some surprise. I had assumed that under a dictatorship, politics were abolished, that differences of opinion disappeared with free elections. It was now clear that there still remained the same kind of palace intrigue and interdepartmental jealousy which goes on in other kinds of government. Perhaps it was even intensified. Again, as in all palace intrigues, the leader himself can do no wrong. It is only the intriguing scoundrels of the opposing faction who get the ear of the leader, and give them bad advice.

When Schultz exhausted this topic, someone asked me how I spent my time as a journalist. "Mostly wandering around Berlin," I answered. That afternoon I had spent at least half an hour staring into the windows of the big toy shop on Friederichstrasse, looking at its Christmas display and toy soldiers. They were the best I had ever seen.

"But that shop has always been there!" said Schultz almost angrily. "It has no more soldiers now than when my father bought them for me there when I was only ten. He was a Social Democrat and that was under the Republic." So I hastily explained that I had intended this as no criticism of the Third Reich, but only in praise of German workmanship.

At this point Mrs. Schultz brought in what would be in America a light eleven o'clock snack. For rationed Germany, in 1939, it was a bounteous feast of rye bread and various cold sliced sausages, both of which were strictly rationed, beer and ersatz coffee. There was even sugar. It was clear that Schultz had obtained from his ministry some extra bread and meat tickets for the purpose of entertaining foreign journalists in his home. When first he had invited me to lunch at the Bristol Hotel, he had explained, only half in joke, that he wanted to bring his wife, not only to meet me but because at the hotel she could get a full and nourishing meal, as they had a baby coming. For this reason, I now ate sparingly of the bread and sausages. At least half of them went back to the kitchen.

And now came the pay-off. Casually, Schultz reached for his brief case on the table.

"I have something here which might interest you," he said to me. "I told the ministry I would check them out so you could see them this evening and then I would bring them back tomorrow. You have heard, of course, of the atrocities that the Poles committed against our people who lived on their side of the border? Hundreds of people murdered, many women and children."

I nodded.

"Well, these pictures were taken by our official Wehrmacht photographers. Now I suppose," he went on defensively, "that you will say this is only propaganda. Anyway, I have told the ministry I would show them to you."

"I haven't yet said they were propaganda," I said. The pictures showed piles of bodies against stone walls. There were close-ups of dead children. The work of a mob is never pretty, not even when it is our mob.

"The British are now trying to tell America that these are the bodies of Poles murdered by the Gestapo, who then took these pictures for release, saying that they were Germans killed by the Poles. But these are Wehrmacht photographs—see, here on the back of each is the stamp—taken as our armies entered."

"I believe you," I said, looking at the photographs. "I think the British are wrong. Of course it was the Poles. Why wouldn't it be the Poles? But why do you call these people Germans?"

"But you can see that from their faces!" said Schultz.

"Weren't they Polish citizens?"

"Technically. But their language was German. Germans have lived in this part of Poland for centuries. In some towns a majority spoke German."

"But until Hitler they were content to be Poles," I said. "Then you spread your propaganda among them, telling them they should by rights be Germans. You have the same propaganda in America."

"But they are Germans. Why should they have not welcomed our armies?"

"And why shouldn't the Poles treat them as traitors? I'm sure the photographs aren't faked, but why should you be surprised that this would happen? It would be the same in America or any other country. What would you do to any German citizens with Polish names who helped an invading Polish army?"

"I thought you would say something like that," said Schultz weakly. "Anyway, I told the ministry I would show them to you."

Schultz was, I reflected, a poor propagandist. He was anxious to do a good job for his country, but those two years in America had shown him the other side. Good propagandists must believe deeply and sincerely all of what they say, at least for the moment.

The serious Nazi engineer, who had understood none of our conversation in English and who had never been out of Germany, was looking at the pictures, one by one, with real pity and genuinely righteous indignation.

On the way home I reflected that the evening had not, from Schultz's standpoint, been a complete loss. For in the kitchen there remained for Mrs. Schultz and the coming baby at least half a platter, both of bread and of sausages, bought on the ministry's ration ticket. Perhaps that had been its real goal.

Only once did Schultz object to any of my stories. One day I picked up a copy of *Der Stuermer*, Jules Streicher's violently anti-Semitic sheet, which contained an attack on Mrs. Roosevelt. It published a picture of her taken as she was being escorted by two uniformed Negro cadets up the steps of a small Negro college which she was inspecting. *Der Stuermer* added in prose a few remarks to the effect that since it was well known that the First Lady was a Jewess, whose family name was Rosenfeld, it was understandable that she should frequently consort with Negro men.

When I made a digest of all this to send back to America, Schultz became excited and I think sincerely aggrieved.

"Why must you emphasize things like that!" he protested.

"Well, there it is in a German paper."

"But no intelligent German reads *Der Stuermer*." This was by and large true. Its newsstand sale was relatively small. But, by government order, it was posted on public bulletin boards, and it was required reading for certain Nazi units. So I said:

"Can I quote you on that? Remember, Hitler endorses it."

He gave a humorless laugh. "No, you can't quote me. But what I say is still true. It gives Americans the wrong impression of what is in the papers that most Germans read."

Of the anti-Jewish mythology which, as a teen-age boy, he had absorbed through the Hitler Jugend, surely something must have remained. But if those two years in America had not removed most of it, they had made him ashamed of what was left. It was something, he knew, of which no intelligent man should be proud, and he was rather self-consciously a world-minded intellectual.

So when American correspondents would ridicule the official anti-Semitism of the Nazis he would sit glumly silent, making no attempt to justify it, although once, when we were perhaps a little too self-righteous, he remarked defensively that he had noticed some anti-Semitism in America; there were even college fraternities and sororities which did not admit Jews. It was, I felt, a fair rejoinder. But it was a subject which he tried hard to avoid, unlike the more rugged Nazis who would scornfully accuse us of writing as we did of their country only because it was demanded by the Jewish advertisers who, of course, controlled our newspapers.

If you wanted to avoid the subject of anti-Semitism in Berlin and confine yourself instead to writing only of the "constructive" side, you could do this as easily and quite as honestly as American fellow-traveler reporters in Moscow avoid the subjects of forced labor camps and police terror, for in neither capital were there many outward and visible signs of it. The victims of totalitarianism are seldom paraded through the streets; both the GPU and the Gestapo preferred to make arrests at night.

Outwardly, Berlin was a normal, if somewhat cheerless, city. Occasionally there would be a sign on a restaurant door— "Jews Unwanted"—but not on all. They were, for instance, free to come to the Hotel Bristol, where I was staying, and one day at teatime Bill Shirer pointed out to me a group of half a dozen somberly-dressed dark men with sensitive and infinitely sad faces, seated together at a table. They were, he explained, the leaders of Berlin's Jewish community, the most important rabbis, gathered for their weekly meeting.

I later learned that the Nazi regulations governing Jews were constantly changing. Various taxes and fines were assessed against them. They were allowed no clothing stamps, nor could they buy legally any of the more nourishing kinds of food. Then, as now, immigration into Palestine was limited. The American quota had a long waiting list. I was surprised that the Soviet Union, in spite of its frequent and loudly expressed public horror for Hitler's racial doctrines, was admitting none whatever, except of course for a few key Communists who crossed by devious underground routes. But this was no help because, Nazi propaganda to the contrary notwithstanding, the overwhelming mass of German Jews were not Communists.

These tragic-eyed rabbis gathered at the table in the Bristol while the orchestra played, represented, by mutual agreement between themselves and the Nazis, Berlin's Jews. Nazi regulations were explained to them, and they passed the information on down to their people. If a heavy fine were imposed on German Jews, in reprisal for something which happened abroad, the Nazis informed these men of the total sum, and they divided it among their people according to their ability to pay. This saved the Nazis considerable trouble and was easier on the Jews because the sums would be more justly apportioned.

I doubt that at this time the idea of mass extermination camps existed, even in the minds of the top Nazis. The first premonition of them came more than a year later when Bill Shirer emerged to write the then almost incredible story of the first death injections—the report that the Nazis were quietly disposing of "useless" people, victims of incurable cancer, tuberculosis and insanity, rather than give them expensive care. There was also the horrid suspicion that perhaps this category of "uselessness" might be extended to include the régime's political enemies—Communists, Social Democrats and even Jews, but in 1939 the suggestion seemed almost slanderous.

It is worthy of note, I think, that the Nazis went to considerable pains to keep secret these death injections, as well as the later extermination camps, not only from the outside world but from their own people, possibly on the theory that most Germans would be as deeply shocked by this as would the outside world.

Presently it came time for me to go. I had planned with Joe Harsch a visit to Czechoslovakia, but suddenly the Finnish war broke out and I decided to run up to Helsinki for a few weeks (no one believed the Finns could last long) and then return to Berlin, saving Czechoslovakia for later.

When I first mentioned this to the Schultzes, they were greatly excited. If I passed through Denmark on my way back, could I possibly bring some things for the coming baby—for instance, a warm wool blanket for its crib? I told Mrs. Schultz to make me a list. He suggested that I might also have room to smuggle in some Danish butter or bacon—fats were scarce because of the war, and the mother must be well nourished. I told them to put it all on the list.

And when, a few days later, it came time to get my exit permit, Schultz was most helpful. There was much red tape in connection with it, and my German was limited. I wanted it clear that, although I was leaving, my German visa should not be canceled as I intended to return soon. It meant many telephone calls, but in the middle of them his attitude changed and there were several little things which I did not completely understand.

On my last day it was necessary for me to go in person to the government bureau which issued the exit permits. Upon opening one door in this building, quite unexpectedly we came upon what was, in 1939, a shocking sight: a long, patient line of sad-faced Jews, waiting for exit permits which would take them into exile. It was the first of many such tragic lines that I was to see in Europe in the next few years. With a curious, embarrassed expression on his face, Schultz hurried me on by the shabby line. It was not an aspect of the New Germany which he wanted me to see, nor do I think he enjoyed seeing it himself.

Schultz also took me to the station. On the platform, as we waited for my train, he seemed reserved. I brought up the matter of the things I was to bring from Denmark, but he seemed to have forgotten all about the list which had been so important only two days ago.

"It doesn't matter," he said. Then he said, "My being down here with you is almost like the scene when a journalist is asked to leave Germany, isn't it?"

I smiled. "Why is it?"

"Someone from the Propaganda Ministry is always assigned to escort them to the train and see that they get on."

"Well, I suppose it is, then." It was a joke. He was smiling, so of course I smiled again. Then his face clouded.

"But even if you did not come back here," he said, "you would not go to England and speak over their radio to America, telling the things I have told you, or perhaps attacking Germany the way Oswald Garrison Villard did?"

Now I thought I understood. He was afraid I might publish the fact that he, a government official, had asked me to smuggle food in to him from Denmark.

"But I'm not going to England," I said. "I have no British visa."

"But if you should change your plans, you would not do as Villard did, would you?"

"What did Villard do?"

"Attacked us over the British radio from London after accepting our hospitality. He had been taken everywhere and shown everything."

"Did he really? Well, Villard has always been unpredictable. He is a very well-known liberal." That didn't commit me to anything. But, of course, I did not intend to go to England at the time.*

At the Prussian port of Sassnitz, today held by the Soviet army, I took the boat for Sweden. Just as I was about to walk up the gangplank I was stopped at the passport control desk. The tough-looking, young Nazi functionary brusquely took my passport and, opening it to the page containing its German visa, stamped "INVALID" over the page.

"But wait a minute. You shouldn't have done that!"

"I have, in your case, had special instructions from Berlin today."

I took the passport. "But this means I can't come back."

* A few months later I made exactly this type of broadcast over the BBC from London. This was back in those dimly remembered days when a reporter who, emerging from a dictatorship, then "violated its hospitality" by pointing out and criticizing its lack of freedom, was wildly applauded in the liberal press.—WLW.

"That is correct," he said. "Get on the boat."

It was now clear that Schultz had discovered that his superiors in the ministry, not being traveled men, had not been amused by my dispatches.

And a few hours later came the bright lights of neutral Sweden and that overwhelming feeling of relief that one always feels on entering a free country after leaving a totalitarian one.

Behind me was Berlin, darkened in fact for the war and even more in spirit. Behind me were those sinister swastika buttons and the arrogant, shrewd and coldly purposeful men who wore them, ruling a silenced and frightened people.

Behind me was the "Hitler Blick"—a phrase we correspondents had picked up from this frightened folk—that quick glance over your shoulder before you finished a sentence. It went with the feeling that you were watched, that your telephone was tapped, that you never knew quite who you could trust.

It affected not only us foreigners, and the frightened anti-Nazi majority of the German people, but even those of the half world, like Schultz, for I was sure he would not have dared drop his party membership. How could he, reacting confusedly to his mixed background and now caught in the cogs of this war machine, be sure that I would not ruin him with a few careless and casual paragraphs in the American press? No wonder he had blustered so unconvincingly on the station platform.

Most of my opinions on Germany had been founded on what had been written by liberals in the 'twenties and 'thirties. My visit to the country in 1939 changed these opinions only a little. In the 'twenties everybody agreed that the problem of world peace depended on how the "German problem" was handled, but there were sharp differences on how it should be done.

There was, first of all, what might be called the French view, although it was not held by all Frenchmen and many Englishmen and Americans supported it. This was that the Germans were an incurably warlike people, arrogant in victory and cunning in defeat, that the world's only hope of peace lay in a permanently disarmed and subject Reich, and that the League of Nations should be used as an instrument to achieve this.

The opposing "liberal" line was that the Germans were a people like any other, reacting to their environment, and that the way to world peace was to help them to equality with other peoples. Liberals pointed out that the Versailles Treaty saddled Germany with heavy reparations payments, and then made these impossible through the imposition of tariff barriers on German goods. Liberals felt that the machinery of the League should be used to correct other injustices imposed on the Germans by the treaty. Most liberals, for instance, favored a union of democratic Austria with a democratic Germany in the 'twenties, since both nations clearly wanted it. Liberals would also concede that the Versailles Treaty contained injustices to Germany in that many Germans, both in the Tyrol and Danzig areas, were under foreign rule; the League was the instrument which should correct them.

Furthermore, although the treaty disarmed Germany, the League promised that other nations would also disarm, and this had not been carried out. The liberal solution to this particular German grievance was to push for general disarmament, and this had not been done.

And why did the League fail? Liberals felt it was largely because America stayed out, leaving England and France as its dominant powers.

Had our detached judgment and potential military might been behind the League's decisions, the League might have been quicker to redress those German grievances and more firm to check the tendency of Germany or any other power toward aggression.

Since we had stayed out, the other Allies had in general from 1919 until 1933 followed the French policy of enforcing the Versailles Treaty to the letter, and holding down a democratic Germany. But when German resentment against this resulted in Hitler's rise to power, the confused British and French then reversed their policy, weakly yielding to his blustering by giving to an arrogant Third Reich everything which they had denied to the polite pleadings of the democratic Weimar Republic.

Reparations had been abolished. Germany had begun to rearm. German troops had reoccupied the Rhine's left bank. Austria was united to Germany. So was the Sudeten, and England and France had finally gagged over Danzig when it was too late.

Had the Allies, during those two decades, consistently followed the liberal line and adjusted the real grievances of a democratic Germany, that would have kept the peace.

Or had they consistently followed the "French" line and marched into a disarmed Germany at Hitler's first show of defiance, that would have worked.

But they had done neither. They had ignored the pleas of the German democrats, only to yield weakly before Hitler. By ignoring the grievances, they had created Hitler. By yielding to him, they had taught the German people that only force gets results.

What other conclusions could this unhappy people possibly draw?

Fashions in ideological millinery change rapidly. It is curious now to remember that prior to the war European and American liberals felt that Hitler was the result of confused policies toward Germany, and were disposed to pity the German masses who were in his power, rather than to blame them.

I believed this fervently in 1939, and rather regret that it is now so badly out of fashion, for most of it I still believe.

CHAPTER II

THE WAR FROM
HITLER'S HEADQUARTERS

I GOT my first glimpse of ruined Berlin in 1946 as the plane dipped a wing for a landing and we could look out over the shattered walls. I had never liked the city or its people in 1939. In the intervening time I had lived in London during the blitz, when the Germans were mercilessly dumping their stuff on us. All right, now they had had it. But hadn't they asked for it? So from the air I tried to pick out the ruins of the Kaiserhof Hotel, and the Propaganda Ministry, and the Foreign Office, where the party boys had strutted so arrogantly with those menacing celluloid swastika buttons seven years ago.

The next day I took a tour in a jeep. I had a good set-up for gloating, for my ragged, polite jeep-driver had been a captain in the Luftwaffe. But presently, as we rode down once familiar streets, it began to get me. I barely recognized my old 1939 hotel, the Bristol, now a roofless wall. One couldn't miss the Chancellery ruins. But the shop on Friedrichstrasse where I had bought my Leica, the candy store at which I had ignorantly bought and in ten minutes eaten my entire month's ration, these were gone without a trace, and one jagged wall looked like another.

The whole downtown area was deserted except for an occasional underfed pedestrian walking slowly down the middle of the street, avoiding the rubble. It was as though someone had wiped out all of Brooklyn and the Bronx and Manhattan below 210th Street, leaving only the residential sections of the Upper Bronx and Queens; or as though all of downtown Chicago were flat until you got out almost as far as Evanston.

And this was true not only of Berlin, not only of every other larger German city, but of most of Central Europe as well. The whole mid-continent has been gutted, in the sense that taxidermists use that word. Only farms and villages are still there. It is true that, given a few generations free of war, the people might rebuild them. But what of these Germans—sixty or seventy millions of them—hopelessly foraging for wood in the parks or for food in the country?

Now there is, of course, that very comforting doctrine of democratic responsibility—the theory that a people by and large deserves the government that it gets, and must bear responsibility for any régime it tolerates. It is a theory which can smugly and self-righteously be held by us Anglo-Saxons—we dwellers on islands or rich, underpopulated continents—we who so far have been so well insulated from the population pressures of the rest of the world by wide channels, broad oceans and strong navies.

It enables us to say comfortably that a people which deserves its freedom will get it and will then preserve it, or, if they do not, then they must suffer the consequences; they cannot whine that it was all the doings of their leaders and none of their own.

But are all Germans and all Russians to be condemned because they fell into the hands of dictators who could plunge them into alliances and wars without consulting them? Are the people of Spain and Yugoslavia to be despised because they cannot rid themselves of Franco and Tito? And are we—comfortable, free nations who have never felt the iron talons of dictatorship in our flesh—qualified to sit in stern judgment on them when they fail?

I wonder. And, there in Berlin, remembering the terror-ridden propaganda-drenched Germany of 1939, I wondered still more.

Because what is any people—Americans, Germans, Jews, Anglo-Saxons—but the product of its geography and its past? That had certainly been true of the Germany which I had seen in 1939. Molded by those twin forces, the Germans were then still recognizable as human beings.

For the better part of a century the German nation was industrially the most highly developed nation on the continent of Europe; culturally they were second only to the French; scientifically none was superior to them. The little nations which surround them, and which have no reason to be sentimental about them, agree that Europe cannot be reorganized without them.

And what were they like now? I felt that in 1939 I had known and understood them. But I could not say what they were today until I knew what had happened to their thinking in those intervening years.

During the war we had had only distant glimpses of their reactions to the great drama of history in which they were playing so tragic a rôle. Now and then a Swedish journalist would emerge from Berlin to write an honest book, but for the most part the picture had been distorted either by the Germans' own wartime propaganda or by ours.

I decided I was not interested in their newly-emerged politicians, or in the squabbles between their rival democratic parties. In the first place, these had no real power, for this was vested in the victors, with the Germans themselves onlookers at the disputes among the conquerors as to what should be done with them.

In any case, if Germany were to become a democracy, its power would presently stem from its people, so the answer lay here. And since they would be a product of their past, I realized that I must first get those missing pages of their story—what had happened to their thinking since 1939.

And as I thought on how to fill in these missing links, naturally I remembered Albrecht Schultz, as, in fact, I had thought of him many times during the war—wondering how he, in Berlin, was taking the news of Pearl Harbor or Stalingrad, or the July 20th attempt on Hitler's life, or the crossing of the Oder, wondering what had become of him. Were his wife and family buried under some pile of Berlin masonry? Was he rotting in a gray uniform near Vitebsk?

These were the probabilities, the answers I expected to hear when, at the Berlin press camp, I brought up his name to a correspondent who also had been in Berlin in 1939, and now was back again.

"Schultz? Oh, he's still around. Looks about the same, only thinner. Think his family's gone back to America. He comes here to the Press Club a good deal. You'll see him."

The next evening I did, and he was pathetically glad to see me. I could not help noticing that he had on the same plaid tweed jacket he had worn when I first had lunch at the Bristol with him and his newly-arrived American wife. Only now it was frayed at the cuffs, out at one elbow and spotted down the front, for there is no cleaning fluid in Germany. His necktie and shirt collar were likewise frayed.

First came a gush of immediate news—the cable he had had from his wife that they had arrived in the States—his hope to earn money for them and then, somehow and somewhere, to join them again, news of his mother and where they were living, news of the people we both had known in 1939—correspondents and Germans—and, of these last, which had survived the war.

It was only the next day that I could sit down with him and start to fill in those missing pages by getting his own story of what had happened to him and to his thinking during the war.

"Let us start," said Schultz, "with 1940, just after you left Berlin. Previously the people had been told there would be no war, but at last the government admitted there would be one. This came as a shock to many. But, in February, many honest German intellectuals who had been against Hitler—in fact, practically all of them—now started saying:

" 'We will have to get back of him because, since we are in the war, we do not want to see our people go through the tragedy of defeat, and only through unity can we avoid this.' Many honest intellectuals stuck to this thesis until the very end.

"My American wife did not like the war. In March of 1940 I was sent on a trip to Poland, which had been conquered by our armies the September before, and I got permission to take her.

You have asked how much the German people knew of what was really happening. I can say truthfully that very few Germans knew of the liquidation of the Polish intelligentsia, which was going on at the time of our visit. Poland was run entirely by party functionaries and not by the army. Even while we were there, they were rounding up all Polish intellectuals, sending the men into labor camps and their wives and families into other sections, boasting that all teachers were being removed, that no leaders would be left in Poland. Young German officials told me privately of how this was being handled. There was still a certain decency among them. For instance, while we were there, a man in the German labor service had gone berserk and, walking down the street, had shot at every Pole he could see. The German general in charge said: 'What are we going to do? Such crimes must certainly be punished, but it is not under my jurisdiction. I am powerless.'

"However, if one single German soldier was shot by a Pole, in reprisal they shot a hundred Poles. During this trip I interviewed a German police commandant in Warsaw who told me that there was no selection—that whenever a German was killed, they would go to the nearest movie house and collect the first hundred Poles who walked out of the darkness, blinking at the lights.

"This man wasn't a calloused monster. He had on his desk a picture of Frederick the Great (not the Führer), also of his own wife and children. He seemed to be torn between the two symbols, and suffering much from what he had to do. He showed us a photograph of himself which was taken just before the war. Now his face had become lined and his cheeks hollow.

" 'But what can I do?' he said. 'I would much rather be in some other post, but I am here to uphold peace and order. I am sorry that these are the measures which I have been ordered to take.'

"There was in Warsaw much talk of how the Russians were behaving in their half of Poland. How they had stripped the houses of furniture and carpets, even removing electric sockets. Among the Germans, this was talked of as an atrocity.

"Although I heard then no talk of extermination camps, already they were rounding up the Jews of Warsaw and Krakow into ghettos, and a part of my duties was to interview the *Eltestenrat* of the Warsaw Jews. We were taken to the ghetto, my wife, another German journalist and I, in a car by a young German press relations officer who was assigned to conduct us.

"The ghetto was then not walled off. But it was a sad sight. My wife and I would, of course, shake hands with all of the Jews to whom we were introduced, but we noticed that when we raised our hands they shrank back in fear.

"This greatly amused the other German journalist who was with us.

" 'You would think that they were going to be hit,' he said. 'How very Jewish of them!'

"My wife thought it was anything but funny. 'Maybe they have been hit,' she said. They seemed to her like frightened caged animals, watching our every move. Just as we came out of the ghetto, our car pulled up for a moment, halted by a Wehrmacht regiment which was marching smartly down the boulevard, in a column. My wife nudged me.

" 'There go your pals!' she said, a little bitterly.

"There was a curious sequel to this trip. Our press relations officer was a typical blond, blue-eyed German, a party member with very orthodox views, who had never before been out of Germany. He showed us the pictures of his wholesome-looking *Frau* and *Kinder*. To compliment me, he told me that my wife didn't look in the least American. 'She seems typically German,' he said. This was his highest praise.

"Well, after we left I learned that suddenly life had hit this very orthodox, very Hitlerian young German—so Nordic in his thinking—because suddenly and inexplicably he fell madly in love with a Jewish girl who was singing in a Warsaw cabaret, and she with him.

"Every night he would wangle a pass to go to the cabaret and they would then spend the night together—sometimes he would go with her to the ghetto, or she would come with him to the Christian district of Warsaw. They were both completely heedless of the consequences of all this.

"Then suddenly the SS found out about it and he was arrested. He made no defense. He was too honest to lie. He told them that the greatest thing in his life was this girl, that he no longer believed any of the things he had previously been taught, that his career meant nothing to him any more, and they could do with him as they liked.

"He was, therefore, tried and convicted of having had intercourse with a Jewess. I assume, of course, that later he was shot, although I never heard definitely.

"But it shows how powerful life can be; that it can reach through and touch even so conventionally-minded a little Nazi officer, so that his whole world explodes.

"The first great shock to German opinion," Schultz continued, "came a little later that spring, with the attack on Norway and Belgium. I know it shocked me. I remember at the time that I told one American correspondent that Germany would now lose the war, because world opinion would be against her, as it was after our invasion of Belgium in 1914.

"But when these two campaigns both ended, with success in the north and the unbelievable victory over France in July, the people could hardly believe it. The whole feeling was accurately expressed by Hitler's frantic jig before the newsreels, which you saw even in America. That was our popular mood. It was also mine. I remember telephoning my wife the news that Paris had fallen. I couldn't understand why she wasn't glad because, to me, this meant that the war would soon be over. It was very confusing to find that she thought the war had only begun.

"After this came the spoils of war—butter and bacon from Denmark, wines, perfumes and silk underwear from Paris—things that Germany hadn't known for years. Everybody thought the war was fine. Very few of us were looking forward to the future. We were sure that now there would be a compromise with England, and then peace—very sure of this.

"But my American wife was most unhappy. She wanted to be with Americans and so applied for a job with the American Embassy. This was arranged at a cocktail party given by Louis Lochner of the Associated Press, in honor of his son's coming marriage. She went to work in the prisoner of war section because America, being neutral, represented the British and the French in matters affecting those of their men we had taken.

"Before she could get this, I had to ask permission of the press section of the Propaganda Ministry, where I was still working.

"But in September, Karl Boemer, my boss, called me in to tell me that she would have to resign. The war, he explained, was going to be over in fourteen days or less. America would probably be called in to arbitrate between Germany and England, according to the Fuehrer's plan, so if my wife, married to a German official, was working in the American Embassy, we might be embarrassed in the use of this important diplomatic channel.

"He told me this just a few days before the air battle for Britain began.

"On the day of the first big air raid on England, Boemer called us together and said that England would give in very soon. He made it clear to us that this was not just something released to improve public morale, but that he got his information confidentially from the very highest top levels.

"It was a long time before we realized that this air battle for England had failed. Even the top level people had believed the Luftwaffe's figures on the number of British planes shot down; and if these were true, the Royal Air Force no longer existed. Except, curiously enough, there always seemed to be some in the air.

"Our people were also sure that the Luftwaffe attack on England was only a preliminary to an invasion of the country. When week after week went by and this did not come off, enthusiasm for the war began to cool.

"The German people never realized the effect of the bombings on London. Of course, our German papers carried accounts of it which our correspondents in America had picked up and cabled back to Germany. But as soon as the newsreels in German theaters began to show burning houses, the German people began to stay away. Their conception of war was that of the paintings of our victory at Sedan in the French campaign of 1870. Burning houses and refugees wandering on crowded roads were something quite different. Our people didn't want to believe that this was part of war.

"A part in this was also played by Goebbels' order to the newsreels that no dead German soldier, nor even a piece of smashed German equipment, could be shown on a German movie screen. For the people were not to think of the dead; they were to think only of victory.*

"Goebbels also would not allow pictures of German soldiers with their tunics unbuttoned. Reality was kept from our people as much and as long as possible.

"Realism, of course, came home to them in the winter of 1940 and 1941, when the Royal Air Force began coming over Berlin. The raids, of course, were light, compared to what came later, and most people didn't even bother to go to shelters. But the fact that British planes could raid Berlin at all broke their intellectual security. They all remembered that Goering had said, 'My name will be Meyer if any British planes get to Berlin.' Yet what was now happening to them brought with it no feeling of pity or horror or grief for what the Luftwaffe had previously done in London and Coventry. The bombing of England still wasn't real to them.

"After we returned from Poland, I was given a new duty in

* In the early part of the war, our American War Department had an almost identical regulation. No picture could be released from censorship which showed a dead American soldier.—WLW.

the Propaganda Ministry—the task of preparing for Hitler a digest of the news from outside stories. I would condense the news from England and America as we got it via Stockholm, Lisbon or Switzerland, underline in red pencil those parts which were most important.

"You remember, of course, the *Auslandsklub*, which was maintained in Berlin for foreign journalists? Well, one day Goebbels himself happened to drop in there and, of course, the American correspondents, headed by Louis Lochner for the Associated Press, gathered around him and he answered a few impromptu questions. It made a good story for Lochner, who cabled it to America, and the interpretation put on it there was that Goebbels was putting out a peace-feeler.

"This must have worried Goebbels. It appeared in the Swedish papers. But next day I got instructions to omit from my digest of world news any mention of Goebbels' interview to the American press. Of course, it had not appeared in the German papers. Clearly, Goebbels did not want Hitler to know of it.

"On the whole, however, confidence returned. What with the victories, living got better in Germany; there came a period of speculation and many peace rumors, particularly in April and May of 1941.

"Even after the Yugoslav war was finished, troop trains continued to move east. Tank commanders were telling their families that they were being trained to go thousands of miles. Many people thought not of war against Russia, but of a war with Russia against England by way of India.

"It came as a great shock and surprise to the German people when, on June 22, 1941, they found that Russia was being attacked. Yet it was a popular war. There had been no happiness when we entered Norway and Belgium. Many Germans were ashamed. But for years an anti-Bolshevik feeling had been built up in Germany, and now came the stories telling the people that the Russian armies had been crouching on our frontiers ready to attack.

"I remember the very first day of war against Russia. I was in the Tennis Club near Berlin and heard a foreign office official, sitting at the swimming pool with his feet dangling in the water, say that he had it direct from Hitler's headquarters that it would take only four weeks to beat Russia.

"It was explained to our people that Napoleon had allowed the Russians to draw him far into the interior of the country while they retreated ahead of him, whereas our strategy was based on the *Kesselschlacht*—quick encircling movements which would trap the Russian armies before they could withdraw.

"The first surprise came from army officers returning from the front, saying that it was clear that Russia had not been preparing for an aggressive war. We had, in fact, marched all through the Baltic States, hitting only tiny bodies of defense troops and failing to find any large masses to surround.

"Only when we got as far as Dunabürg, on the push toward Leningrad, did we encounter the first really tough Russian troops.

"The first shock to our people came when Rostov was retaken by the Russians and we realized that they still had the power to hit back. There were, of course, many boastful speeches—the first by Dietricht and later, on October 30th, by Hitler, in which he said the Red Army no longer existed. General Halder, who commanded the northern front, had planned a winter drive. But it was Hitler who forced the advance onward toward Moscow, where the Germans were beaten almost at the outskirts of the city. With this defeat, there came bitter criticism of his statement that 'I will command the armies according to my intuition.' Our counter-propaganda explained the defeat to the German people by saying that winter had come too soon, and that our German vehicles had been running on summer oil. But, by now, there were many intellectuals in Germany who were saying that the war was lost, that although we might make another *Putsch* and perhaps even a third, eventually we would be driven back, because there was no chance of beating Russia.

"Meanwhile, I had been having family difficulties. In our

home my sister was constantly denouncing my wife because she trained her child in the American way, not at all like German *Kinder*. Finally my wife resented this and began to talk back. My sister said she would denounce us both and that we ought to be put in concentration camps. So in September 1941 I sent my wife to Italy. She was not well, the second baby was due very soon now, and the climate of Italy should be good for her.

"Actually, I wanted to get out myself. I had been hoping that, perhaps with my experience in China, I could get sent to Shanghai to work in the consulate there and take her with me. But, of course, the Russian war had stopped this dream. Up to now I had, on the war, what you could call the viewpoint of an American isolationist. It was just another European fight for supremacy, in which I felt almost neutral. And yet, in spite of this, I was also under emotional pressure to try to justify my country.

"For, who knew? Perhaps Hitler's New Order would really mean a new kind of European unity, with a new status for everybody—a Europe in which each nation could develop its genius, in which Danes would intermarry with French; there would be no more boundary lines and a real harmony.

"I even believed it so strongly that I would have fights about it with my wife, who could see nothing coming out of this war but bloodshed and misery.

"All of my hopes were shattered by Pearl Harbor. On that particular day I happened to be visiting a German naval officer in the Department of Foreign Navies, which had the task of keeping score on the strength of enemy fleets and where their units were located. Also, of course, convoys and their dispositions.

"As I was talking to him, his telephone rang and he got the news that the Japanese had just attacked Pearl Harbor.

"His first reaction, as a naval man, was that the Japanese were

damned fools, were operating too far from their bases, and
would not accomplish anything.

"But something else was now clear to him. Hitler was not
as big a fool as we had thought. There had been some sense
behind his boastful speeches about how Russia was beaten to
her knees. He had been trying to coax the Japanese into the
war, feeling that if the war were only broader, there might be
a better chance for him.

"But for me, the last light in the world had now gone out.
I went home to write my wife in Italy that from now on I
could promise her there would be no arguments between us. It
happened that our second daughter was born on December 8th
and, therefore, my wife was not told that her country was at
war with mine until the 11th.

"If I had had any lingering doubts, they were settled on the
11th, for that was the day that Hitler made his answering
speech. If he had had any real vision, he could have offered
Europe a new charter of freedom, could have appealed to all
its peoples to rise up against the old, outworn capitalism, and
thus bring about better days. He did none of these things. All
he could say was that Roosevelt was born with a silver spoon
in his mouth, whereas he, Hitler, was a poor man, but would
nevertheless beat Roosevelt in the end.

"When I got down to Italy so see my wife in January of
1942 I found that our German consul in Florence felt exactly
as I did—that all hope of victory was gone.

" 'What shall we do?' he said, and then, 'I can only stay
here at my post and do what I can for Germany.'

"After Pearl Harbor I knew that the war was lost, and openly
said so, among groups of friends that I thought I could trust.
But I was not too discreet and, later, was to pay for this. Already in 1942, the generals were discussing the possibilities of a
coup d'état. The trouble was they had no strategy. They knew
they could kill Hitler, but what then? All we had was two
groups of them—one saying we should fight in the East and

make peace in the West, the other saying we should fight in the West and make peace with Russia.

"All knew the war was going badly. When Leningrad was not taken, the Nazis said that Hitler could win over the peasants, but the proletarian cities were strongholds of Communism which would have to be completely destroyed. We were also not doing well in France politically. Of course, we had Laval, whom the French people hated. But we had tried to win over Pétain, whom we thought all of them would trust, and found that we could not. The old man was wily and stubborn.

"Meanwhile, I was trying to find out about how the war was affecting America. When the *Saturday Evening Post* came in from Lisbon, my friends and I would read articles avidly. *Life* was even more satisfactory in giving a picture of the country's frame of mind. We were very much impressed by the first pictures of MacArthur. Germans had always admired America for her gadgets, for good living, for nice magazines, and as being a place where you could write as you pleased. But we had always been told that America had no military guts.

"But here was a man who was clearly a real soldier. We began to study democracy from a different angle. We thought that now that America was in the war, of course the country must also go totalitarian. But this did not seem to happen.

"Meanwhile, I had a plan. I told my superiors that I would like very much to be assigned to duty in Lisbon, explaining that this would put me close to my contacts with foreign news. To one man, whom I thought I could completely trust, I hinted a little more of my plans.

"Instead of immediately granting my request, the press department of the Propaganda Ministry fired me in May of 1942. But they said that after I had completed my army training, then they would let me go to Lisbon.

"The training was completed in September of '42 and I

then went back to the Propaganda Ministry to see the official there, called Stefan, who had promised me the Lisbon post. He was, incidentally, an ardent Nazi. He now said that he had an even better job for me. I was to be given the rank of captain and would then be assigned to Hitler's headquarters, where I would have the privilege of writing dispatches for Hitler's own eyes and, therefore, from a completely objective standpoint.

"I was badly flustered. I thanked him for even considering me for such an honor, but told him that I felt I should decline and take the little Lisbon position instead—first, because the other responsibility was too great for me and, second, because I felt that the climate of Lisbon would be better for my wife's health.

"Now he became not only very angry but suspicious. There had been rumors about me, he said, which he had not wanted to believe. But any man who refuses a job in Hitler's headquarters for one in Lisbon wants to go to Portugal only because he has decided to change sides in the war.

"I protested that this was completely untrue. But he now said that I was to report for duty at Hitler's headquarters as a private, and if there were any more bad reports about me he would see to it that I would peel potatoes for the rest of the war, if indeed I did not land in a concentration camp.

"I should now like to get ahead of my story to tell what eventually happened to Stefan. Immediately after the collapse he went into hiding in a farmhouse in the British Zone. After a few months he emerged and began, under an assumed name, to organize a new 'democratic' party there. But his identity was revealed and he is now himself in a concentration camp.

"The following winter, 1942–43, brought the battle of Stalingrad, and after that it was not only the intellectuals and the generals who realized that Germany could not win. The year 1943 was also the beginning of the wholesale extermination of Jews, although it actually began at various times and for different reasons in various places. It was started, for instance, in the wake of the armies as they entered the Ukraine. But suddenly the Gestapo discovered that most of the skilled artisans and craftsmen—carpenters, saddlemakers and so forth—in those regions were Jewish, and the economy of the country would not function without them. Then somebody cried: 'Stop! Make them work for us!'

"I personally had heard rumors of extermination camps as early as 1942 and I think that most Germans who now say they never knew of them until they were brought out at the Nürnberg trials, are fooling themselves.

"But it had not been in the original plan. At first the party leaders intended, when Russia was beaten, to divide up all of that country this side of the Urals and to set aside one state for the Jews. But when it became clear that Russia could not be beaten, of course that was out. It was a wave of hysteria which swept through the Nazi party. Early in the spring of '43, sometime in advance of Hitler's birthday, the papers carried the story that the *Gauleiter* of the Berlin district had announced that his birthday present to the Fuehrer would be the fact that his particular *Gau* would then be *Judenfrei* (free of Jews). Presently others took it up and pledged this same thing for their *Gaue*. Jews were always taken away unobtrusively. All Germans heard that they were being removed, but many presumed that they were not going to be taken too far.

"You ask what was the driving force behind it—was it the little party functionaries or were they only following secret orders from the top? I still cannot answer that. I only know that the higher you went into the intellectual hierarchy, the more people you met who knew that this was a shameful thing and should not be done.

"And I also know that a war brings out lots of native sadism. I remember one day when I was doing my army training a group of us, off duty, were watching a ragged, hungry, Russian prisoner of war who had opened the door of an incinerator and gone inside to scrounge the last bit of potato peeling which might still remain there.

"And a German private—ordinarily a normal, good-natured boy—thought it very funny to slam shut the incinerator door, leaving the Russian inside. Somebody had probably been kicking the private around, so it was fun to kick the Russian around.

"Then the argument started. Some of us said: 'Let the man out before he smothers!'

"And then others would say: 'What does it matter? After all, he's only a Russian.'

"This same sadism was operating in relation to the Jews. And also there operated, so far as the petty Nazi functionaries were concerned, a perverted kind of 'orderliness.' For they had been drenched with propaganda to the effect that the Jews were not human and were unclean, and it did not matter what happened to them. Also, as defeat grew nearer, they were suddenly afraid that the few Jews who were left would foment dissension within Germany and, when at last they knew it was inevitable, they said among themselves, 'Now that we're defeated, at least let's finish the job: kill all the remaining Jews, and destroy as much of Europe as possible.'

"It was as Hitler had told Rauschning: that if he lost, all civilization would go down with him. But then, in 1944, among ordinary non-party Germans, another idea began to grow up alongside this one. They said it would be a good idea to help a Jew because after the war then you could protect yourself, prove that you were not guilty.

"My mother and I first learned first-hand how horrible conditions were from a girl whose husband had been a corporal in my company and who was living with us in Zehlendorf. She had a vacation from her job, which was as secretary in the law branch of the German military government in Lemberg.*

* The Poles, who used to own it, called it Lwow, and the Russians, who have since annexed it, call it Lvov, so take your choice.—WLW.

While she was there, early in 1944, 60,000 Jews were killed in that town in several weeks. Sometime previously, the Jews of Lemberg had been crowded into a ghetto by the SS, but then a tunnel was built through the ghetto wall into the gentile section near the opera and Jews would escape in that way.

"She was never able to find any specific reason for the Lemberg pogrom except that the SS, she said, suddenly seemed to go berserk and started killing all the Jews.

"It took several weeks. Only Germans were allowed to ride on streetcars in Lemberg and often, during their lunch hour, the other German secretaries would take a streetcar sightseeing trip to watch the SS troopers shooting the Jews. Then the secretaries would return to tell about it at lunch over a cigarette—the bloody corpses of dead Jews lying in the gutters of the Lemberg ghetto.

"They told her of the body of one Jewish woman which was hanging out of an upper-story window. Apparently she had been shouting for help, when she was killed by a gun butt which came down on her skull from behind.

"In the gutters there were corpses of both men and women and also even of two- and three-year-old children with their heads bashed in, so the other secretaries cheerfully said. This girl was so horrified that she could hardly listen, let alone go to see for herself.

"She said the SS would assemble the Jews in the ghetto and then would herd them in great droves down to the railway station, where they were ordered to undress completely on the platform. This she had seen herself one day when she was passing the station. This clothing was to be sent to Germany to be distributed to the poor in the *Winterhilfe*.

"The naked Jews then would be packed into gas trains, which would move out of the station, and the Jews would then be gassed on the open road.

"The thing was so extensive, she said, that it even had a serious effect on the black market. While it was in progress,

Polish farmers would pay very high prices for suits or dresses of any kind, exchanging butter and eggs for clothing.

"This was because frequently some of these naked Jews would succeed in escaping from the gas trains after they left the station. They would do this either by bribing the train guard or, if the gas mechanism for some reason failed to function, then when the guards opened the doors expecting to shovel out the dead bodies into the ditch by the side of the railway, the Jews, still alive, would make a break for it, rush the guards, and then run naked out into the open country.

"There they would appeal to the Polish peasants for clothing to save their lives, and most of the peasants gave it freely. She did say, however, that a few of the Poles were not greatly opposed to what the Germans were doing to the Jews.

"As soon as all the Jews of Lemberg were dead, she said, the black market immediately reacted, for the price of clothing dropped sharply since the Polish peasants were no longer buying it to replace what they had given to the Jews.

"This girl, of course, was deeply and terribly shocked by what she had seen and heard. But it was, after all, the doings of the notorious SS, and she was still more profoundly shocked by something which happened on the train from Lemberg back to Berlin.

"Two officers entered her compartment. One of them was a railway official and the other an officer in the military government of Poland. Neither one seemed to be a member of the Party.

"Presently the two officers fell to discussing the topic of gas trucks. They were very calm about it and, presently, the discussion grew technical. The railway man said that it was a shame that the trucks had not been developed with more technical skill because, he pointed out, after the Jews had been killed by the gas it was still necessary to lift their bodies out by hand.

"This, he felt, was extremely stupid. Each truck should have had a dump apparatus with a hydraulic lift so that, simply by pulling a lever, the chauffeur could pour the dead Jews into a ditch or pit unaided, thus saving many man-hours of precious labor.

"It was a well-known device, he pointed out; the engineer who designed the present trucks should have employed it, and should now be severely censured.

"And, to the girl, this was the most shocking of all. What had her people come to, when two ordinary-looking, middle-class Germans who had never known each other before should talk in this manner in a second-class railway compartment, with no feeling of shame for what was being done?

"The girl was also thoroughly disgusted with the sloppiness of procedure in the legal office where she worked, and pointed out that the clerks, many of whom felt as she did about what was going on, would often sabotage things, either by mixing the files or by hiding them. She herself sabotaged, not from Marxist principles but from liberal principles. Others, she said, would sabotage because they were paid by Poles who were accused of crimes and, therefore, wished the records lost.

"During this period I was still in contact with many foreign correspondents whom I had met while I was working in the foreign press department of the Propaganda Ministry—there was still a number of Swiss, Swedish and Danish correspondents in Berlin. There was less risk to me if I gave stories to the Danes for, since their country was occupied by a German army, I knew that they would write the story guardedly and in such a way that it could not be traced back to me. It was more risky to give things to the Swedes or Swiss, because their papers were published in a free country and sometimes they would write things which might get me into serious trouble.

"I decided, however, that the outside world should know of this girl's story. I told it to a Danish correspondent and also to a very well-known Swiss one; in fact, I invited him to lunch so that he could hear it direct from the girl herself.

"This particular Swiss correspondent had an excellent German cultural background and was a great lover of Goethe and Schiller and all the old German traditions. He listened to the girl's story in silence but I could tell that he had been tremendously shocked by what he had heard.

"After the girl left he was silent a long time. Then he told me firmly that he was not going to write her story at all, not even after he got back to Switzerland, because he didn't really believe it.* Obviously, he said, the girl exaggerated greatly and was a victim of war hysteria.

"So, what was the use?

"In August of 1944, the British and Americans broke out of Normandy, where they had landed and where the high command hoped they could be contained, and by the middle of the month had overrun all Brittany and were starting the drive to Paris. The Russians seemed ready to cross the Vistula into Warsaw. It was in this week that Colonel General Jodl summoned a meeting of the officers of the High Command to make the speech which was never published. Because I was attached to Hitler's headquarters I managed to smuggle myself in, but afterwards was told to keep mum about it.

" 'We know,' said Jodl, 'that we can't beat America. But Germany must remain *a power in being,* so that when the Russians and the Anglo-American bloc split apart, something of Germany will still stand, no matter how weak or how small. If even only a little remains, this will give her bargaining power when the rupture comes.

"Of course it was not a speech ever intended for the German people, but presently rumors of it began to leak out into the Nazi party and they had a curious effect. Presently the SS began accosting party members, asking them why they no longer wore their party buttons in public. Each had an excuse

* We see exactly this type of reaction in those American intellectuals who have a strong emotional attachment to the Soviet Union, and whose otherwise honest minds reject all evidence of the extent of Soviet concentration camps and what goes on in them.—WLW.

but the obvious reason for all was that it had become un-popular, and the men who had strutted with them most openly during the victories were now the first to hide them away.

"I had a friend, a German journalist, who had never joined the party because, when war broke out, he had been in London where he held a most responsible job. On his return he was told that his superiors had enrolled him in the party several years before and that now he must pay up his back dues. This he could not refuse to do, even though he was never a party sympathizer.

"This man, although previously he had never worn the but-ton, said in 1944, 'Now that others are throwing theirs away, I believe I will start wearing mine.' And afterwards he never appeared in public without it. This was to show his contempt for the stinking cowardice of the real Nazis, who only wore their buttons in the days of victory.

"We had many talks about the war because our ideas were alike. But we also had some arguments.

"I told him that I thought Germany deserved to lose the war, if only because of the war crimes.

"He said this was nuts, and called it neurotic self-castigation, because if Germany was defeated it would be the end of the nation, and as far as war crimes were concerned, what about the British bombing which was killing hundreds of thousands of German civilians who were quite as guiltless as the Jews?

" 'But,' I said, 'what will happen to you if Germany does win and the Nazis bring out their buttons again and strut the streets in victory?'

"He admitted that maybe the Nazis would want to set up a super-state, but 'our German officers who have seen the world and who have come back from the war with anti-Nazi ideas will take care of them,' he said. 'In one quick revolution we will throw the blond gangsters out.'

"No one knew quite what to do, but there were many who hated the Nazis and yet who still did not think that defeat was an answer. In July, the army tried to get rid of Hitler, but that failed and bloody purges followed.

"Meanwhile, I had succeeded in getting my American wife and our two little girls into Denmark, where the food was better and where they would be safe from the bombing. And, finally, I even wangled a brief leave to go up and visit them.

"When in Denmark, of course, I wore civilian clothes. And since my wife and I always talked English, we had many curious experiences.

"Waiters in restaurants always assumed that I was a British agent who had been parachuted in to direct sabotage. But they took this as a matter of course, brought us extra large helpings of everything, and never once did anyone object to our speaking English or threaten to denounce us. Surely the war was drawing to a close, and they thought my appearance was just another sign of the beginning of the end.

"There were a few other changes. In Germany, the extermination of the Jews, which had begun in 1943, was considered completed in 1944, and the party then started on what was left of the Jews in the countries which German armies still occupied. But the Danes gave every help to their Jews and succeeded in smuggling most of them out to Sweden in spite of the SS.

"But they had tried to make a clean sweep in Germany. There was even one man I knew of mixed parentage—a 'Mischling' the Nazis called them—who had hoped to atone for his mixed ancestry by serving in the army, but now he was denounced as a Jew, kicked out and sent to work in the quicksilver mines.

"And now we come to the beginning of the end. It really falls into two periods. The first one was when the Russians, at the end of a terrific drive from the Vistula River in Poland, in only two weeks reached the Oder River, fifty miles from Berlin, in early February. We all thought it was the end and, since it was bound to come, many said, 'Let's get it over with now.'

"The advance through Poland and Prussia had been so fast that the Propaganda Ministry had not caught up with events. Our newspapers were still pounding on the theme that the Oder River must be defended at any cost, even after the Russians had crossed it. There had been no time to build up the slogan: 'Defend Berlin or die.'

"Then suddenly the ice broke on the Oder, and the Russians seemed to be stopped, although they managed to hold a few bridgeheads.

"Now the party people said: 'A miracle has once more saved Hitler. It will be a long time before the Anglo-American Allies can cross the Rhine. We will have time to re-form.'

"It also meant that Goebbels could regroup his propaganda line. First, there were slogans that Berlin must be defended at any cost, and then this was backed up by a campaign to build dread of the Russians. A propaganda tour for foreign correspondents was arranged to a city in Lower Silesia, which had been retaken from the Russians. Swedish, Swiss, Danish, Dutch, Hungarian, and Belgian correspondents who were still in Berlin returned with atrocity stories on the Red Army, backed up by affidavits, and these were also printed in the German press, with the result that many people who in early February would have welcomed speedy liberation by the Russians, now began to dread the future although they knew it could not long be avoided.

"With the Russians just across the Oder, even High Command privates, like myself, were drawn into an organization to defend central Berlin. My outfit, consisting of five officers and four privates, had charge of compiling every day that report on the foreign press which went to Hitler's headquarters and to a few other high officers. Now we were also assigned to defend a sector of Tiergartenstrasse, a hundred meters long.

"To this end, they issued to us a rifle each, two bazookas, two tommy guns, and four hand grenades. With this equipment, the nine of us were supposed to hold that hundred meters against the Red Army.

"Now, the hard facts were that we were office workers. While we had had some basic training in the rifle, the other weapons were at the best useless, while the bazookas were an actual menace because, lying there on the floor of our office, one of them might get nicked by a bomb fragment during an American air raid and blow us all through the roof. So, unobtrusively, we put them in the empty cellar of a nearby bombed-out house.

"Berlin, as the end approached, was filled with many rumors, and now and then one got a glimpse of what was in the minds of those at the top. A friend of mine, who was one of Goebbels' confidential secretaries, one day told me that the previous afternoon he had found Goebbels pacing up and down his private garden in deep thought.

"It seems that he had just reread *Gone with the Wind* and it had now suddenly struck him that this book proved beyond any doubt that, following a war, no nation can ever hope to return to its prewar status—not even in its thinking.

"Not only was this true of the vanquished, Goebbels said thoughtfully, but also of the victors. Win or lose, the old ideas were gone forever. At least, said Goebbels, that was the lesson of this book and it was, therefore, a dangerous book for Germany. Perhaps its German translation should be immediately banned, because any German reading it, and thinking of this war, could not help coming to that conclusion.

"Because of the dearth of reliable news, we in this little office assumed great importance. We were known to be in possession of all facts from the outside world. So majors and colonels would drop in casually, start a conversation with me, a mere private first-class, and say:

" 'You know more than I because you get these radio reports from abroad. Are we going to have strength enough to hold off the Russians? Will the Americans reach Berlin first?'

"They even wanted personal advice. One night during an air raid, a major asked me if I thought he should get his wife and children out of Thuringia. In my opinion, 'would it be taken by the Russians, or by the British and Americans?'

"Although no one was supposed to think of the possibility of defeat, tremendous interest was concentrated on reports from abroad that one of the decisions at Yalta had been the lines of demarcation between the future Russian, British and American zones of Germany. No word of this had been published in the German press but all the high people had heard rumors, and would come to me, a private, saying they understood the British papers had published a map showing these zones and did I, by chance, have a copy?

"What did we ourselves think? More or less as we always had. Those of us who had previously been against the Nazis were still at it. One lieutenant in my outfit said:

" 'I am not going to fight to the last man. If I were on the other side and it was in danger of losing, I would go on to the bitter end. But not for this régime.' He said this to me, a private.

"On the other hand, the one Nazi we had in our outfit was continuously saying that, any day now, the Allies would split in two, and thus give Germany a chance to survive.

"Yet even this man did not protest when saner heads suggested, as a means of getting out of the ridiculous duty of defending the Tiergartenstrasse, that we change our offices by moving out of the High Command building into a vacated school in Dehlen, a Berlin suburb far removed from the inner defense circle which was to be held so strongly.

"Organization was already so bad that when we checked out of the defense organization in the High Command building, no one thought to assign us any defense duties in the new suburban area, and I doubt that anyone remembered to assign other men to our hundred-meter stretch in the Tiergartenstrasse.

"Meanwhile, well-authenticated rumors of furious palace intrigues began to leak down from above. It appeared that Goebbels and Himmler, who had been at swords' points, had finally made friends and were discussing the possible ousting of Hitler, in the hope that what was left of Germany could then join the Western Allies in fighting the Russians under the leadership of Field Marshal Tschoerner, who was suddenly being built up by Goebbels' propaganda machine as the 'savior of Germany' because his defense line in Silesia seemed to be holding for the present, and he had even retaken a few villages.

"I also noticed that many underlings whom I had known in the Propaganda Ministry and who in the past had always slavishly followed the party line, now for the first time and as if by order, were speaking unflatteringly of Hitler, telling stories that he had had several nervous breakdowns and was constantly trembling, unable to stand erect and always having to hold on to a chair or a table.

"Germany's world was crashing and yet, curiously enough, much of life went on as usual. In February and in March, the food was all right: many of the things in the shops were available as usual, except in the center of Berlin where, on February 3rd, the most terrible raid of the war completely flattened the government district.

"From then on, the city communication system broke down. And since the government was unable to start the streetcars running, it covered up this failure by building anti-tank walls across the boulevards, presumably for defense. By now, even old men and boys were being called into the *Volkssturm* and there were tremendous appeals to defend the city.

"And suddenly, for the first time, signs of a sullen underground began to be apparent, because all over Berlin appeared the single word '*Nein!*'—chalked, painted or scrawled in huge letters on walls or shop windows.

"This needed no explanation to Germans at that time. It meant we should refuse to defend Berlin.

"Goebbels, at first, was at a complete loss. Finally, he ordered

his men to paint a second *'Nein!'* under the first, explaining that
this now meant we would never surrender our capital city. But
it was a feeble answer.

"At about this time I was approached by a German sergeant
I had known, who asked me to join a secret group already
working under the command of a Russian major who even now
was sitting in Berlin, with plenty of money to build his organization.

"When I asked him its purpose, he explained that it was 'anti-
Western' but this didn't mean we would have to fight the
English and Americans. Instead, as soon as possible after the
surrender, it wanted to see an independent Germany which
would, nevertheless, be very close with Russia.

"He explained that while he himself had never seen the
Soviet major, the group was already well organized and financed.
Their members were all in the German army but their secret
organization provided them with forged travel orders to get
about the country, and also supplied them with printed pamphlets.

"For a minute I should like to jump ahead of my story to
tell what happened to him. After the surrender, but before the
English and Americans came to Berlin, he and I together went
to the Russian commandant of Zehlendorf, asking permission to
start a German paper. This was refused because the Russians had
already started the *Tägliche Rundschau*. Later he joined its staff
as a reporter. Still later, the Russians ordered him to go to
Moscow where he would be trained in journalism, to become a
German member of Tass, the Soviet news bureau. This he
has tried to avoid, feeling that there are too many orders to
be taken, and afraid that his life will depend too much on
the personal impulses of his employers.

"But, back to Berlin in April. In the first week began the
general exodus of all ministries. Day and night papers were
burned as one branch after another left the city, and the public
began to feel very uneasy. A part of the foreign press—for in-

stance, the Japanese correspondents—left for Bavaria. Yet, in many ways, things went on as usual. Rations were distributed as before.

"But there were many curious scenes. Of course, you remember Joyce, whom the British called Lord Haw-Haw and who, even when you were here in 1939, used to broadcast in English from Berlin. He was still talking bombastically over the air of a great regroupment of forces, of the German army's rallying again for a huge pincer offensive which would extend from Silesia in the north to Pomerania in the south. It was the official government line and many who heard him believed it.

"But not those who saw him broadcast, shaking with fright, nor those who saw him afterwards at the bar of the *Auslandsklub*, where he sat every night slumped over, trying to get stinko, drowning his fear in cognac, but the fear was too strong; his wife trying to keep up with him, drink for drink, reassuring him, comforting him, telling him Germany was still so strong that she could never be beaten!

"While many believed that the Russians could be held, all felt there was no hope of stopping the Western advance. In fact, because of the general fear of the Russians, the British and Americans were now viewed as liberators. For instance, I knew one man in the *Sicherheitsdienst* (in America you would call this the FBI) who had supplied me with passports and visas when I was taking my family to Italy in 1941. In these last days, I ran into him one evening on the elevated platform.

"He told me that he had just been ordered to go to the Saargebeit, where he was to take command of a 'Werewolf' organization which would resist the Western Allies.

" 'I will go since I must,' he said. 'But as soon as I arrive I will offer my services to the Americans and tell them everything I know of this organization. If the Americans want me, all right. If they don't, then it's bad luck for me. But I will not be foolish enough to pretend that this war is not lost and forever finished.'

"The average man felt this way, but not those at the top, where things were sharply divided. The High Command, for instance, did not want to let the Western powers in, although already we were getting stories that our soldiers did not fight as well in the West as those who were holding back the Russians. But at the top the actual line-up was Goebbels and Himmler on one side, who favored resisting the Russians and letting in the West, while on the other side was Ribbentrop, who had the idea that if we resisted in the West but allowed the Russians to advance, this would frighten the Western powers into negotiating a separate peace with us.

"Between these two factions was Hitler, who favored first one and then the other, and seemed to change his mind every minute. And that was Germany's leadership as the war was closing.

"Among the people it was different. When, toward the end of April, the Americans crossed the Elbe, we all hoped that this meant that they would make a speedy tank dash toward Berlin, and everybody was saying that no one would fight the Americans. Their spearhead advanced and we even heard that one patrol got within sight of Potsdam. No one could understand why this spearhead presently pulled back across the Elbe. Perhaps the big dash for Berlin would not come until a concerted offensive could be started from both sides. No one in Berlin believed that the conquest of our city would be a Russian job alone. But, of course, none of us knew then of the agreement between the Allies. Even had we heard, we would not have believed it because we would not have wanted to.

"On April 14th Potsdam was bombed and, with nearby burning ammunition dumps exploding all through the night, the rumor raced through Berlin that British and American parachute troops had landed—a rumor born only of the wish.

"Finally, on April 16th, the big final Russian offensive started. On the 18th it was clear that they had broken through our defense lines southwest of Berlin. Hitler's headquarters had been in special underground bunkers in Zessen, southwest of Berlin, which contained a whole cement village, mostly underground, where the General Staff had worked.

"This was now moved to Wandsee. But by now our communications were terribly disrupted. A colonel who stopped by, in the hope of picking up some information from me, told me that co-ordination was so bad that the few fighter bombers which we had hoarded to strafe the Russian spearheads were, by mistake, bombing our own counter-offensive spearhead.

"But by now I had my own worries. On April 17th, the second day of the drive, a warrant for my arrest by the Gestapo arrived at my home in Zehlendorf. Curiously enough, because of the confusion and the shortage of men, they had been able to spare no one to arrest me, so the warrant was delivered by mail with instructions that I report immediately.

"At last it had come. My family in Zehlendorf got word to me in Berlin of this warrant. But since I knew the bombing on April 14th had undoubtedly disrupted the machinery, I took the chance of pretending I had never heard of the summons, but carefully stayed in Berlin and away from Zehlendorf until the 19th, when I got in touch with my mother who told me that so far no one had showed up.

"I learned, however, that someone else who had received a similar warrant by mail, had reported to the Gestapo and was told there that a number of warrants had been mailed out at that time, charging various people with the serious offense of dissipating the state morale. However, the Gestapo explained apologetically that since then their files had been blown up, and so other summonses would be issued later.

"I wasn't greatly worried for now the Russians were only thirty miles from Berlin, and everybody in the city knew that the big final push was on. All knew that tremendous changes, great convulsions, were ahead for us. And yet, if you ask me what I remember most vividly of those last days when the Third Reich was dying, I can only answer quickly that it was the weather. That made everything unreal, and we seemed to be moving in some fantastic dream.

"No one longer feared the Hitler terror. All realized that what was left of our Germany was only a rapidly shrinking island, that foreign armies in great waves would presently sweep over what was left of it into Berlin itself, that great changes were ahead for our people, that nothing of life as any of us had known it could ever again return—all of that, we knew, was true.

"But the first lovely, warm, radiant days of spring had just come to Berlin. The maybelles and magnolias were blooming on every lawn, and all around was the fresh green of the new grass. The young girls were walking springily down the street in gaily-colored dirndls, with their white socks and bare calves and fluffy golden hair.

"In the evening people would move their wicker furniture down off their porches into the garden, to enjoy the soft warmth of the spring night and the sultry smell of the magnolias. No Russian fighters or bombers had yet come over Berlin. We would sit in the stillness of the spring evening, just as you and I are sitting tonight, only then we would hear the guns in the distance. We knew, of course, that what was left of our army was fighting without hope Germany's last battle—knew it but could not believe it, for the only real thing was the spring.

"At my office work went on as usual. We would take our turns at getting the foreign news, and more and more we had to depend on the BBC and the Voice of America.

"At night we would tune in Radio Moscow for the Russian communiqué, and then *Soldatensenderweste,* the big Allied propaganda station addressed to our armies.

"According to his political beliefs, each individual officer on duty would accent the news. For instance, our one Nazi lieutenant would try to ferret out any hint of Allied discord from either the London *Times* or *Pravda.* The *Times,* incidentally, still came in regularly from Lisbon. The rest of us, instead of trying to conjure up imaginary disputes between the Allies, were more interested in what we could gather of their plans for Germany after our defeat.

"Although the Propaganda Ministry claimed the power to censor us, actually we were on our own in those final days. At the very end we were reduced to two lieutenants, one captain and myself, plus a sergeant who acted as stenographer and another messenger who brought us material from DNB.

"Our final routine was to write one complete report every morning which went to various high officers, plus an hour-by-hour news flash report telephoned directly to Colonel Krummacher, who passed it on to Colonel General Jodl at Hitler's headquarters.

"By now the general disorganization had become so great that Hitler's headquarters would even telephone us, asking what Radio London was saying about the drive into the Harz Mountains or Wurzburg.

"At one time we were alarmed to discover that our little group had slightly changed the course of the war. For instance, we put special emphasis on a United Press report that Patton was making a quick thrust in the direction of Munich. Actually, it turned out to be only a small task force sent to liberate a camp for war prisoners, in which one of Patton's relatives was confined. But Hitler's headquarters, having no other information on the situation and following our lead, sent a special élite Panzer force to counteract Patton's drive. The tiny task force was badly beaten up but, in the meantime, Patton's real push, which was farther north, succeeded in breaking through to get as far as Kassel.

"Finally, the confusion deepened until nobody knew anything. Although this, understand, was never quite admitted to Hitler.

"And at the close, one of our messengers came back with the story that Hitler was still in his Command Bunker frantically issuing orders over the few of his many telephones that still were working, giving precise commands that divisions which actually had surrendered should now be ordered to retire to towns which the enemy had held for many days—fighting a paper war with men and guns which existed only in his mind.

"At the very end I went out to Zehlendorf to be with my mother there when the Russians came, since I was the only man of my family.

"The occupation was nothing: we simply woke up in the morning to see, out of the windows, a Soviet regiment marching by, and presently patrols came from house to house, making sure there were no arms. After a few days, I was rounded up into a civilian internment camp but when, at the end of about three weeks, my record had been examined and nothing was found against me, I was released.

"There were, of course, a good many rapes but I also think these have been exaggerated, and I know that some of the girls who still do the most talking about it are actually the ones who resisted the least. It seems to me that these girls, who still tell anyone who will listen, are as bad as the Russians who did it.

"During that period, between the time the Russian army entered Berlin and two months later when the British and Americans were allowed to enter, there was much uncertainty and uneasiness. For instance, there was the case of the Kaiser Wilhelm Institute, which contains all our top scientists and physicists and would be like your Rockefeller Foundation, if that were a state monopoly. In June, many of these were offered fine jobs in Moscow with promises of good houses, summer places in the Crimea, and high salaries. Many accepted. Some might not have wanted to go, but they did not know where else to turn, nor did they know what would happen if they refused.

"To the rest of us, this gave reason to believe that Berlin would soon be occupied by all four powers, even before the official announcement was made.

"Then we started guessing what sectors of Berlin would be assigned to the various powers. And we had certain aids in our guesses. When we heard that the Russians were removing machinery from the Telefunken Building, and when we saw they were taking the electric motors from *S-Bahn* trains which ran through this district, and also machinery from the Zehlendorf Station, then other Germans would say to us who lived in this area:

" 'Aha! This means that your district will be in the British or American zone! Congratulations!'

"Until the other Allied troops arrived, and particularly during the early part of this period, the pretty girls either stayed off the streets entirely or would only venture out wearing dark glasses and with their hair combed very tight back and held in an ugly knot. This was probably unnecessary but most of them enjoyed hoping that it wasn't.

"Of course, none of us knew what to expect, but when, on that first morning of occupation, a Soviet major knocked loudly on our door, we were all very much afraid. When we opened it, he began to ask us questions, but since he spoke no German, we did not know that he only wanted to search the house for arms.

"When he discovered that my aunt spoke Russian, of course he then addressed himself entirely to her. They talked for quite a while and soon it became clear that he was trying to persuade her of something to which she would not agree. My aunt is a very stubborn woman.

"Then, glancing around impatiently at the rest of us, he said something to my aunt and almost pushed her toward the stairway. As she went up, she called very fearfully back to us that this was what she had always feared, this was the end.

"I was the only man in the house. Although I knew what would surely happen to me, I went down into our cellar and there finally found a hammer, which was the only thing that looked like a weapon.

"Hiding this under my coat, I went back to the first floor. As I fearfully and quietly climbed the stairs, I was surprised to hear no screams or sounds of struggling; nor was there a stillness, which would have been even worse. Instead, through the half-open door of my aunt's bedroom, I could hear voices, apparently arguing.

"I found them sitting side by side on her bed, and she was shaking her head violently. Very earnestly and patiently, the Soviet major was trying to persuade her that only through the Marxist philosophy could the great masses of the people find real happiness. My aunt was telling him indignantly that he was a very young man who never before had been outside of Russia and, therefore, could not possibly know what he was talking about.

"I believe I have already said that my aunt is a very stubborn woman and extremely set in her ideas."

CHAPTER III

U-BOATS

HAVING, in the Berlin of 1939, watched the sad-faced leaders of Berlin's sad, dwindling Jewish *Gemeinde* sitting at a table in the Hotel Bristol for their weekly meeting, I was amazed to learn that there still existed in Berlin a *Gemeinde* of Jews who somehow had managed to stay in the city all during the war, surviving deportations, extermination camps and Allied bombings.

The community center of this forlorn little *Gemeinde* was in what had been a large, comfortable suburban residence. An electrically lighted Star of David glows over its entrance, and light comes through its bay window, for there are no restrictions on electricity for Berlin's surviving Jews, as there are on other Germans. Likewise, a roaring furnace kept the big house pleasantly warm all winter, in this city where no German had a fire for which he did not chop the wood from trees in the city's park.

Inside it was pleasantly furnished, and in the big living room were rows of folding chairs which faced the table on which was another Star of David, and at which religious services were conducted. It was here that I talked to Mrs. Sophie B., who was one of so few to survive.

She was a short, plump, pleasant-looking little woman in her mid-forties, with brown hair and brown eyes, and in the normal place and time would have lived out a pleasant and placid life as a suburban housewife.

When I told her that I would like to hear the story of the Jews who survived the war in Berlin, because I remembered seeing their leaders meeting in the Bristol just at the start of the war in 1939, she nodded her head slowly and without smiling.

"There is much guilt on some of the leaders of the Jewish *Gemeinde*," she said. "So many people were being killed! Each Jew was, after all, a man. And some thought, 'If I help the Nazis, perhaps I will save myself.'

"Of course, our best leaders had left, our truly great ones. Before the war in Berlin there were two *Gemeinden*—one liberal, and one orthodox. The liberal leaders had very big words in their mouths, fine-sounding liberal words, but they saved their own lives first. Of course, they promised as soon as they got to America, everything would be done for us here. But nothing happened.

"The orthodox left also, and as they left they also had big words for us. Their big words were about holding to the faith of our fathers and in hope for the future. But they likewise saved their own lives and left us here. Mind, I do not blame any of them! But nothing happened from any of the big words.

"Yet, we had one great man, Dr. Karlbach of Hamburg, a deeply religious man who, in 1939, had a chance to leave but did not.

" 'I belong here,' he said. 'Here is my people.' Still later he had another chance to leave, but would not. Already the trucks were leaving for the death camps, but he said his place was in Germany to comfort his people, and so went out himself on the last truck on the final day. He had a great soul!

"And now I am one who is left out of so many! There is today in Berlin only this tiny *Gemeinde*—we who were able to hide during the war. Of the many tens of thousands who once lived in Berlin only 7000 remain, and this is counting quarter-blood Jews, half-Jews, and full Jews. Of these last, only 1600 are left.

"Of this 7000, only 25 are children, and none of these children are full Jews. In fact, there are only 100 left between

the ages of 20 to 22. All the rest of the children, and all of
the aged, were taken away to be killed—as useless Jews. I can
remember in the deportations of 1943 when a little child was
taken from the apartment in which I lived. The mother at
the time was very sick, and I shall never forget the screams
of the little girl when the storm troopers threw her into the
truck.

"In addition to these 7000 who are now in Berlin, another
1700 have returned from concentration camps. Then, outside
of our *Gemeinde*, there are about 4000 true *Mischlinge* who
wish to get in today.

"These *Mischlinge* have a little Jewish blood, but they were
baptized as Christians, have never belonged to the *Gemeinde*,
and during the Hitler régime were proud not to be considered
Jewish, boasted that they were not.

"But since the war has ended, these *Mischlinge* are the first
to go to the Jewish welfare organization and say that now
they must be helped, because they are really Victims of Fascism,
and have suffered terribly under Hitler!

"In all there are now 12,000 (and most of these are not
even *Mischlinge*) who today claim that they have at least a
trace of Jewish blood and are entitled to be considered Jewish.
They remain in the Protestant or Catholic Church in which
they were baptized, but are applying for certification as Jews,
demanding Jewish aid, asking permission to emigrate to America,
and expect that the Jews should advance the money for their
transportation!

"To get back to myself: when the war began in 1939 I was
living in our nice little flat with my daughter, who was then
15. Two years before I had sent my son away, when he was 16.

"You say that it is your impression that in 1939, at least
70 per cent of all Germans were against what Hitler was doing
to the Jews? It is also mine. It may even have been higher, but
it was at least that. Of this I am sure, because I have talked
to many Germans who did not know I was Jewish, and so I

could get the truth. Those who now say there were never any good Germans are most unfair. If there were not many good ones, I would not be alive today.

"The trouble for Jews in Germany all started with Hitler. When I first came to the country from Poland with my father, as a little girl after the last war, I hardly realized that I was Jewish. The Germans had always had class differences—between rich and poor, between those who were *Hochgeboren* and those who were not, but not differences of race.

"There were in 1939 many German people who had never liked Hitler, and still others who had seen that what he did was not right. These helped us whenever they could, sometimes at great risk. There were many German intellectuals, educated people with great souls. These were very much all right.

"But of course it was not all of them. There was a man in our apartment house who was an enemy to the Jews, but did not know that I was Jewish. He was well educated, and was an SA. He had been taught to believe that the Jews were the worst people in the world, and quoted from the Bible to prove this. When I would defend the Jews, he would say:

"'No! It is not enough, what we do to them!' So if there were good Germans, there were also others whose souls were small and mean. All too well have I learned both of these things.

"Things were not so bad for my daughter and me until October 1941 when I got a letter from the Jewish *Gemeinde*, saying that we must leave our flat and come that very day to their office. We did not know until we got down there that it was for evacuation. But all the other people who got those letters on this day had to leave that very week.

"My father had been a Polish Jew, and all of these had been evacuated as early as 1939. Now they were evacuating Germans. But because my husband, who was also Jewish, had lost a leg fighting for Germany in the other war, we were allowed for the time being to remain. However, we were told that we must move out of our nice apartment and into a small flat in an apartment house which was a 'Jewish house.' Our previous apartment had not been a Jewish house. It had nine rooms and now we would have only three, and into these we must also take three other Jews.

"Now began a terrible time for us, dreading every ring of the doorbell or the telephone, because almost every day the Gestapo would search us. Even if we were not taken ourselves, each of us felt the pain from the other people and feared as they did.

"Our food cards had a big 'J' on them, which meant that we were allotted no fruit, no butter, no eggs, no fish, no meat, and no vegetables, but could only buy bread, margarine, sugar, and noodles, and also could not appear in a queue at the food store until after four o'clock. By this time most of the food had already gone.

"Yet, we lived only because each Jew had at least one gentile friend. It is true that some of these 'friends' only brought you something because they knew they would get something back. But more often they expected nothing at all. Sometimes complete strangers were our friends. They would come in the night and leave vegetables and eggs, and you would never know who had brought them.

"Even in the shops, the people would frequently give us something which was not allowed, and for which they would be severely punished if it were found out. Our butcher would send us meat in the night, when he easily could have sold it for more on the black market at less risk. Of course, in better days I had always been a good customer in his store. Maybe it was friendship, maybe it was business, maybe it was both.

"Yet we were never safe. If the Gestapo, in searching our rooms, would find even a tomato, they would take away an entire family, because fresh fruit was forbidden to Jews. Each day we would either hear or read of one suicide after another.

Former Senate President Lindenau, seventy years old, tried three times to kill himself and succeeded only on the fourth.

"My daughter, who was then 18 and working in a Jewish hospital, told me of this, and also said that every day a new suicide attempt would come in. Also, the Gestapo was coming there to take away even those who were sick in bed.

"Only after the war did we know that they were being sent to the crematorium. We heard rumors of this, of course, but we did not believe them. We thought that they were being sent away to work.

"Some Germans knew of the crematoriums, of course, but I think that we Jews believed it even less than did the Germans, because we did not want to.

"For instance, in the shop where I worked the proprietor had a young son whom I had known since he was a baby. One day he came back on leave from the army, and I saw that his hair was grey. When I said, 'Why, what has happened to you, Hans?', he began to cry.

"Because I had known him since he was a child, I took him by the arm and led him home. Finally he said the reason was 'that I must shoot so many Jewish people!' But still I could not believe it. I thought he had said this only as a joke to frighten me. But if it was a joke, why should he cry?"

"Don't you think," I asked Mrs. Sophie B., "that you could not believe it only because you did not want to, but that most of the German Christians really knew that it was so?"

There was a long silence. Thinking she had not understood my clumsy German, I began again.

"Don't you think—"

"I know what you mean," she said, "but I can't be sure." There was another long pause. "The SS, and people like that, of course knew." Then there was still another pause. "But it would not be fair to say that a great many knew. Many, of course, like me, heard the rumors, but decent Germans would not have wanted to believe them any more than I. They wanted to think well of their people.

"For almost three years, when I was in hiding, no one knew that I was Jewish. I had a lot of friends—some of them in big uniforms, who could not believe that I was not for Hitler, and always talked freely. I could not honestly say how many knew, but I know that many did not, even until the very end.

"While in 1939 it was true, as you say, that at least 70 per cent of the German people opposed Hitler's Jewish policy and would give help to the Jews even at risk to themselves, as the war went on this percentage began to grow smaller. In 1940, with the big victories in Norway and France, it dropped to 60 per cent. It now seemed to many Germans that Hitler had, after all, been proved right about many things, so perhaps he was also right about the Jews.

"Nineteen forty-one brought more victories, in Yugoslavia and in Greece, and of course the big advance into Russia, and with this the percentage dropped to about 50.

"Nineteen forty-two brought still greater advances into Russia, the Nazis seemed unbeatable, and the percentage then dropped to its lowest point, which was about 40 per cent. From then on it was to rise, and by 1943 it had returned to 50 per cent for and against the Jews, because the people had now seen that the things Hitler promised were not coming true. The German nation began to awake from its sleep, its humanity was reawakened, and it saw that there had been a great injustice against the Jews. From then on, until the end of the war, it was never less than this; at least half the German people were glad to help the Jews when they could.

"Also, many more were beginning to realize what was happening to the Jews. Each German family had at least one member in the war, and many of these would come home to whisper of the things they had seen done, but say, 'It would be my head if anyone heard I had told it.' So no one had the courage to speak up, for the Gestapo spies were everywhere.

"The darkest days began for me in 1942, and this is when I have learned to hate many of the German people. On February 28th the Gestapo came and fetched many people from our house. My daughter and I happened to be out at the time, but as we were returning the housekeeper met us down the street and said:

"'Do not go to the apartment, because the Gestapo is waiting!' So we turned and went in the other direction, to find friends who would shelter us.

"It happened that that night there was a big British air raid, and a bomb which landed in the street destroyed much of the front of the apartment house, but the back stairs could still be used.

"However, I decided that now it would never be safe to go back there, because the Gestapo had already come for us once, so now we must go into hiding, living however we could and with whoever would take us in, under false Aryan papers instead of Jewish papers.

"I did not even dare to go back to the flat. As for the furniture, I knew a Christian widow with three children who I thought was a friend of mine. When she had been in trouble I had loaned her two hundred marks,* and I now told her she could go to the flat and take the furniture away.

"About six months before I had already succeeded in getting false papers for my daughter which showed she was Aryan. I was helped in this by a very fine German, at great risk to himself, not for money, but only to help us. He was killed by the Russians on the last day of the war.

"My daughter's false papers, however, showed that she was three years younger than she actually was. They were the papers of another girl who had been killed in a bombing. As a further protection, my daughter had joined BDM (the Hitler Youth for girls) and because of this difference in age they thought she was very clever for her age and wanted to make

---

* About $40.

her a leader. This, however, she refused, explaining that she was not worthy of it.

"For the time being my daughter seemed safe, but they were terrible times for me. We Jews who were living undercover in Berlin were called 'U-Boote' (U-Boats), because most of the time we were submerged, and only now and then dared come up to look around. In the last months of the war I had false Aryan papers, but from 1942 to 1944 I lived without either papers or food cards.

"Sometimes, even at eight o'clock in the evening, I would not know where I would sleep that night. During this period I would frequently meet friends on the street who would tell me where two or three other Jewish friends lived, but of course I would never write down the addresses, for fear they would be found on me if I were arrested. We who were living as 'U-Boats' did not really want to know the addresses even of our best friends. In case of torture, it was better so.

"Of course, we had good German friends whom we could call on the telephone. One such man owned a liquor factory, and every week he gave me a bottle of *Schnaps*. This was not allowed, but he knew that I could trade this *Schnaps* for bread.

"Also I was getting food from a Polish labor camp. Because my father had come from Poland, I could speak their language. The prisoners were good to me and gave me work there. But one day a German overheard me speaking in Polish and for this I was denounced because, as a German, I had lowered myself by associating with Poles.

"I was now desperate for a food card, when I heard the sister of the German widow to whom I had given my furniture the previous year, had a job in the food card distribution office. I thought perhaps she could help. One day I telephoned the widow, making an appointment to meet her in a coffee house.

"It happened at the time that my daughter had got diphtheria and had been taken to a hospital, so of course food was no problem for her.

"When I got to the coffee house the widow seemed very happy to see me.

" 'I feared you had been deported!' she said, and then also explained that she should have paid me the two hundred marks she owed me long ago and was sorry she did not have the cash with her. When I asked her if her sister could help me get a food card, she said she would surely do this and that I was to telephone her next week. I told no one, of course, where I lived. But then I made one mistake.

"She asked after the health of my daughter, and when I told her that she was then in the hospital, she said that it would be nice if we sent the girl a postcard wishing her speedy recovery, to which we would both sign our names. This we did—I writing on the card my daughter's name and the address of the hospital, as she watched me.

"Three days later I got a mysterious telephone call from my daughter in the hospital.

" 'Mother, think of it!' she said in what was intended to sound like a joking tone. 'Over here they believe that I am Jewish! You must bring me papers proving that I am not!'

"When one lives as we had had to live for years, one learns to think fast and shrewdly. I addressed three envelopes to fictitious addresses in the city of Cologne, but instead of putting letters in them, I put only pieces of old newspaper, stamped and sealed them, took them to the post office, sent them by registered mail, and got a receipt for each letter.

"The next day I went to the hospital to see my daughter, and was allowed to speak to her through a window. In whispers she told me that the hospital had just received an anonymous letter saying she had entered the hospital under false papers and must be reported as a Jewess.

"I now went to the head nurse, who was a great lover of Hitler and terribly firm.

" 'You must bring papers at once!' she said. I explained to her that our family had come from Cologne, and that I had already written three letters asking for copies of the papers (I showed her the registry receipts), but that due to the bombings which had disorganized the mails, perhaps the answers would not come for a week.

"This gave me time to plan. Of course, I had poison which I could take myself if I were caught. But I knew that if my daughter took it, they would pump it out of her at the hospital. So I went with this great trouble to a German friend. She listened to the story and then insisted on taking me to another friend of hers, to whom I should tell this story.

" 'For although she is a party member and a great lover of Hitler,' explained my first friend, 'nevertheless she is a mother, and perhaps she will help because you are also a mother.' It was my last hope, and so together we went to see the party member at her home.

"As she, in turn, listened to my story there was no change in her face. Then she was silent. At last she said:

" 'As a German to a Jewess, I should not help you. But as one mother to another, I will do what I can.' And she asked us to come back the following day.

"When we returned she had everything planned. First she handed me a paper on which was the address of a house which had been recently bombed, and in which had lived a Christian woman and her daughter who had both been killed. She told me to memorize these, and then to go to the food office in which worked a particularly stupid clerk, whose name she also gave me and to whom I was to explain that my daughter and I had lived in this house, but had been bombed out, and that I now wanted a certificate, saying that we had been evacuated from that neighborhood.

"The problem now, however, after I had done this, was how to get the information to my daughter giving this new address. I knew, of course, that her mail would be read. So I wrote her a letter which began, 'Dear Daughter, Our nice house in such-and-such a district, such-and-such a street, has been bombed, and our landlady, giving such-and-such a name, is dead.' This she could give to the head nurse.

"But the next day, when I arrived at the hospital, I found that there was still so much contradiction in our story that the head nurse had not believed it, and she told me that I must report to the doctor in charge of the hospital. I knew that he, of course, would be a party member.

"I noticed that he had a very intelligent face. Suddenly he interrupted my story by pulling out a piece of paper.

" 'Do you recognize this writing?' he asked.

" 'Why, yes,' I said before I thought. Then my heart almost stopped beating, for I realized that it was the handwriting of the German widow who owed me the two hundred marks and who had my furniture. It was, of course, she who had written the anonymous letter.

"So then, pretending to look more closely, I said quickly, 'No, I find I am mistaken. I do not know it.'

"The head doctor was looking at me closely. Very faintly he smiled, and I saw that he did not believe me. Then he said:

" 'You look pale. Don't you want to sit down in this chair?'

"I did, and he gave me a glass of water. I could not help noticing that he wore his party button in his lapel. After a minute he held up the letter again.

" 'What it says is not true,' I said.

" 'It is an anonymous letter,' he said and, folding it, he began tearing it into pieces.

" 'We never pay any attention to anonymous mail,' he said, dropping the pieces into his wastebasket.

"I could hardly believe it. Then I said:

" 'My daughter tells me she has passed the negative test for diphtheria, which shows she is now over the disease. Can I have her back now?'

" 'Not yet,' he said. 'She is still weak, and should stay three or four days longer with us.'

" 'Please!' I said, and he saw that I feared that if she stayed longer something else might happen. So he said:

" 'Very well. She may go now if you wish.'

"I must now tell something which happened in Berlin only last week. From a friend I have learned that this Nazi doctor who pretended that he believed my story has been removed from the hospital, on the charge that he was a member of the party, and put to cleaning streets instead. When I learned of it, I wrote out this whole story and sent it to another doctor in the hope that it would help this man. Because even if he was a party member, he was a man of great soul."

"And the widow who wrote the anonymous letter?" I asked.

"The last I heard she had gone to Silesia during the war because of the air raids in Berlin. Because I thought she was one of my best friends, I had given her my furniture, but later she realized that if my daughter and I were sent to an extermination camp, then she need never repay me those two hundred marks.

"And this," she said bitterly, "is the German soul! Or at least it is the soul of some of them.

"Those were terrible days for us. And because I had false papers and no one knew I was Jewish, they talked freely and I could learn both the good and the bad.

"And the bad were not all Nazis. Once during this troubled period I returned to the district where we had first lived. One of our neighbors had been a Christian woman, with whom I had had a lawsuit, and after she lost her case she hated me, ever since. This woman had, incidentally, a Jewish husband.

"Suddenly, on the street, I almost ran into her. When she saw me, she wheeled on me, stared at me, put her hands on her hips, and said:

" 'What! Look! Look!' and then, pointing at me, cried loudly, '*You* are *still* here!'

"I was terribly frightened. Suddenly I saw a tram, jumped aboard it, changed three or four times, and for two weeks I did not stay in the same house for two nights.

"This woman's Jewish husband now gets packages from the Joint Distribution Committee. *She* does not. I don't doubt, however, that she has applied.

"I know still another woman, who is half-Jewish and who, during the war, denounced many other people as Jews, but who has now applied for aid to the Joint Committee because, she says, she has suffered so much at the hands of the Nazis.

"In 1944, when the Hitler luck was over, began the period of discontent in Germany. There was no more extra food, rations were cut, and more sons and fathers were killed. Now you would hear openly very bad words against Hitler. Also, you would hear Germans say:

" 'It is an unhappy, a tragic thing we have done against the Jews.'

"When the bombers would come over, people would say:

" 'Had we kept the Jews in Germany and put them in the fifth stories of the houses, perhaps the English would now keep away.'

"They were not saying this as a joke. Others would say:

" 'Now it must go badly with us, because of how we have treated the Jews. If we had helped them, perhaps it would not be so bad. But in England and America, the Jews are united against us.'

"And those of very small souls would say:

" 'We must have victory because, if not, we will have to give back to the Jews what we took from them.' But even this shows that many of these small people believed that if the Allies won, the Jews could be brought back, not realizing that Hitler had already killed almost all of them.

"With such people it was not love of Fatherland that made them fear defeat; they have no big souls and no honor, these little people. Yesterday they cried, 'Heil Hitler!' and now they cry, 'Heil Moscow!' I have learned to hate many of the German people.

"In November 1944, the last official transport left Berlin, loaded with Jews, and the Nazis announced that their removal was complete. However, several thousand of us were still left in the city, all of us underground. The Nazis suspected this, and presently informers got around among the Jews who were left. For instance, an Austrian Jew disclosed the hiding place of eight hundred Jews who had been sleeping in air-raid shelters. When it was discovered who had told, the other Jews wanted to lynch him.

"Then there was another that we all hated—a young girl, very beautiful, blonde with blue eyes, who was actually a Jewess although she did not seem to be. She went the rounds of the various coffee houses and cafés of Berlin, and she had a keen eye for a Jewish face.

"She was always with a Gestapo man. When she would see someone she remembered, she would nod or speak and then give the sign to the Gestapo man following her, who would say:

" 'Come, show me your papers!'

"Her name was Stella. We all heard rumors of her and greatly feared her. Only a few days ago they caught her in hiding, and the story of her arrest was in the American papers here in Berlin. She now says that she did this only to save her own life. But was her life worth the lives of so many? And yet, to take hers now, will not bring back the lives which are gone.

"She also says that she did not know that those whom she denounced were being sent to crematoriums, but thought only that they would be deported. And who knows? It might well be true. After all, in those days I did not know myself."

For a minute she was silent. Then she said:

"As soon as the war ended and we were free, the first thing I did was to put in a frame and hang on the wall the yellow star which I had been compelled to wear. I did this so that I would never forget those terrible days. Yet I have forgotten them, and now I find I am very glad that I have forgotten so much."

After a minute she said, "It is good to forget. That is the only way."

✦

And now a few final paragraphs on the relations between the German Jews and Christians in Berlin.

The first story I have from a German friend concerning a distant relative of his family—the penny-pinching old widow of a careful, thrifty, Prussian bureaucrat, who now produces proudly from the depths of her shabby black handbag a well-worn anonymous postcard written to her many years ago, just before Hitler took power, and warning her against buying at a certain Jewish-owned department store.

My German friend, who has a keen sense of humor, says that his miserly old aunt had traded there, not out of any sympathy for Jews, but because their prices were a few *pfennig* cheaper, or anyway so she thought.

Today, with the swastikas gone and the four Allied flags flapping in triumph over Berlin, the old lady with quiet pride produces this card, which she has kept carefully hidden for a decade and a half, explaining:

"I always thought that some day this would come in handy."

It is her credentials as an anti-fascist.

In the old days here there used to be many stories about Jews and half-Jews who, either through persuasion or bribery, obtained from the registry clerks of small German villages certificates proving that their parents, grandparents, or great-grandparents had been baptized as Christians, thus putting them outside the operation of Hitler's Nürnberg Laws, which classified as Jewish anyone having less than two Christian grandmothers. There were many jokes about this.

Today, the wheel has again turned full circle, and the gossip is that many people who are either full-German or part-German are now attempting to bribe or persuade the district clerks to give them certificates proving that they have either one or more Jewish ancestors, thus entitling them to the extra rations and privileges such as help in getting out of Germany to America.

Berlin jokesters are as busy with this new situation as they were with the old one.

"Have you heard," they say, "that so-and-so, the former Nazi *Gauleiter*, still wants to keep on fighting the British, and so has bought himself two Jewish grandmothers and is leaving for Palestine?"

The jokesters also insist that there is a black market in Jewish grandmothers, with daily quotations; if the Russians move more troops into their zone the price rises, but if rations are increased, then it falls.

They also pretend to have read in the want-ad columns: "Will exchange grand piano in good condition for guaranteed Jewish grandmother."

The only significant thing about these jokes is that they are an exact parallel, in reverse, of the ones of yesteryear.

Jokesters also insist that there exists, for those who cannot afford Jewish ancestors, a "poor man's market" where one can buy letters proving that during the war the purchaser has defended a Jew.

The kernel of truth behind this not-too-pretty jest is that German Jews who have survived have sometimes been more generous than discriminating in giving testimonial letters to German Christians who might have helped them in the past, but I never heard it seriously charged that any such letter was ever sold.

However, sometimes they were issued to German Christians who may have helped some Jews but denounced others, and Berlin's Jewish *Gemeinde* moved to correct this situation by passing a most sensible rule under which no individual Jew should issue such a letter until after the case had been investigated by the *Gemeinde* and found to be worthy.

My final witness on the subject of the Jews at present in Germany is a Christian German *Geheimrat*, who deservedly occupies a trusted position with the Allies because his anti-Nazi record is solidly based on service in a concentration camp during part of the war. The *Geheimrat* reported that there no longer existed in

Germany what even Hitler himself could call a Jewish "problem," and that this was largely due to the decent behavior of the German Jews themselves.

At the time of the collapse, most Germans expected that when the Allies took over, Jews would immediately start moving into the foreground and pushing into big jobs, but this didn't happen. Instead, the German Jews who emerged from hiding or returned from concentration camps showed a real understanding of the German problem, and a complete realization of the fact that many Germans had been quite as strongly opposed to Hitler as they were.

However, continued the *Geheimrat*, there did seem to be a minor Jewish "problem" in the American occupation and particularly in the Counter-Intelligence Division, which included many German Jews who left for America in 1937 or 1938, and were now back in American uniforms. Some of these behaved, the *Geheimrat* thought, as though there could be no such thing as a good Christian German, and he said that their reports to Washington might unfavorably influence American policy toward Germany and hinder a growing understanding of the true German situation. He also added that this was not only his own observation, but he had heard Americans say the same thing.

I have heard Americans make remarks similar to those of the *Geheimrat*, for there is in the American Army in Germany a certain amount of anti-Semitism, and a good deal of this is focused on former German refugees in American uniforms, the critics insisting that when they were mustered in, captain's commissions were passed out to them on one day and naturalization papers the next.

Actually, the situation, as I saw it, was a mixed one and would point to the conclusion that Jews are only human beings like the rest of us, a platitude which everyone but Hitler seems to have accepted all along.

It is true that a few of these former refugees from Germany seem to have returned to gloat rather than to govern, a behavior-pattern which is understandable if it is not admirable. On the other hand, far more others, because of their real understanding of German character and conditions, are furnishing our American Army with its most intelligent guidance. While they waste no maudlin sympathy on Nazis, they surprise the average German by treating him with understanding as well as with true dignity. If anti-Semitism is eradicated in Germany, it will be through the fine example set the Germans by this last group, rather than through the feverish efforts of the first.

I have a final and sad little note on race relations in the Fourth Reich.

Under Hitler the usual insult of small boys quarreling on the school grounds was to call each other *"Du Jude!"* (You Jew!) Now, completely without any official admonitions from above, this has been abandoned, and instead they now say, *"Du Neger!"*

One of the new de-Nazified schoolteachers gave her little class a talk on this, saying that the new term was no better than the first, because it was thoughtlessly cruel to emphasize race differences, and as undemocratic as it was unkind.

The following day a little girl raised her hand in class: "I told my *Mutti* what you said yesterday," she said, "and *Mutti* said, 'Your teacher must have an American Negro soldier for a boy friend.' "

"So what can you do with them," said the teacher, throwing up her hands helplessly, "if you do not have the parents with you?"

CHAPTER IV

WANDERERS

BECAUSE I had seen in Warsaw the start of the mass migration of Eastern European Jews out of the Soviet zone toward Western Europe, when I got to Berlin I was anxious to see the second step in this tragic mass movement, and so visited the big Jewish refugee camp established by the Americans and in charge of Harold F. Fishbein, whose better-known brother is secretary of the American Medical Association.

The outside of the camp was not prepossessing and I would guess that it had formerly been an old military barracks, built at least thirty years ago. But it was clean enough, there were no guards at the gate, and the sad-eyed, undersized and underfed-looking inmates did not seem overcrowded and are free to go and come at will. There was about the whole place an air of easy informality and I was not surprised to find that even the door to Director Fishbein's simple little office was standing ajar, and assumed that someone had carelessly left it open.

Harold Fishbein is plump and not too tall, with that type of large round head which anthropologists describe as Alpine. He is Jewish in race and Christian in religion, and speaks with a slow Midwestern drawl, as unshakably American as apple pie à la mode.

Having, since 1939, seen some of and read still more about the war, I have increasingly of late been wondering what it was about. There was originally the now unfashionable theory that it was a struggle between the "have" nations and the "have-not"; that Germany, Italy and Japan, being late-comers in the sphere of world empire, were demanding a revision of colonies or spheres of influence as an outlet for their rapidly expanding population and their energy.

In 1939 the British would have told you most earnestly that the war was to prevent the spread of dictatorship, and to preserve the freedom of small nations. A glance at the map would seem to prove this theory hardly less outmoded than the first.

However, most of the people on our side felt that it was a bloody struggle to keep such qualities as kindliness and friendly understanding from being swept off the earth; limited and hazy objectives, if you like, but not less important for that.

However this may be, anyone who steps through the open door of Harold Fishbein's office is pleasantly surprised to find the hackneyed qualities of friendliness and human decency so very much alive in that dingy little room and in his kindly face, and it is refreshing to realize that many simple-hearted boys on our side, who were naïve enough to think that it might even be worth dying to preserve such things, have perhaps not died in vain.

But first, a little background on the camp. It was started early in 1946, after the world was taken by surprise by the sudden mass movement of Jews out of Soviet-controlled Poland, and its population of transients at the time of my visit was 1300. The exodus had begun in the fall of 1945, with the Jews traveling any way they could, moving in bands for protection. As a result of the outcry and to fill a real need, this and other camps were set up.

Where were these people going? Their first destination was the Palestinian Brigade, stationed near the Belgian-Dutch border, but the real goal of almost all of them was Palestine itself. Many were questioned in this camp, and only 50 out of 5000 expressed any desire to go to America. From this camp they were taken in truck convoys across the Soviet-occupied zone of Germany, in which they feared to travel alone. Arriving at the border of the British zone, they left the trucks and made their own way.

So far this mass exodus has been in two waves, Fishbein explained. The first one consisted largely of Jews who had managed to survive the German occupation in Poland. They were, for the most part, skilled and trained workers whom the Germans had locked up in camps and used in war production.

"And our biggest job," said Harold Fishbein, with great earnestness, "is to make these people back into human beings again. Because for six years they were taught that organized society was their enemy, and every man against them. None of them could have survived who did not develop the cunning of a wild animal, for that was how they were treated.

"Our hardest job is to explain to them why it is no longer necessary to carry over into this new life the ethical patterns they learned under the Germans in Poland. For instance, if the Germans arrested any Jew, it was a matter of honor for the others to get him out of jail.

"But now, however, they are not arrested because they are Jews, but only for such things as black market offenses, which are offenses against all the people. At first, the Jews who came from Poland felt honor-bound to get their people out of jail, no matter what the offense. I had to explain to them that our trials were fair trials, conducted by Allied military courts, and that only the guilty would be punished. It was not as it had been under the Gestapo.

"Formerly they had to steal from the Germans in order to live; it was the only way. Now I explain to them that when they steal food or clothing from the stores we have here, it is not like taking it from the German government; they are really stealing from each other. When they finally understood this, our camp was free from any theft.

"But it was hard. At first they could not understand why I would not help them when they were arrested for minor offenses.

" 'But you too,' they would say accusingly, 'are a Jew!'

" 'No,' I would say to them, 'I am an American official. If you have done wrong, I should not help you just because you are a Jew. Whatever I would do for you, I would also do for a gentile.'

"Here we must teach them all over again that at last they are once more a part of society. The law is once more their law, the courts are their courts, the army and the police are not here to hound them, but to protect them.

"But, after six years, you cannot blame them for being distrustful, when at the border most of them have been robbed by either the Russian or Polish frontier guards, and even when they get into the American zone, they are sometimes robbed here. Only last night two who recently arrived from Poland were held up and robbed in a subway station of 20,000 marks by two American soldiers. They are of all classes. We now have six men in the camp who, when they lived in Poland before the war, were worth half a million dollars each. Today they are as miserable as the rest."

56173

At this point there were footsteps in the corridor, and in through Harold Fishbein's open door came a boy in his teens, led by a bearded Jew of about 50. The dialogue was in Yiddish, but since this is very close to German, I had little trouble in understanding, and Harold Fishbein occasionally translated a phrase I did not know.

"'*Herr Direktor*,' said the bearded Jew, 'this boy claims to be a Jew and wants admittance here, but he has no papers to prove it, and also he has not been circumcised.'"

I looked at the boy. He was slender and handsome, with clear blue eyes, a small straight nose, and very light brown hair. It could be true, of course, that he was Jewish; it could also be true of Greta Garbo. The boy seemed uncertain and frightened. Through the open door we could smell the soup kettles of the noon meal.

"My son," said Harold Fishbein, "how old are you?"

"Fifteen."

"You say you are Jewish?"

"My mother told me she was Jewish," said the boy. "She is now dead."

"And your father?"

"I do not know where he is," said the boy, "but I do not think he was Jewish."

"You have observed Yom Kippur?" * asked Harold Fishbein.

The boy hesitated. "What is that?" he asked.

"You have heard of Rosh Hashana?" *

The boy shook his head. "I do not understand that either."

The bearded Jew shook his head skeptically.

"Why do you want to come to this camp?" asked Harold Fishbein.

"Before she died my mother told me I had a grandmother in New York," said the boy. "I want to go there to see if I can find my grandmother."

"Where were you born?" asked Fishbein.

"In Breslau," said the boy. He explained that he went east with his mother, and after she died had spent most of the war at a Russian work camp in Poltava in the Ukraine. The Russians allowed him to leave November 2, 1945.

"You went to school there?" asked Harold Fishbein.

The boy said that he had had eight years of school in Breslau, but there had been no school in the Soviet work camp, and very little to eat. Only work. But after seven o'clock at night they had been free to do as they liked. After the war he had returned to Berlin and had been living at the mission. No, he had no papers or anything to show that he was a Jew, but he wanted very much to go to America to see his grandmother. We could see that he was very worried.

"Well, my son, you can go over to the office, and we will register you," said Harold Fishbein, after a thoughtful pause.

For the first time the boy smiled. The bearded Jew, frowning and shaking his head doubtfully, now led him out through the open door and down the corridor past the room where the soup kettles were bubbling.

"I always give them the benefit of the doubt," said Harold

* Holidays as well known to Jews as Christmas and Easter are known to Christians.—WLW.

Fishbein. "Of course, many try to get in who do not belong. Probably we make some mistakes. But after all, they are hungry and miserable human beings or they would not come here, and it is no great crime if we feed a few by mistake."

"Are mistakes such a problem?"

"I can tell you of one. As you know, the Germans this year are very hungry. Shortly after our camp opened, a girl arrived and asked to be registered as a Jewess. But her identity card showed that her religion was Evangelical Lutheran. She explained this by saying she was the daughter of a gentile mother and a Jewish father who had not been married, and because of this she had been put in Theresianstadt concentration camp. When we started to check on this, she explained that possibly her records might now be missing, because she had not been there during the whole period of the war. But because we try to err on the side of right, I took her in.

"But after a short time the policeman whom I had appointed for the camp came to me, telling me they were sure the girl was a liar and should be thrown out. It developed that she was a nymphomaniac, infected with gonorrhea, and that she had infected others in the camp.

"When I questioned her again, she did not seem so sure of her previous story, but asked if she could not be allowed to stay anyway, saying that she could be very useful to us as a spy to smell out Nazi collaborators from the Baltic States who might have attached themselves to us, claiming that they were Jewish.

"I felt we should keep this sick girl in camp, at least until she was cured. However, my policemen, who were now very angry with her, had searched her room and discovered pictures of her with her father and her brother, who were all dressed up in Nazi uniforms.

"When we confronted her with these, she caved in completely and got out of camp as fast as possible, not even waiting to be cured.

"But back to that boy. He is representative of the second

wave which has come through this camp. They are for the most part Jews who fled ahead of the Nazi armies, starting in 1939. First many of them fled into Lithuania, then into Russia. After 1941 the Soviet government moved these Jews into central Russia. Now that the war is over they are returning from the steppes of Russia. I wouldn't call them anti-Communist, but they have a negative attitude toward Communism; they don't like it. Also, they have felt the manifestations of anti-Semitism in Russia—from the Russian people, but not from the Russian government. So they are moving west again, seeking the security of Jewish surroundings here."

At this point another ragged man shuffled through the open door. He had a minor request to make of Harold Fishbein—something about a change in sleeping quarters—and then, for my benefit, Fishbein questioned him. He was twenty-seven years old and had formerly lived in Poland. When the Nazis entered, his wife went to Latvia and he went first to Esthonia and, finally, they were reunited and lived for a time in Vilna.

And how did he like it under the Russians?

"Well, even though they fed me, I still did not like the Communists. It is not where I would want to live."

"And why not?"

"Because," he said, "it is not a good system, for if a man has earned something and bought it, then that thing should belong to him—it should be his to keep."

"Why did you leave Poland?" asked Harold Fishbein.

"But why should I stay there? When they see I have a large nose, they will kill me!" He shakes his head. "It is very bad in Poland. I would not go back there for anything." Then he goes out.

"One of the big troubles we have," explained Harold Fishbein, "is that these people bring with them, even after all their suffering in the war, the racial conflicts of the people among whom they have lived. I have to settle angry disputes between Polish Jews and Lithuanian Jews. Both of these groups are usually against

WANDERERS   103

German Jews. And, of course, all Jews are against the *Mischlinge*, those of mixed blood, part Jewish and part gentile.

"For instance, we have here a little hospital which is largely run by our people in the camp. Three of the girls working in the hospital were Polish Jewesses, not trained nurses. When we asked them to carry out the urine, they refused, saying:

" 'Let the Germans do it! When they were in Poland, didn't they make us clean the toilets with our tongues? Let them come in and do it now!'

"But one of the nurses in the infirmary was a German Jewess and this infuriated her. She said these girls were fools, that the SS in Poland had done many horrible things, even as it had in Germany, but there were also many good Germans who had helped the Jews against the SS; if this were not true, she herself would not be alive today, and that such an attitude toward all Germans was not only silly but dangerous because it would make future trouble for all Jews. It was the old conflict between Polish Jews and German Jews. Finally, I explained it to the three women in terms of responsibility, saying that this was our camp and it was our duty to take care of it."

At this point two more shabby figures came through the open door, and Harold Fishbein explained that they were the two who were robbed by the American soldiers in the subway the night before. They were very thin, and clad in greasy rags, with their trousers held up by knotted ropes instead of belts. They had uncouth, long, black kinky hair and quickly-shifting, nervous black eyes which were piercing as gimlets and, at the same time, fearful. Six years was a long time.

They came in to inquire if anything had been heard of the 20,000 marks of which they were robbed by the two American soldiers the previous night. Their names were Jacob Kliger and David Josephovich. They had just arrived from Poland and were on their way to Palestine.

"Why are you leaving Poland?" asked Harold Fishbein.

They both shook their heads. "The Russian system is not a

good one for Jews," explained Josephovich. "Also, there is anti-Semitism even in Russia, and we think it will come every place. That is why we want to go to Palestine."

"What do you think of the government in Poland?" asked Harold Fishbein.

"Well," said Kliger, "the government is a good one for the Jews. It has many Jews in important places."

When Harold Fishbein expressed doubt of this, Kliger insisted, "Yes, there are many Jews, although many of them are under Polish names.* In fact, they wanted me to take a good position in the government, but I refused. I wanted to leave."

"And why?"

"Too many people are opposed to the government there," said Kliger, shaking his head. "There are too many gangsters who shoot at people from behind trees."

"There are gangsters in every country," said Fishbein, "reactionary elements among all peoples."

Josephovich now said that they were glad to get out when they did, as there was a new ordinance which provided for five years imprisonment for illegally leaving Poland, and that recently fifty people were arrested for crossing the Oder.†

But Josephovich and Kliger were still concerned about their stolen 20,000 marks, which they said they bought from Russian soldiers near the Polish border. There was, of course, little hope that they would ever see them again, but Harold Fishbein patiently explained that the American Military Police had been notified, and also pointed out that these German marks would buy nothing anyway.

* This does not check with my own observation. None of the Jews I met in the Warsaw government was using any such subterfuges, and none was ashamed of his race.—WLW.

† Again I don't believe this, or rather it could be true if the fifty were gentiles, for in Warsaw Jacob Berman assured me that Jews were free to leave Poland, and I have never heard it since denied. It is possible, however, that Polish frontier guards, trying to extort money from the fleeing Jews, could have lied to these people by way of asking for bribes.

"One could have bought a suit of clothes with them," insisted Kliger.

"Then you haven't lost anything," said Fishbein. "Because we'll give you both good clothing here in the camp."

"But what will happen when we come to the British zone without money?" insisted Josephovich. "We hear there is very little to eat there, and one must sell one's clothes and belongings in order to live."

"In the Jewish camps there," exclaimed Fishbein, "you will get more margarine than the English even in England are allowed to have. So you see," he said soothingly, "you have really lost nothing at all. You will be taken care of."

After those six years it was clear enough that Kliger and Josephovich still were not sure of this, but they went out.

"For so long they have been able to trust nothing," explained Harold Fishbein, "and it takes time to get them out of old ways. For instance, not long ago I started a drive against the black market. I called them all together and explained that these laws had been made by their friends, and it was now their duty to help us stamp out the black market.

"When they understood, they agreed to help me and, after talking it over among themselves, one group came to me and said they had decided to start a real drive against such activities; there was much enthusiasm for it, and they were going to begin the operation with a big banquet, at which plans would be thoroughly explained, and asked me if I would let them have, out of our stores, fifty packages of cigarettes for this banquet.

"When they told me how many people would be there, I suggested that perhaps twenty-five packages would be enough. They said of course this was true, but they needed the other twenty-five packages so that each man could have *Schnaps* to drink at the banquet, which they could easily get by trading the extra cigarettes for it at the black market! So you see I must be patient.

"But if you want to see the whole story of this camp, come back next Thursday morning. Then they will be loading a hun-

dred of them into trucks to start out across the Soviet zone into
Hanover. You should see their faces when they climb into those
trucks! All that they have with them is worthless German money
as they go out into the unknown. But they also have courage,
and now the confidence that everywhere along the road there
will be Jewish helping hands.

"When I see their faces as they climb into that truck, I can
forgive them anything that they do."

I told him I would try to come on Thursday, thanked him and,
as I left his little office, started to close the door.

"Don't do that!" He spoke for the first time sharply, and then,
"I have a reason for it. You know, we give these people food
and clothing here, but that isn't what they really need. I leave it
open so that they always know they can come in and talk to me.
They need someone who they feel is interested in them and to
whom they can tell their troubles. For the past ten years no one
has cared what happened to them, and now it's the most important thing I can do. Their faces may look thin to you, but what
they are really starved for is love."

I thanked him again and, at the end of the corridor, I turned
to look back at Harold Fishbein's open door, and it occurred to
me that perhaps the cynics were wrong, and that a lot of friendly
open-hearted boys who failed to come back from this war may
not, after all, have died in vain.

CHAPTER V

WHAT DO GERMANS THINK NOW?

IT IS hard for a white Southerner in the United States to find out what a Negro really thinks, for an Englishman to learn what a Hindu thinks, a European to learn what an Arab thinks, and particularly difficult for an American now to discover what Germans really think, for the reason that all oppressed or subject peoples never tell their rulers quite all of the truth, but instead tell them what they now want these victors to believe they think.

From the start I realized that this would be what I would get if, in American uniform, I wandered about Germany asking its people what was now on their minds. So in order to get the truth I engaged three German legmen, two of whom were well-trained reporters and all of whom, I think, were dependable. Their assignment was simply to circulate among their friends or people they happened to run into at bars, to try to work into the conversation casual questions such as: What do you think of the Americans and the Russians? When did you first decide that Germany had lost the war? When, during the war, did you first hear of the extermination camps?

I also asked my legmen to bring me a little biographical background on each subject so that I could have some kind of picture of what kind of man it was that had the opinion, but promised them that when it came to print, the real identities would be disguised.

One of these scouts was Schultz, and after he had been working for a few days he came in with a puzzled look.

"I must take back something which I told you the day you first arrived," he said.

"And what's that?"

"You remember I said that we were all guilty, although now we did not want to believe it, that all of us knew at least something of the atrocities?"

"Yes."

"That was true of many like me, but after all I worked in the Propaganda Ministry and gathered foreign news for Hitler's headquarters. I listened daily to Radio London where all such things were broadcast in great detail. Sometimes I talked with important people, or at least talked with others who had spoken with them. I could not avoid knowing most of the truth. It was part of my job. But since I have been talking to ordinary Germans, as you said, I am surprised at how many of them knew very little of the atrocities and did not then believe what they heard."

"Because they didn't want to believe?"

"That is true, but I find there was still another important reason. All Germans remember and resent the First World War propaganda when the British accused us of cutting the breasts off Belgian nuns, crucifying Canadian soldiers on barn doors, and even boiling the bodies of our dead soldiers to get fat for soap. All of these things the British propagandists sent to neutral countries where they had some effect at the time, and although after the war it was all disproved, it made the Germans very angry."

"I remember it well myself."

"The German people remembered it even better. So, in this war, British Intelligence got many accurate reports of what went on in concentration camps, and of the extermination of the Jews. These were broadcast to Germany over the British radio, but Germans who heard them, or who were told of them by other people, often only laughed and said, "The British are again up to their old propaganda tricks.'

"For instance, only today I talked to a friend about the crematorium, and he said, yes, he had heard such reports during the war but did not believe them; he thought they were only echoes of the British radio.

"He tells this story. You know, we have in Germany a brand of soap called 'Kernseife' which is as well known as Ivory or Palmolive in America. One day this man, with another friend, was in the washroom of the Hotel Kaiserhof, and the second man happened to be washing his hands at the basin with a little bar of *Kernseife*.

" 'You know,' said the first man, 'that *Kernseife* is now made out of the pulverized bones of Jews.' Whereupon both men laughed."

"Why did they laugh?" I asked.

"Because neither one believed it. They thought they were making a joke at British radio propaganda which was then saying just that sort of thing. Since I have been asking people your questions, I find that people like this are more numerous than I had thought, so I would like to modify, a little, what I told you on that first day."

Without any more preliminaries I present the most interesting and representative of these case histories which these three men gathered.

The Case of Hermann L.

He is a dentist, now back practicing his profession after demobilization. He has never had any Nazi party affiliations. If he had had, the Allies would not now permit him to practice dentistry, and he would have to be employed at manual labor.

He says he knew nothing about the gas chambers for Jews, until the war ended and he read the story of the Nürnberg trials.

"I had a number of Jewish friends among my classmates at the University of Berlin. In 1930 I planned to marry a Jewish girl, but she objected." (Here he took from his desk a letter from the girl, which he showed to my scout; it read, "You know I am Jewish. I feel that I would be able to bridge this gap. However, my parents don't see it this way, so nothing can be done about it." Therefore they separated.)

"Most of my Jewish friends disappeared during the early

years of the war, some of them managing to emigrate from Germany. Where the others went, I didn't know at the time. I knew that concentration camps existed, but I did not know how bad they were. I thought that in them every action had to be done 'on the double,' that the food was poor, but I never heard of gas chambers.

"However, I did know that some very peculiar things were going on, and I learned this as early as 1941 when I was an army dentist in Narvik, Norway, with our occupation troops. I was stationed there from 1940 to 1943.

"Of course, I could not listen to Radio London, as I lived in the officers mess and this was prohibited.

"But occasionally I would hear it when I was on furlough in Berlin, stumbling onto that wave length more or less by accident, rather than desire. I didn't happen to hear any atrocity stories when I tuned in.

"But, in 1941, as I have said, a curious thing happened in Narvik. The SS brought into the harbor and unloaded a shipful of Croats and Slovaks, civilian internees who were immediately put behind barbed wire. We of the army heard that the reason for this was that they were infected with spotted fever.

"Word of this got down to headquarters in Oslo and a few days later a high army doctor arrived at our mess. He said he had come to inspect the camp, to make sure that our soldiers and the Norwegian civil population were safe from this epidemic.

"But at first the SS guards would not let this army officer into the stockade. He waited around for several days and at last was given permission to enter. Walking through the camp, he was amazed to find that it was now completely empty and that a lot of used cartridges were strewn around. He was then ushered into the SS commandant who, with a curious smile, assured him that the prisoners would not be a danger to the German army or the Norwegian civil population, and that they were well taken care of by the SS. That was all the SS commandant would say.

"When this army doctor came back to our mess for the night, he told the story in whispers to the head surgeon of our hospital, who later told it to me.

"I hated it, but what could any of us do?

"When did I know the war was lost? In the winter of 1942 and '43. Actors and entertainers, coming out from Berlin to entertain our troops in Norway, told us of experiences they had had when they were entertaining troops on the Russian front, told us of things which soldiers and officers serving there had told them. This was about the time of the battle of Stalingrad.

"After I heard these things, I knew that Germany could never hope to win."

THE CASE OF WILHELM B.

Before the war he belonged to the Nationalist party, which was strongly right-wing and originally opposed to Hitler. He was by profession a journalist, but was kicked out of his job in 1933 when Hitler came to power. After a while, however, this past seemed to be forgotten, and he was able to get a job as one of the editors of Transocean News Service, one of the German propaganda agencies abroad.

He was opposed to the war but, after it started, he thought it would be a war for German survival, and that he should therefore do all that he could to help. Every day he read the news from all over the world, but didn't believe the atrocity stories, knowing from his own job how easy it is to manufacture propaganda.

However, late in the spring of 1943, he got a shock which changed his mind. An acquaintance of his, who was an old Party member entitled to the special button (meaning that he had been one of the first 100,000 to join), came to him one day and said he was badly worried. The Party member explained that the year before when the army was advancing into Russia, the SS had killed 35,000 Jews in one particular Russian town (he thinks it was Kiev) and buried them in a mass grave.

Now, continued the Party member, the German army was retreating and presently this area would fall into the hands of the Russians, who would be certain to discover what had happened, advertise it to the world, and it would go bad for Germany.

"I was greatly shocked to hear this," said Wilhelm B. "But then I asked my Party member friend:

" 'How long have you known this?'

" 'For almost a year.'

" 'But weren't you shocked when you first heard it?'

" 'Privately I was shocked,' confessed the Party member, 'but then I realized that the Party must have had sound reason for doing this, and of course my private feelings are of no consequence and I could not consider them in a matter which involves the state. And I tell it to you now,' continued the Party member, 'not to arouse your private emotions, but because if this is discovered, it will go hard for Germany; it is a matter of grave concern for all Germans.'

"And that," says Wilhelm B., "is typical of the Nazi mind. The man is a human being and when he first hears of such a deed he has emotions like the rest of us. But he thinks he must keep them separate from his duties to the Party. I will never understand them."

During the war he would have liked to go into opposition to the Hitler régime, but after the "unconditional surrender" announcement by Roosevelt and Churchill at Casablanca, he realized that Germany should fight to the bitter end, because this meant that England and America would have no mercy on the country even if it could overthrow Hitler.

When asked if he knew what the real Nazi policy was

toward the Jews and when the order for extermination was given, he says that he didn't know because he was not allowed to see certain publications of the Party. And even for party members, he says, there was an inner circle into which outsiders could not penetrate.

In 1944, Transocean fired him because someone had dug up a lot of facts about his past and they didn't want to keep him. He was therefore drafted into the army. He says that he decided the war would probably be lost when he learned that Hitler had lied to Goebbels about the "buzz bomb," saying that it would be ready in the fall of 1943 when, actually, it came nearly a year later.

But Goebbels really believed, at that time, what he was saying in the propaganda about a secret weapon. And had it been ready in that year, the war might not have been lost.

After the Normandy landing succeeded, then Wilhelm B. knew that all hope was gone. He got a bad leg wound in the fighting in Silesia, which has kept him in bed for almost a year, and since then he has done a lot of thinking.

He now says that although he was a convinced rightist, he no longer thinks that Germany either can or should be a dominating force in Europe. The war, he says, has proved that Germans are not mature enough. It has also proved that even when Germany pulled together with all her might she has not enough power to be decisive in the world. So she should step back and try to build a happy little country in the middle of Europe, which he thinks she can do.

But he doesn't think that people like himself, who were once frankly nationalist, should now be punished when they have sincerely changed their minds. He is not talking, he says, about criminal cases—men like those on trial at Nürnberg should be punished; they can't say that now their viewpoint has altered.

But those who have been good brave officers and are still proud of their bravery, but now doubt the wisdom of the military attitude, these should be accepted in the rebuilding of Germany.

As it is now, he complained, you must prove that you have been in a concentration camp or that you have disobeyed a Hitler order, before you will be accepted.

THE CASE OF RUPRECHT K.

Before Hitler he was a member of the Centrist party and an official in the Foreign Office under Chancellor Brüning. When Hitler seized power in 1933, he resigned. But presently he was taken back on the staff of the Foreign Office by the Nazis in a subordinate position. A little later they offered him a job of secretary of the German Embassy in Paris. He made quiet enquiries and found out that if he took this he would have to join the party, so made excuses and got out of it.

He doesn't believe that many Germans knew the full truth of what went on in the concentration camps and crematoriums. He himself only knew it from foreign sources, such as the BBC.

And he is still bitter because the British and the French, in the 'thirties, recognized Hitler.

"If Chamberlain trusted Hitler in 1938 at Munich, and Stalin trusted him the following year," he says, "how can the ordinary German now be blamed for not realizing that Hitler's real aim was a war of world conquest?"

And he has a number of criticisms to make on the American occupation.

"From what I have observed, I believe that the American authorities here are more tightly controlled by directives than the Germans were under Hitler. The orders they get are more specific, and entail more red tape than ours did.

"Also, American officers don't seem to have any inclination to get around directives when these are obviously against common sense. A German anti-Nazi, serving under Hitler, would do everything in his power to avoid enforcing orders which he thought were unreasonable. The Americans never do this, even though they will tell you they think the order is wrong. Yet now they ask us Germans:

" 'If you thought Hitler's orders were bad, why did you obey them?'

"However, it is certainly true that the American government does not demand them to do anything so obnoxious or cruel as did the old German state."

He thinks that American regulations are particularly unjust in dealing with the cases of borderline Nazis. Such a man is barred from practicing his profession, and this means starvation for himself and his family. He says that the difference between this and the treatment of Jews by the Nazis is only a matter of degree. He also feels that Americans have been so indoctrinated against the Germans that they have no human interest in them. Whereas many Germans, in spite of Hitler's propaganda, continued to have a human interest in the Jews, and fought to avoid the official directives so that these Jews could survive and get food.

BAR AND GRILL

One of my scouts spent an hour at a small German *Bierstube* which, in America, would be called a bar and grill, and recorded conversations with his foot on the brass rail.

The barkeeper, who owns the place, says that American soldiers often come there.

"They have no discipline," he complains. "Once an American officer was sitting at one of those tables with a blonde German girl who was not exactly beautiful, and an American corporal, who happened to be passing his table, said loudly:

" 'My, what a goat you've got there!'

"I'm glad that this could not happen in the German army," says the barkeeper. "If soldiers have discipline, that isn't necessarily militarism. But soldiers can't behave like private citizens, even when they are off duty."

My scout now asks the group if, during the war, they heard anything about atrocities.

The first to answer is a former German sergeant who now has a job working for the Americans in the transportation division.

"I never heard anything like that when I was in the army," he says, "but since then I have been reading the testimony of the Nürnberg trials, and I believe every word of it is true, including what they say happened at Belsen."

"I didn't know about it either, until after the war," says the innkeeper, "but I can now tell you about it first-hand, because one of my best customers was imprisoned in Belsen. He tells me a lot of things that didn't even get in the newspapers.

"For instance, that woman, Irma Griese, who was in charge of the women's section of Belsen. The lowdown on her is that she was really a Lesbian. She was the one who always walked around in camp wearing riding trousers and carrying a whip.

"My friend told me that she would always look over all of the newcomers, and pick the one that she liked. If the girl refused, she would be sent right away to the ovens to be cooked. However, if she consented, that only got her a little time, because pretty soon Irma Griese would find one she liked better and order the previous girl sent to the ovens. She kept changing all the time, and always cooking them afterwards.

"I asked my friend if she did this because she had no regard for human life, and felt that these people were only rats. He said no, that the killing after the loving was a part of her pleasure—the two went together.

"After hearing this from my friend, I was sorry when I later read in the papers that the Allies had hanged Irma Griese, because I wish we Germans could have had the pleasure of doing it instead."

"I hope they leave a few for us to hang," says the sergeant.

"When I went into the army as a private, my sergeant was a nasty guy. In civilian life he had been a storm troop trainer, and although he didn't quite kill any of us, it was only because he didn't have any ovens. We later found out that he had got himself syphilis in Greece and had nursed his case along, keeping it alive, so that he could continue training men behind the lines, and avoid going to the front."

Next to the sergeant at the bar is a small man with ink-stained fingers.

"A curious thing happened at our shop in connection with Irma Griese," says the ink-stained man. "I am a printer and I work at *Der Berliner*.* When the story about her came out, we printed Griese's picture and the caption under it was 'So War Criminals Look!'

"We had just started the presses when we got an order from the British censor to stop and remake the first page. That caption had caused all the trouble. The British said that of course Irma Griese was a terrible woman and everybody knew she was guilty. Nevertheless, it had not been proved yet in court, and she should not be called a war criminal by a newspaper until after she was convicted.

"This change represented much work for all of us, but we saw the point and we liked it because it was so different from the old days when, if a man was arrested, you knew that he certainly would be convicted and maybe he would not even be given a trial at all.

"We had forgotten what it is like to be fair. And we liked it even better the next day when we read the Russian papers and saw that they were accusing the people on trial of all sorts of things, some of them going beyond what was in the indictment. A man should be held innocent until he has been proved guilty; that is important!"

My scout said that now the talk turned to the Russians.

* This is the German-language paper published in Berlin and licensed and censored by the British there.—WLW.

"At Nürnberg," says the barkeeper, "they are trying Germans for having taken things away from occupied countries. Maybe that's all right.

"But now, what are the Russians doing? I ask you that! Everybody knows that they are taking out of Germany everything that they can. Why doesn't somebody put them on trial? On the other hand, I am against those Germans who are now complaining, 'Why don't the Allies give us this or that?' Why should they? Did we give anything to the countries we occupied? We only took things away. We have no right to expect the Allies to give us things now."

THE GERMAN ENGINEER

He was formerly employed in the development department of the Henschel plant. Since the war he has been working in the railway repair shop, trying to develop designs for a new modern type of railway car. Now he realizes that there is no hope for this because no new railway equipment may be built in Germany in this generation.

Therefore, he wants to emigrate. He could go to Russia, where they have offered him a villa in the Crimea. But he prefers China or an English-speaking country.

"When did you realize the war was lost?" my scout asked him.

"Early," he said, "when the Allied bombers came over and it was apparent that they could not be beaten off. From a purely mechanical standpoint, I am convinced we could have won this war if Goering had not been such a fathead. He deserves the *Kriegsverlustkreuz*.* Goering would not allow inventive genius to have full play. He did not assemble a technical staff which would have realized the industrial and inventive possibilities of Germany. That is why we did not have better fighters and bombers. Inventive genius was not free."

---

* This is a joke. It means war-losing cross, as opposed to the well-known German decoration *Kriegsverdienstkreuz*, or war-winning cross.—WLW.

"But," argued my scout, "it was not free because Germany was not free. If we had been free, we would never have started this war."

"That is also correct," said the engineer.

Then my scout asked him when he first knew of the extinction camps.

"I didn't know much until the Nürnberg trials," said the engineer. "And I don't think many others did either. For instance, a good friend of mine comes from a family in which there is some Jewish blood, and so part of the family was taken away to a Jewish camp and part of it was allowed to remain. But not even those who were left behind believed that extinction camps existed. When they heard that their mother had died, they convinced themselves that probably she had died a natural death."

Then the engineer said he still couldn't understand why the Allies went in for the aerial bombing of German cities.

"This did not really shorten the war, which could easily have been done if they had concentrated on our fuel plants instead. But, by bombing cities, they only built up future hatred."

My scout thinks this is wrong, and that the bombing of cities actually did shorten the war. For instance, he says that, as a soldier on the Russian front, he heard other soldiers say: "What is the use of defending the Fatherland here when it is being destroyed by Allied bombers at home?"

He also says you now hear Germans say, "Why did they destroy civilian houses?"—forgetting that in the beginning it was the Germans themselves who were so sure that terror was the only way to bring peace.

However, he says that he has decided that air raids have taught the Germans no moral lesson, and maybe air raids are not the way to teach moral lessons. In any case, many of them still say, "Yes, war is terrible, but let's beat the Russians." They seem to be more for war now (or at least some of them) than they were when it was going on.

THE INTERPRETER

This man knows several languages, and before the war was an interpreter. After it broke out, the Nazis investigated his case several times to see if he could not be used as a spy. He fooled them by playing dumb, telling them, "My English isn't good enough." He is now making his living by speculation on the black market.

"When did I know the war was lost?" he said. "The day it started. My reasons were not military or mechanical. But I thought that the party had committed so many crimes and had taken our nation so far from the path that we should have followed that, if there was a God in Heaven, such a war could not be won.

"Not even in 1940, when so many Germans became jubilant, did I depart from this conviction. But I don't believe the mass of Germans knew the whole terror of the concentration camps or the extent of the crimes which were being committed. Radio propaganda from Moscow and London seemed beyond belief, and so by and by our ears were closed to things like this. The war itself was so much of a horror that people looked for escapist entertainment. We drank, danced and talked. We did not want to know.

"But, still more important, nobody dared repeat what he knew of terror in concentration camps. Even the word 'Gestapo' brought a terrible fear beyond anything which is comprehensible today. A friend of mine was sent to a concentration camp in 1942 but one day he reappeared among us. He had been given a six months' parole and had pledged his word to return on the dot.

"While he was out on furlough, he would not say one word,

even to his family, of what he had been through. This also he had promised before he left.

"And when the day for return came, he was there at the gate of the camp on the dot. Why? Because he knew that if he did not, his whole tribe would be wiped out. This he has told me himself since the war.

"The English and Americans, of course, will not believe it now, but nevertheless it was true—even those who had been in the camps were afraid to talk of it.

"I have still another friend, an engineer who spent three years in America before the war, who got into trouble while he was in the army, and was given ninety days' punitive treatment in the fortress of Torgau.

"Many months later I met him again. He called me aside and asked if we could talk in private. He had to tell someone —he couldn't stand living alone with the memories of what had happened.

"We went to a small restaurant and for hours he talked. He said it would help him get rid of the memory. I remember one thing he told me: that in Torgau German soldiers were put into cages and would then be ordered to put out their arms through the heavy wire mesh. Then, while they were standing there, someone on the outside would strike a blow which would break their wrists. After this, guns were put into their hands and they had to drill with these cracked wrists.

" 'Imagine,' he said, 'they did this to German soldiers, while publicly Hitler and his gang were calling them the best in the world!'

"If they survived Torgau, these men were then ordered to punishment battalions where, if they proved themselves particularly brave, they would be exonerated. Such battalions were always sent to the most dangerous parts of the line, and everything had to be executed on the double.

"My friend said that he was assigned to an advance observation post on the Russian front, from which 'I was supposed to direct our artillery fire by field telephone. It was so dangerous that no officer ever inspected the position. Occasionally at night they would bring me food and ammunition.' The ammunition, he would either fire into the air or throw into a nearby creek. Also, it gave him great pleasure to misdirect the German artillery fire—sending the salvos either 100 meters too short or 100 meters too long.

"After about a month of this duty, he said that he was exonerated, was told that his original offense and trial would be forgotten, and all references to it removed from his record. Of course, they did not know that he had been misdirecting the artillery fire.

"Yet this man would talk of these horrors only to me, his closest friend and in confidence. So it is no wonder that such things were not generally known.

"Of course, people in cities larger than a hundred thousand knew that Jews were being deported, although they did not know where, or what happened to them. In Berlin, for instance, knowledge about Theresienstadt was common. But in small towns and villages, frequently such things were not known at all."

Mathilda J.

She is a very intelligent newspaper woman now working for a Berlin daily licensed by the French. During the war her husband died in a Gestapo prison, but she says she never will remarry. She belongs to no political party, but her politics are strongly liberal and democratic. My scout first asked her when she first learned of atrocities in concentration camps.

"My husband and I had no idea how lawless this régime was," she said, "until we found out by bitter experience.

"In 1938 we went on a trip to America, which we arranged through the North German Lloyd. Very recently I was called in and cross-questioned about my *Fragebogen*＊ by a German Jew who left this country in 1937 and has come back as an American officer. He wanted to know why we hadn't stayed in America, instead of coming back.

"The only reason we came back was that we didn't find any hope of getting a job, to take the chance of staying. I wanted to stay anyway, but my husband could not see how he could make a living. Anyway, we didn't have the cash to wait in Cuba for an immigration visa, so we had to come back.

"The day war broke out, I cried harder than I have ever cried before or since, thinking of all the misery and deaths and hardships that would come to so many. My husband and I both knew that Germany would lose, and we stuck to this knowledge even in 1940 when everyone was so confident, and most of our friends were then saying:

" 'We can't visit with Mathilda and her husband any more, they are so defeatist.'

"But I had no idea of how horrible this régime could be until we experienced this in our own family. Suddenly, my husband was arrested and I could not find out why. I thought perhaps it was because of our American trip.

"Later I found out, through devious channels, that he was accused of having been in conspiracy against Germany on a recent business trip he had taken to Switzerland.

"While he was in this Berlin prison, he succeeded in smuggling out to me a note in his own handwriting which said briefly, among other things, that they were whipping him. Now, the curious thing is that still later, when I got permission to speak with him for a few minutes, he completely denied either

＊ The *Fragebogen* is the questionnaire which all Germans must fill out, listing all positions they may have held in political, military or welfare organizations, as well as any titles of nobility their parents may have had or any articles or books they may have written. If all the answers are not satisfactory, they may be barred from holding any important job or practicing any profession. The questionnaire has been most useful in uncovering concealed Nazis. A number of injustices have also resulted.—WLW.

the whipping or sending me the note, although no wife can fail to recognize her husband's writing. This was because the terror was so great. He had decided it was not safe even for me to know what had happened, for fear that I might tell and this would in turn get me into trouble.

"Prison regulations allowed the wives of inmates to come for their dirty clothes, and bring them clean ones. These last the prison guards used to inspect in the yard, to make sure that we were not smuggling in anything.

"They would hold up each garment, look at it and, when they were through, shove the whole pile back towards each wife, telling her to wrap it up again. Actually, I was able to smuggle tobacco to him in the following way. I would empty the tobacco out of cigarettes, tie it up into a neat little thin paper package about the size of a cookie, and when I was putting the clean clothes back into the bundle I would slip these tiny packages in with the garments.

"I was never caught at this although, as we were wrapping the packages back up, the loud speaker in the courtyard would blare:

"*'Achtung! Achtung!* Do not believe that your packages will not be checked once again. If we find anything, we will give the punishment to your husband, *Du Judensau!*' *

"I was not Jewish nor was my husband, but I learned that this was the common name by which the Gestapo addressed all wives of political prisoners.

"When first I asked the prison officials permission to talk to my husband, they refused and cursed me because I came back several times on the same day hoping to get it.

"'Who do you think you are, you *Judensau*,' they said, 'the wife of a rotten traitor who does not deserve to be called German!'

"I finally managed to talk to him by making use of a

* The translation is: "You Jewish sow!"

friend who was, in turn, a friend of Himmler's private physician."

(My scout here points out that the two men in this chain to Himmler were undoubtedly big-shot Nazis, and they have probably by now come to this girl, asking her to sign statements saying that they had aided her and that they were always secretly opposed to Hitler's régime.)

"Through the same channel I was able to get a date set for his trial, after which I am sure he would have been released, for nothing was actually proved against him. But as a result of the treatment there, he died just a week before the trial was to have taken place.

"Now that it is all over, the Americans and the British who have never been through such a thing, cannot know what a terrorizing influence the Gestapo had on German minds. People were afraid even to know too much. On the other hand, young people who for years had been trained to see only vermin in Jews or in anybody who was in political opposition, finally became utterly callous toward them and their suffering.

"For instance, I know one family where the daughter, a member of the *Bund Deutscher Mädel*, denounced her own parents to the political police for saying that Germany would lose the war.

"Also, I know two other sisters of good family whose parents were taken to concentration camps and killed there during Christmas week. But the children, who were Nazis, cared so little that they gave for their friends a big New Year's Party which lasted until the 2nd of January. They were only seventeen and nineteen years old. And after that, they didn't want to have anything to do with their parents' former friends, refusing even to speak to them. Formerly they had been quiet simple girls, but now they were out craving excitement, absolutely abandoned to pleasure, and very promiscuous.

"It is amazing how people can change. I used to wonder about this when I would arrive at the prison early in the morning with the fresh clothes for my husband, and as I watched the police employees arrive.

"When they were on duty they would curse us, referring to all of us wives of political prisoners as Jewish swine. But as I watched them entering the building, none of them looked brutal. They all seemed to be only respectable, middle-class German citizens, who had kissed their wives dutifully before starting a day at the office—so serenely bourgeois!

"And still I wonder why! It must be that Germans somehow get themselves mystically involved with certain ideas, to such a degree that in the end they become unbalanced. This is the only explanation that I know."

A final note on this girl. My scout tells me that, as a wife of a political prisoner who died in confinement, she is eligible to join the "Victims of Fascism" and thus get extra food cards, an allotment of fuel for the winter, and many other privileges which are denied to other Germans.

However, she has never joined this organization, and says that she never will. Her point is that the entire German nation is a victim of fascism, that those families who did not lose members in concentration camps have lost sons and fathers killed in the war, and that she will have nothing to do with something which would set her apart from other Germans, as a member of a privileged upper caste.

CHAPTER VI

AN UNRECONSTRUCTED GERMAN

FOR several days I had been badgering my scouts to bring me an unrepentant Nazi.

All of their stories so far had been about Germans who had never wanted the war in the first place, or Germans who may have wanted it at the start but changed their minds toward the middle or at the end.

I did not question the truth of these stories, nor did I question the fact that they were typical of the feeling of almost all Germans. But was there not, somewhere, a Nazi who was still glad that the war was started, still sorry that it was lost, and who would do it all over again, only better, if he got the chance?

Surely there must be at least one, I insisted. I also told them that if they could find one who would talk frankly, giving me his true point of view, I would not let him down. They could assure such a Nazi, I told them, that I was not a police agent but a reporter trying to get representative German opinion. It was his viewpoint I wanted, not his neck. And now, get the hell out of here and bring me in a Nazi!

All three were faithful boys and they worked hard. But they could only report that all of the really important Nazis had fled Berlin ahead of the Russians and most of them were now rounded up in British and American stockades. The lesser ones who had been left behind now felt that Hitler had sucked them in with tall talk and fake promises. While there might be a few of these small fry who still believed in him, they were too wary to say so, even to Germans in confidence.

After some days of this hectoring and badgering, my little red-headed scout finally announced that if the others failed to bring in a bona fide Nazi, he thought he had a man who would be second best. Of course, his man was not a Nazi, had in fact always refused to join the party, "although," said my scout hopefully, "I believe he does have some prejudice against Negroes."

However, the man was, he promised, an unreconstructed German nationalist who, although he had never cared for Hitler, now disliked him even more for having lost the war, but did not hesitate to say that everybody would soon see that Germany had done a far better job of organizing Europe than the Allies showed any promise of doing.

Moreover, this man, while he admitted that very bad things were being disclosed at the Nürnberg trials, said that the Allies were, in addition, trying to foist on to the German people a lot of hysterical exaggerations seldom equaled even by Goebbels at his best.

Lastly, said my red-headed scout, I might have a particular interest in meeting this man because, during the war, he had been a German war correspondent, covering practically every battle front. One of his stories had, in fact, been printed verbatim by an important American magazine early in the war. It was an eyewitness account of the capture of Crete by parachutists from the viewpoint of one of the men who had made the jump, describing the whole thing.

Actually, said my scout, this particular story had been a re-write job. Friedrich Neumann had not himself made the jump; in fact, had not at this particular time even completed his military training. But Neumann's story was so skillfully put together from the accounts of men who had actually made the jump that when it was filed, to be cabled to the United States, it had fooled even the Berlin censor, who had held it up, feeling that anything so vivid must surely contain military information which the enemy should not have. It was only released after the explanations were made.

Neumann was, so my red-headed scout said, a great admirer of the work of Ernest Hemingway and, in this particular story, had copied much of his style. He had been born in Hamburg and before the war was a top reporter on one of its larger papers. After the surrender, he came to Berlin in the hope that he could get a job on one of the American, British or French papers published here. However, he had failed to pass the American *Fragebogen* since his work as a war correspondent was automatically classified as propaganda.

If I wanted to see Neumann, said my red-headed scout, it must be soon for already he had applied for permission to return to Hamburg, where he would spend the next three months writing a book about the war from the German standpoint.

I said I was most anxious to meet him, not only because he might do for a Nazi in case we failed to get a real one (we did fail), but also because it would be most interesting to talk to a war correspondent who had covered the other side. So, what about making the date for eleven o'clock tomorrow in my rooms, where we would not be disturbed and where he, the red-headed scout, could be available as translator if need be, since he had already explained that Neumann, while he spoke excellent French, knew not one word of English.

The date was made for eleven but it happened that on this morning a general gave a prolonged press conference, so I was late for it.

I now present an unreconstructed, unrepentant German.

Neumann turned out to be a tall, handsome, extremely well-built man of about 35, with a very light, clear, pink-and-white German complexion, straight dark brown hair and brown eyes. Across one of his cheeks there was what might have been a dueling scar, or possibly a mark from the war.

At the outset (indeed through all of our talk), he seemed mildly distrustful of me, looking at me warily with a chip on his shoulder. I have seen the same proud, wary look on the face of a Harlem Negro intellectual who has been invited out to a party with white people and is on the lookout for any kind of snub, sometimes imagining one when none was intended.

I first apologized for the fact that my suite contained no comfortable chairs. My red-headed scout then explained to Neumann that I had been told I could have all the furniture I wanted, but had preferred to keep this wicker stuff which was already in the room, because asking for more would only mean that it would be requisitioned from Germans living in the neighborhood.

Neumann was not, however, disposed to hand me too many metals for this forbearance. He nodded and said that there had also been, among the German officer corps, many such sensitive intellectuals who, when they had been part of a German army of occupation, had exercised the same consideration for the people among whom they lived.

I said I was sure this had been true.

Then, quite naturally, we began to talk about the war, of which he had seen much more than I. Although he had not been in Crete, he had covered the German landings in Norway. Later, he had been with Rommel in the desert, and still later on the Russian front.

He had also covered our Normandy landings from the German side and had been present at the questioning of American prisoners. They had seemed to him, he said, to have been excellent troops. Some of them were green, of course, but their behavior under fire showed that their basic training in camp had been sound, and their morale was high.

I said the same could be said of German morale among the prisoners we took.

Our nearest mutual point of contact seemed to have been during the battle of Britain, when he had inspected the long-range, cross-Channel guns near Calais at approximately the same time, so far as we could figure out, that they had been firing at me in Dover.

I then said that, returning from England, I had flown in the regular seaplanes from Bournemouth to Lisbon, and that it had been my understanding that there was a tacit deal between both sides that the British would not molest the regular German planes which flew from Lisbon to Berlin if the Luftwaffe would refrain from shooting down British flying boats on the route which I had traveled.

"I have also heard of this unwritten agreement from our side," said Neumann, "so certainly it must be true. In fact, I think it was violated only once, and then by us, when we shot down the plane on which Leslie Howard was traveling. We had got a false report from our intelligence agents in London that Winston Churchill would be aboard. I was very sorry it happened, not only because we missed shooting Churchill, but because we got Howard by mistake. I always thought him a truly great actor with real sensitivity."

I said I could agree entirely with his estimate of Howard.

Although we had just begun our talk, it was now time for lunch, and this presented the usual delicate problem. I was bound by the rigidly fixed hours at which meals were served in our mess, and told them how much I regretted that I could not ask them to join me.

Neumann said I must not give the matter another thought, since he had often been in similar predicaments in countries which the German army had occupied.

There was, however, a way out. We were in the middle of the large residential suburb of Zehlendorf and the nearest restaurant in which Germans could eat was twenty blocks away. I could take them there in my jeep, wait while they ate a hurried German meal, bring them back to my quarters, and then step around the corner to the Press Club still in time for my American meal.

It then also occurred to me that I could, in addition, play

an angle, in this city of angles. On the way back from their restaurant we could pause at *Onkel Tomm's Hutte.* Actually, this is a Berlin subway station named many decades ago after Harriet Beecher Stowe's novel, which was the rage in Germany at the time. The subway station has since been fitted with an attractive underground arcade in which there were many shops. All of these have now been taken over by our army, and a large section is occupied by the American Red Cross which sells ice cream at the nominal price of a penny for a small, paper-wrapped bar.

The point is, however, that this establishment is almost unique in Berlin as being the only American canteen where one is permitted not only to buy ice cream, but to take it off the premises. Which means, of course, as every American in Berlin knows, that you can then give it to Germans. On our way back to our quarters, I would stop here just long enough to buy ice cream for the three of us and then, after I had finished the main course of my press camp meal, would return to my room where we three would eat it together.

When we got to their little German restaurant, it was crowded. There were, in fact, a few Germans standing and waiting for tables. My uniform attracted the same kind of not entirely friendly stares which a white man would get in a restaurant in Harlem. What was I doing here? Was I slumming? Furthermore, since a good American meal was provided for me at my own mess, why did I come here to help eat up the meager food supplies allotted to Germans, with food tickets which had probably been bought on the black market?

Some of this slightly hostile curiosity I felt, and probably imagined the rest. I was not, of course, planning to eat here; only to sit with them until they finished.

Again because of my uniform, the proprietor hustled three Germans through the end of their meal to make places for us. But still other Germans were standing. I did not intend to eat, so I explained to the other two that when they were through I would be outside, and went out to sit in the jeep.

It was really more like Harlem than even I had guessed, because my red-headed scout later told me that as I walked out Neumann said to him:

"Aha! So that is his limit! He will talk to us in his room, but he is ashamed that some other American will see that he is eating with Germans!" My scout then loyally explained that this was not my reason.

Now I'm sure that Neumann, when he was in occupied France, was reasonably decent and considerate of the natives, and yet I still wonder how many Frenchmen or Jews he had occasion to dine with in those days.

When they finished, we got in the jeep and presently pulled up in front of *Onkel Tomm's Hutte*. Just in front of the jeep, waiting at the curb by her bicycle, was a very beautiful German girl. She was about 20, with a peaches-and-cream complexion. Her soft golden hair, which had been recently washed, fluffed out in a cloud; she was wearing a freshly-ironed green and white dirndl, and also bobby socks.

My two companions, being Germans, were not allowed in the enclosure, so I had to leave them in the car.

Since the ice cream bars were small, I thought we ought to have at least three apiece. Just ahead of me in the line at the counter was a tall, muscular, very smartly-uniformed Negro corporal. He was wearing paratroopers' boots which had been freshly polished, and there was not a wrinkle in his carefully-fitted, recently-pressed uniform. As a purely African type, he was quite handsome, being a much darker version of Joe Louis. He seemed quite sure of himself, and was being most courteous to the German girls who were waiting on us.

But he was buying really a fantastic amount of ice cream bars. They were wrapping them into a couple of packages, each of which must contain at least thirty.

We have a good many Negro troops in Berlin and I suddenly remembered a little incident on the last day of my visit to Germany in 1939. I was wandering around the streets of the little Prussian town of Sassnitz, killing a few hours while waiting for my journey to Sweden, and paused in front of a notice board on which government propaganda was posted for the natives to read.

They had, first, a photostatic reproduction of a then recent article from one of the more sensational British tabloids. The article first referred to Hitler's racial doctrines, and then went on to say that it might be a good idea, at the end of the war, to include plenty of Negro troops in the army of occupation. This would serve the Germans right.

There followed a translation into German of the British tabloid's article. At the very top, Goebbel's Propaganda Ministry had put a caption in huge type: "GERMAN WOMEN! GERMAN MEN! SEE HOW THE BRITISH ARE PLOTTING TO DEGRADE OUR SISTERS AND DAUGHTERS AND DEBASE OUR GERMAN BLOOD!"

When the Negro, with his two huge packages of ice cream, had gone out I ordered my nine bars and got them of mixed flavors, not knowing which my friends would prefer. When they were wrapped, I went back to the jeep and we started off. Now I noticed that we were overtaking two cyclists who pulled over to the curb to let us by. They had been riding very close together. One of them was the beautiful twenty-year-old German girl with the peaches-and-cream complexion and the cloud of freshly-washed, fluffy golden hair. The other was the Negro corporal who had been just ahead of me in line. To the handlebars of each bicycle was attached a metal mesh basket and in each basket was one of the huge packages of ice cream bars, completely filling it.

Nobody in our jeep said anything until we had passed them. Then Neumann said:

"That is something which I do not like to see."

"To me," said the red-headed scout, "it is their own business. They should be able to do as they like."

"I have heard that you would never see it in America," said Neumann.

"You might see it in New York," said my scout. He knew the town fairly well, having been assistant purser on one of the North German Lloyd liners before the war.

"But even in New York, would you see it often?"

"Still you might see it. And what people want to do should be their own affair."

"I am sure it is good ice cream," said Neumann. And that was all that anybody said the rest of the way home.

It did not take me long to eat and soon I was back with the other two and we finished the ice cream.

Now I tackled Neumann. What did he really think about our occupation? And would he please be perfectly frank, and not consider my feelings as an American?

He started off with what he thought about our policy in dealing with collaboration, which covered everything from de-Nazification to the *Fragebogen*. He said that Americans are "naïve on the subject of this old continent."

"All Europeans," he said, "know that any nation must follow the course which is set by its leading group. That when a course of events is started, there is not much chance to escape from the final conclusion.

"The French, who are wise in the ways of Europe, are completely aware of this. Furthermore, they have been occupied and they understand that, under those circumstances, most Frenchmen had to collaborate with Pétain who, in turn, had to collaborate with the Germans. There was no escape.

"Therefore, in dealing with Germany now, the French are free from any kind of false Puritanism in these matters, and waste little time in righteous indignation. Since they had to collaborate with Hitler, they understand why Germans also had to.

"Furthermore, the French, being close to the rapidly changing European scene, realize that no human being should be reproached for not seeing the consequences of his acts four years later. Americans, since they have not had to live in Europe, do not understand this.

"For two months the Germans laughed about the American *Fragebogen*. Then the laugh ended suddenly, because it was found that this *Fragebogen* was a means of guillotining all the managerial material, all the intelligent and competent people in Germany. Because any German of any consequence, if his answers to the *Fragebogen* were honest, could be crucified by this.

"For instance, many Germans who were not for Hitler were nevertheless members of the National Socialist People's Welfare. This was because Hitler had given it a monopoly of all charitable and welfare work in Germany, dissolving all the previous ones and prohibiting the churches from taking any part.

"He then put pressure on all Germans to co-operate with it and it was impossible to avoid this, since this People's Welfare organization had charge of hospitals, the care of children, and so forth. To fail to join it would be like refusing to buy a membership in the American Red Cross in wartime. Yet at the beginning the Americans blamed the Germans even for this.

"Furthermore, Germans were stigmatized if they had belonged to any of the special organizations of war veterans which, the Americans said, proved they were militarists. Many of these, Neumann said, such as the *Stahlhelm*, were founded long before Hitler, and occupied the same position in German life that the American Legion and the Veterans of Foreign Wars do in our country.

"The reason for this American attitude was that you had absorbed the hatred of Hitler brought to America by the first emigrants from Nazism. Getting such a distorted picture, which viewed only the worst aspects of Nazism, the Americans wondered why so many Germans could possibly co-operate with such a régime at all.

"You Americans therefore made two principal mistakes.

"You had heard of only the bad aspects of the Nazi régime and failed to realize that there were, in addition, many neutral aspects and even a few good ones.

"You also failed to realize that in Europe the ordinary man is forced to co-operate with the ruling régime in his country, whether he approves of it or not.

"Take the case, for instance, of a German engineer who, in 1937 or 1938, starts working on a certain process of aluminum. Later this process is used in a military aircraft factory. The Americans see such a man only as co-plotter of Hitler in a war of aggression, and not as a technician doing his routine job with no particular thought of war. And even so, for generations Europe has always been on the verge of war, whether Germany happened to be under the leadership of the Hohenzollerns, Hindenburg or Hitler, and it was the duty of any good citizen to make his country strong whether or not he approved of the régime which was for the moment in power.

"But at least the British and American authorities have finally freed themselves of the myth that political heroism and human bravery were to be found only in concentration camp survivors. They are now more realistic about it.

"When you first arrived, and issued your *Fragebogen*, the Germans, after reading it, said, 'You have to have been born in a concentration camp to be a good German today.'

"And when the Allies formed their new German police force, it was at the beginning a hasty collection of the glorified contents of concentration camps, and still contains many criminal elements which Germans resent. For instance, the proceeds of black market raids are given to the German police as pay. Recently, when I traveled from Hesse to Thuringia, I watched the police on the trains collecting fines of from 50 to 250 marks for which they gave no receipts—all of it went into their own pockets.

"In the schools, the children of these men say innocently: 'Since my father is in the police force, we have potatoes.' And other Germans resent such corruption greatly.

"Furthermore, you were very foolish in your original attitude toward the Hitler Youth. Just after the close of the war, the Allies started rounding up all these kids as dangerous animals, putting a heavy stigma on them and treating them as criminal outlaws, whereas, as a matter of fact, they were little more than Boy Scouts. Most of the Hitler Jugend activities were pretty innocent.*

"In some of these Allied camps, re-education was attempted, but the trouble was that it started out by telling them that everything that they had been taught before was wicked, and that they themselves were criminals who now should be regenerated —neither of which was actually true. And these kids don't need much re-education. Because they have seen the general trend of events. This has made on them a much deeper impression than any propaganda they might have gotten from Balder von Schirach, Hitler's official youth leader.

"These kids now are the strongest persisting element in the postwar migration which is still going on in Germany. They are wandering about the country, looking for their parents and their lost homes. They are uprooted and thus make excellent raw material for gangs of smugglers.

"In addition, in the last days of the war the High Command dissolved some of the bigger army units into small bands, ranging from eight to twenty, which were to operate as partisans after the Allied advance had rolled over them. For the most part, this was done on the Eastern front, and in no place did it really amount to much.

---

* If we take Neumann's broad viewpoint we might conclude that most of the activities of Fagin's school for thieves was only clean, outdoor fun.— WLW.

"However, in this way boys learned to fight in gangs, and this has persisted over into the postwar era. First they traveled on foot and on bicycles, then they hooked rides on freight trains. Now, they ride passenger trains or go about in stolen automobiles.

"The actual crimes these boys commit do not interest me so much as the fact that their anarchical life leads to more serious criminality. And, of course, today the world is turned upside down. Ordinarily it is no crime to bring potatoes from the country to the city. Today it is bootlegging, and they are engaged in it.

"From old people in the towns they get rings, jewelry and textiles. These they take into the country villages, where they buy potatoes which they bring back to the towns in exchange. Many people, ordinarily of good character, are now being forced into this kind of traffic by hunger."

I now brought up the subject of the book which Neumann hopes to write on the war from the German standpoint. It will be, he said, most difficult, because:

"Now that the German Empire is dead, it is hard to bring back the old atmosphere even though, down there at Nürnberg, those tired and hunted old men * sit in the box of that courtroom, and we can still see in the newspapers the now haggard faces of Germany's former leaders.

"It is a dramatic story, to write of the great change from the period of elation which came with the conquest of France in 1940, and on down to the misery in Berlin in 1944 caused by the Allied bombing. I remember one officer, shocked by the growing disintegration as our armies constantly fell back in defeat, who one day said bitterly:

" 'We are now lunching the war backward, vomiting up our victories, and they don't taste as good as they did on the way down.'

* This somewhat neglects the fact that these winsome old characters, in the days when they were not quite so tired, did some pretty vigorous hunting on their own.—WLW.

"And then, with the final collapse, everything was reversed: the peoples we had conquered were now on top of us. Just before the final collapse, every German was extremely afraid that the foreign labor in our country would rise in revolt and start raising hell, looting and shooting. Of course, they did quite a bit but it wasn't nearly as bad as we had imagined. But, occasionally, one would say to another:

" 'I have been mistreated by that so-and-so at Zedanstrasse 50; let's go there and clean out the place.' Yet, on the whole, these foreign workers who had lived with us during the war were not so full of hate for us as were the indoctrinated American and British soldiers who came in from the outside. For instance, in Pomerania and Silesia, there were many farms from which the German men had gone, but their places had been taken by labor imported from France. When the Russians broke through, these Frenchmen, who had been well treated, took the place of the absent head of the house, harnessed the horses, filled the cart with the furniture and valuables from the house, put the younger children on the mattresses and bedding, helped the German woman up on the seat beside them, and then started driving west with these adopted families, ahead of the Russian advance.

"These agricultural workers—you now call them 'slave labor' but we called them 'foreign workers'—had very little resentment of their treatment while they were here, and some had none at all. It should not be forgotten that great numbers of them came voluntarily.* And it should be remembered that what is now being told in Nürnberg of the treatment of some of them is not all the truth. It is not the whole picture, and most Germans would say that it is not even the largest part of the picture, although it is the only part that is ever printed today.

"It is true that foreigners who worked in our factories were not so well satisfied as those who worked on our farms. Never-

* But just what is a volunteer? Is a man a free agent if he can only feed his family by taking a German war job?—WLW.

theless, most of them were content, and got the same rations as Germans during the same period. I do not pretend that we did this out of a sentimental love for foreigners, but only because we had brought them to Germany since we needed their labor, and any fool knows that a man who is not contented and well-fed will not work, or if he does not know this he will soon find it out.

"We had trouble with some, of course, but the percentage was small. These were sent to punishment camps, and it is only such camps that are ever spoken of today, which gives a distorted picture.

"Yet even the worst of this, which is all that is now talked of, came about not through deliberate cruelty, but because of the disruption and confusion in the last weeks and days of the war.

"For instance, at such a camp, the food supply failed, and also coal did not come for the crematoriums. Just after the cessation of hostilities you Americans, in the best Goebbels style, rushed in photographers who took pictures of whole mountains of corpses. The newspapers here were filled with this; it was also printed into pamphlets and posters were put up, headed 'You should know that!' The town *Bürgermeister* was forced to look at this pile of corpses and his picture was also taken.

"Now it happens that just as all of this was being printed the first Germans were being released from your American prisoner of war camps. I realize that you suddenly got hundreds of thousands of German prisoners which you did not expect and were not prepared for. You could not feed them and the weather was below freezing. You do not need to apologize to me because our men died of exhaustion and cold and lack of food. I have a comrade who was in your camp at Kreuzenach am Rhein, where the death rate among our boys from cold, exhaustion and starvation was between 130 and 150 per day. I have heard that the Americans later court-martialed their camp commander for what happened there.

"Now, of course, not as many died here as died at our concentration camps. But your treatment of our prisoners was in
no way better, and surely it could not have been worse. It can
be said that only 130 corpses daily is not much, but if Goebbels
could have photographed them, the pictures would have been
quite as impressive as those you took at Belsen. The point is,
however, that you filled our papers with what had been done
at Belsen, with not one word of what had gone on at Kreuzenach am Rhein, although just at that time our boys were coming
back to tell us of this."

"I confess I have never heard of Kreuzenach am Rhein," I
said. "I concede that many bad things can happen in the confusion of a war's end. Anyway, I am not here to argue, but to
ask something else. Between 1939 and 1945, about 6,000,000
people—most of them either very old or very young—were
killed in those parts of Europe which Germany controlled,
because they had been classified as 'useless Jews.' I understand
that this did not happen at the end of the war, but for the
most part in the years 1943 and 1944." As I talked Neumann's
face changed, and when he next spoke it seemed to me that
he was both embarrassed and nervous.

"That was, of course, a terrible thing," he said quickly, "a
bestial and a savage thing, the worst thing that our leadership
did by far. No one could justify it. Our war leadership would
have said that these people were by then our bitter enemies, even
if we had made them so, and that we could not spare for those
who were unable to work for us any food and clothing at a time
when the German nation was fighting for its very existence, and
every ounce of these things was precious if we were to survive,
which, of course, in the end we did not. That is what the old
leadership would have said.

"But really to understand how such orders could be obeyed
by Germans, you must realize how cheap human life had by then
become. It was at the time of the heaviest British and American
air raids upon our civilian cities when, with our men at the front,

our women and children were being killed night after night—sometimes as many as two hundred thousand in a single city in a single night.

"Of course," he said, looking at me with narrowed eyes and talking rapidly, "I know it was war, but you must realize how cheap it made the value of a human life, so that orders were then both issued and obeyed which at the beginning would have been unthinkable. I suppose it is always so at the end of a war. I remember once when we were falling back out of Russia, I saw a column of Russian prisoners being marched ahead of our retreat under guard, and saw our guards shoot through the head those prisoners who straggled and could not keep up, never giving a second thought to the fact that they were taking a human life. Only after five years of war was such a thing possible. In the first years, the men who did this thing would have been as shocked at the idea as any civilian."

That was his answer, and I should like to stress the fact that it is typical. Whenever one brings up the subject of what happened to the Jews, all Germans are always deeply shocked, usually insist that they knew little and did not approve of what they knew even at the time, and shortly after that the conversation somehow always drifts around to the bombing of their cities.

I always express deep sympathy, explaining that I spent the blitz in London before the Allied bombings of Germany started, so that I know from personal experience exactly what the Germans went through.

That always ends this particular topic of conversation.

CHAPTER VII

THIS IS A FRÄULEIN

OF COURSE past and future are always linked, for the future is only a product of past and present. But perhaps we have spent too much time on Germany's past and you might be interested in looking at one of those who will make her future.

I first met Dorothea Klein in the office of one of the German newspapers, where she was a reporter. She is a very competent newspaper woman, with a keen sense of humor. She finished three semesters at the University of Berlin at the age of 21, and, without being particularly pretty, is most attractive.

It occurred to me that she ought to be representative of that generation in Germany which was formed under Hitler, because when he came to power she was only eight years old. It is also the generation which will take over whatever power is left to Germany in the next twenty years.

So what are they like? What do they think of it all now? And, into this thinking, how deeply has the National Socialist viewpoint been ingrained, if at all?

I asked her if she could spare an afternoon to fill me in on general background about people of her age in Germany: what has happened to them and what they now think about things—not only the girls but the boys who have come back from the army.

I said back home our demobilized GIs were having their troubles and undoubtedly it would be the same over here. She said she'd be glad to help me out, so we made a date for the following day. Of course, since she was a non-canine German, it was impossible for me to take her to dinner. But I set out half a dozen bottles of Coca-Cola on a table in my sitting room, plus some candy bars, a freshly-opened can of almonds, and a package of crackers, all from the PX, which were the only things I could legally share with her, and sent my red-headed scout to fetch her.

Then we opened the Coca-Cola, which was fairly cold from the electric refrigerator downstairs, and also the crackers, and presently got down to work. My red-headed scout stayed around, partly because Dorothea is an old friend of his, mostly because he is unusually fond of Coca-Cola which he learned to like when he was with the North German Lloyd—he now insists that, because of his suffering when he could not get it during the war, he ought to qualify for membership in the "Victims of Fascism."

Dorothea had arrived in an indignant mood because of the story on which she had been working. It seemed that the paper which she represented was the organ for one of Germany's non-Communist parties, although it was licensed by the Russians and, therefore, operated under Soviet censorship.

Two nights before, one of the leaders of this party had been to an afternoon entertainment given by some Americans. There had been cocktails, and in the course of two hours he had taken a couple. At about five o'clock in the evening, he had started walking home. There was, in his neighborhood, an outfit of American engineers who had quite a reputation for rowdyism. He said that all he remembered was that when he was about two hundred yards from his house, he noticed that an American soldier was approaching him on the sidewalk, but he paid no particular attention to this.

The next thing he remembered was that he was lying on his back on the sidewalk with a bloody nose and fast-blackening eye. The soldier, in the meantime, had gone. It probably doesn't matter that the party of which he was one of the leaders was most sympathetic to America.

He finally dragged himself home. All of his German friends who heard the story indignantly advised him to file a protest with the commander of the American outfit, and he agreed to make a report. His next-door neighbor, however, warned him that this would do no good. This neighbor was a German Jew who had returned since the war from concentration camp, and was therefore a member of the privileged "Victims of Fascism." The neighbor explained that he recently filed a protest with this commander against these Americans for breaking two of his windows while playing ball. Glass is very scarce in Berlin. The result of this protest was that two or three days later one of the soldiers knocked on his door and told him that if he ever made another protest they would break every goddam window in his house and burn it down afterwards. The Jew decided that if this unit stayed he would move out of the neighborhood.

Dorothea was indignant, not only about this but because it seemed that German men are often beaten up by our soldiers.

"Perhaps," volunteered my red-headed scout, "he was not really drunk, but just two drinks would make him feel happy, so that he carelessly forgot to step off the sidewalk as he passed the American soldier."

"I myself am not afraid to go on the streets of Berlin even at night," said Dorothea. "because I am a girl. Americans do not hate girls. Sometimes they call out, or take me by the arm, but I only say nicely, 'Please let me go, I am not a bit interested in you,' and they say, 'Okay,' and walk off. But a man should not be out at night, even in the American sector, for he may be robbed or knocked down. Mostly they only knock them down and call them 'damned Dutch.'

"Mostly this happens when the Americans are a little drunk. Then sometimes they stop German men who are then knocked down because maybe they have not understood the thing which the American has said to them. I think that the Americans find it fun to fight with Germans, and struggle with them.

"I have found some Americans who really hate Germans, and this I can't understand. Recently there was an American movie,

Fighting Lady, which I wanted to see, playing at the Titania.*
I had asked an American soldier to take me there—he was ac-
quainted with a girl friend of mine—explaining that I was a journalist and wanted to see the difference between your films and
ours.

"But when we got to the gate, the sergeant in charge said no.
I think he did not realize that I understood English because then
he said, 'Every time I can help a German down, I help them
down.' I said nothing.

"But mostly American soldiers are very kind. I have the feeling that they don't hate Germans at all, so I can't understand why
they knock down our men.

"German men are naturally jealous if their girls go with
American men. A few Sundays ago I was on my way to meet
some German friends who had given me the address of their
home, but somehow I found I did not have the directions cor-
rectly. So I stopped a young man on a bicycle to ask him if he
knew how to find this street.

" 'You take the first left turn, then the next right.' Then he
said, 'By the way, Americans live in that house, don't they?'

" 'No, you are wrong,' I said. 'Germans live there. I'm going
to Germans.'

" 'Oh,' he said. 'There are still girls in Berlin who go with
Germans?'

" 'Why not?' I said.

"Yet many girls in Berlin have left their homes and parents
and now live in apartments which their American boy friends
have taken for them. The boy friends go to German families and
say, 'I will give you cigarettes or money, and you will give me
one room.' Then their German girls live in this one room. When
this American goes back home, naturally the girl tries to meet
another. You see these girls standing before the American barracks, speaking to soldiers when they come out. The soldiers

* This is one of Berlin's largest movie houses, now taken over exclusively
for American troops.—WLW.

take them to their clubs. Often they sneak them into their barracks. If it is late at night and no tramway is going—what else can they do?

"There are, working in your American barracks and messes, many women of society whose husbands had been officers in the army. But now they are dead and our banks are closed, and since people have no money, the widows now work for the Americans, washing dishes and waiting on table, to get food or money for their children. One of them I know well.

"These women who come from good German families, and who now see the little girls waiting for the American soldiers at the barracks doors, have a sad name for them. They call them 'Ruinenmäuschen'—in English it would be 'Ruin-mice'—after the poor little mice which now live in the ruins of bombed houses, feeding from the bodies which may still lie beneath them, or perhaps on buried food, growing fat out of the devastation and decay of our country—and yet not evil, only sad, innocent, weak little things who somehow must eat to live.

"Ruinenmäuschen—a sad little name for sad little people—do you not think?

"At seven o'clock when I come home from my office I take a street car which comes out through the American sector, and it is always full of these little girls, dressed up to go to the American enlisted men's clubs. They are girls who are not accustomed to lipstick, and yet now they wear it. They have nice dresses which the boys have bought for them, and they smoke American cigarettes. It is a special type which I could show you on the streets.

"And, of course, they speak a terrible English which is made up of GI slang and has no grammar. Often they speak a terrible German too, but sometimes they are very nice girls of decent families.

"Most of our people are angry with them. But my opinion is that anyone can do as he likes. If a girl wants to ruin herself, if

THIS IS A FRÄULEIN

she likes 'snow jobs' * and believes in them, if she likes cigarettes and chocolates and is willing to pay the price, that is her
business.

"It is also true that today there are not many German men.
Many were killed in the war, and still more of our boys are yet
prisoners in Russia or in France. Those who are back show the
effects of having been long in the war. They are very serious,
many have been wounded, all of them are worried for their
future, so it is natural that some girls who look only at the outward things in a man say: 'Why should I go with such a man?
I can have a nice one, a good-looking one, who has everything
I need.' These girls take Americans.

"It is not only for the food that they go with them. There
are also other reasons. The second one would be that they want
to amuse themselves, and Americans are gay and carefree.
Thirdly, they have an interest in foreign peoples and are curious
about these foreigners. Fourthly, the girls who have Americans
think that they are better than the other girls, that this is proof
that they are more beautiful and more interesting.

"Do you know what we who are back from the war think of
all this?" asked my red-headed scout. "We have a saying, 'We
stood up for six years against the whole world, but now our
women lie down in five minutes.' "

"But in war there is always demoralization," said Dorothea.
"It was the same way in France when French men were all in
camps, so their women went with our men. And do you know
what some of our women are now saying? They say to the men,
'For six years you were away in foreign countries seeing new
things, doing things you do not tell us about, while we stayed
home and worked. Well, now it is our turn!' "

* This is very new American slang which has originated with our army
of occupation in Germany. A "snow job" is a tall exaggerated story, told
by an American soldier to a foreign girl, about how wonderful everything
is in America, and how rich and distinguished his own family is back home.
The German explanation is that they are so called because if the girl ever
sees the reality, the story she has been told will melt like snow.—WLW.

Now that we were on this subject, I asked Dorothea and my red-headed scout about a story which had several times appeared in the American papers during the war, concerning recreation camps which had been provided by the army for German air force officers on leave. According to this story, each man was provided, during his stay, with a German girl who had had to pass a strict examination, and if later there were any children, these were cared for by the state. I asked Dorothea what she knew of this.

"I think it is complete nonsense!" she said. "Surely if such things had existed, we would have heard of them! * Anyway, I disbelieve it completely because there was no need for it. There were girls enough and in every country who were eager to go with pilots, so that they would not have to be provided by the state. Did your government need to bring girls to your fliers? Mostly they must be chased away!

"It reminds me of a Nazi book that I came across during the war. The University of Berlin had been bombed, and we students were cleaning up the rooms after the attack. It was in about 1943. One of the girls ran across a book called *The Perfect Body from Blood and Soil* and opened it to see what it was about. It was a silly book in which the writer was saying that a special type of German girl should be designated with a number, and then be connected with storm troopers to bring up the perfect German type.

"The girl who found the book began to scream with laughter as she read it, and presently the other girls gathered around, saying, 'What's that? What do you have there?' And when she read them a little of it, they all said, 'But this is *Schweinerei*—read more, what else does this fool say?'—giggling and laughing. You see we students at the University of Berlin were against the Nazis. We wanted to be free, and any normal person would think this was nonsense."

* Not completely convincing, since so many Germans were unaware of the extermination camps, which certainly existed.—WLW.

"Have you ever heard of the fatherhood draft card?" asked my red-headed scout.

"What is that?" asked Dorothea.

"In 1944 I got one in the mail," he said with a grin. "It was printed, and it said, 'You have been selected as the perfect specimen of German manhood. It is essential that your kind should be reproduced, and since there are so many German women whose husbands have been away in the war for years, you have an obligation to the state. For this reason you are ordered to report at such-and-such a Gestapo station at such-and-such a time, where your specifications will be taken down, and you will then be notified of your duties.' "

By this time Dorothea was laughing. "Did you go?" she finally said.

"Of course not," he said, "I could see it was a joke. But many cards were sent out, and there must have been some who took them down to police headquarters and asked what room they should go to for the fatherhood draft.

"I am not even sure that it was a joke. I think it may have been circulated by the underground to arouse feeling against the SS and the party for treating poor German women in such a way.

"After all, in 1940, our propaganda for the French was almost the same. We dropped over their lines many colored pictures showing British Tommies standing over French women, and warning French soldiers that they should return to their homes to protect their family honor, hoping that we could get them to leave the Maginot Line."

"But speaking of camps such as you mentioned," Dorothea said to me, "I have never heard of that, and I am sure that some rumor would have reached us. There were places to which unmarried mothers could go to have their babies—but I think these exist in all countries. There was also a school which lasted eight weeks, to which all girls who were engaged to SS troopers were supposed to go. There they were taught to care for children and

to cook. And probably Nazi propaganda as well—certainly they
never missed a chance for that! But, in general, I do not think
it is a bad thing to train girls for things they will need to know
when they are married.

"There is one terrible thing which they did, and which comes
near to the things that were in that book. Every girl who was
going to marry either an SS trooper or a German officer had to
go to a doctor for examination, and he had to sign a paper saying
that she had no inherited sickness, and also that she would be
able to have babies. That was terrible! You would think that
you were some farm animal, and that the farmer wanted only
healthy calves and cared nothing about you!

"But as for that story which you say was printed in America,
it is possible that such places existed and I did not hear of them,
but I think it is all a propaganda dream."

"Did you hear about the death camps?" I asked.

"Not at first. We heard, of course, that there were concentration camps to which Communists were sent, and where they
were not too well treated, but what really went on we only
began to realize later, when we saw the prisoners being marched
to work, and how they looked.

"The first that I really learned about the death camps I
learned from my uncle. He was—I do not know how you would
say it in English—the chief of a house to which crazy people are
sent—he was the head doctor, and this place was in Silesia. One
day our family visited him, and he said to my father, 'In a few
days this whole place will be empty.'

" 'Why?' asked my father.

" 'Because all these people will be removed.'

" 'But why?'

" 'Because,' said my uncle, 'I was ordered to bring all of these
patients to gas chambers where they would be killed, but I refused to do this, so now the order has come that they are to
be taken to another hospital, and I know what will happen to
them there. The other director will not refuse.'

"When I heard this, I could not at first believe it, and said to him, 'You are my uncle, but you are crazy!' Yet he is an honest man, and at last we had to believe it. This was in about 1943 or 1944. Later, of course, we heard much more about it.

"The crazy people who were under my uncle were, of course, all Germans, but if they would do this to Germans I knew, of course, they would do it more quickly to others, even to ones who were not crazy.

"The Jews? We saw that they were fewer and fewer, so we thought that they were being sent out of the country. At this time I was in the university and had no interest in the news. But there was a big hatred, a real hatred, against the Jews in Germany at that time. Naturally, there were some people—for instance, my parents—who always told me that there are many good Jews and that it is wrong to treat a whole people in such a way.

"They had been very happy in Germany before Hitler came. After the First World War, many had come to Germany from Poland. These knew all about business and they did very well. Of course, there was a little feeling. I know that. Of some hotels, my father would say, 'I do not care to go there, there are too many Jews.' But, on the other hand, there were always Jews who were your friends.

"How is it now? Well, you still find here that, although people do not hate them, yet there is a distance. Not an intellectual distance, but only one of feeling. Yesterday I talked with a Jewish journalist, a girl who had lived in hiding all during the war. She said to me:

"'We don't feel happy in Germany, even though now we are free. We want to leave.' And then she said, 'We have suffered so much and for so long, and for this suffering we now should have special rights. We deserve this to make up for what you have done to us. But,' she said, 'we don't get them. We even live in a worse way than you Germans, because we have been so long out of our jobs. Therefore,' she said, frowning at me, 'we want to leave.'

"That was the first time that I have found Jewish people who spoke to me in such a way. As soon as the war was over, we expected that Jewish people would come in from abroad in big numbers to do business. But that didn't happen, and as for the German Jews who were in hiding during the war or who returned from concentration camps, I have always found them very kind to the rest of us, and not at all arrogant. I even found them a little shy, and I think that they fear this terrible country where they have been persecuted in such a brutal way.

"And there is still much fear of the past in Christian Germans as well as Jews. For instance, the older men who are coming back from the war want to have nothing to do with political parties. They say it is too dangerous. They say that when the Nazis came in, people were punished for being in other parties. Now they are again being punished for having been in the Nazi party. So now they say, 'If we now join your party, how do we know what will happen in ten years? Please let me go. Do not make me join.'

"This is not my opinion. I can understand why people should be afraid to join parties when they are old, when they have seen two wars, and are now weak from hunger and care only for food.

"But young people should be interested in parties because that is the future. And I am glad that my little cousin, who is only sixteen, is very much interested in politics, as are the other boys in his school. So we need not be afraid for our young. The trouble is that the people over forty do not care now for politics. It is they who have had the experience, and it is this very experience which we young people need. Because we have seen only the Nazi times, and can remember nothing beyond this. I, for instance, cannot remember a time when Hitler was not reigning.

"But it is not true to say that our young people have been spoiled by Hitler. A few, perhaps, yes. There is a type of boy, mostly they have been young officers in the war, who already have a soldier's character, and their Nazi education has killed the germs of all other character. Mostly they are now twenty-four and twenty-five. Perhaps those cannot be re-educated. But this type is only a few.

"Of course, very young boys come with a book on the war and they say, 'Isn't it wonderful?' Boys always dream of military heroes at this age. And the way to correct it is not to tell such a boy that all our soldiers were bad people and criminals. He knows better, and if he sees you are telling lies, he will not trust you. The young have a very keen feeling for propaganda.

"Instead, you must tell him that there can be heroes and great men and fine leaders in the ways of peace, rather than in those of war. That he will believe.

"In addition, it is not good to tell him that *everything* that he learned in the Hitler Jugend was wicked, because this again was not true. Actually, it was much like the Boy Scouts except that there was also Nazi education. It is better to say that only this was wrong, rather than the whole. Young boys of this age love to struggle and to dare. You have a nice way of using this desire in the Boy Scouts. But that was a grip which Hitler had on the youth, because he used this thing in a wrong way.

"You can get to children if you tell them how much the Nazis did that was wrong and inhuman. Then they are all ashamed inside, because they have been fooled. They really see that this part of it was wrong, and they confess it."

"What was it like for girls under Hitler?"

"I only remember dimly how it was before. I do know, for instance, that before he came girls were happy in the knowledge that they were equal and could go to school. For instance, I was told that in 1931 and 1932 some women would not allow a boy to buy her beer. She was independent and would pay for it herself. But under Hitler, it was not considered good for women to go to school. Their place was in the home and with the children.

"I knew that I would have to go to a Nazi work camp by the

time I was eighteen, but since I wanted to begin college then I got my high school degree when I was seventeen so that this would give me a year off before college when I could go to work camp, which I would be compelled to attend before I could enter college.

"I told myself before I went that I must keep up my inward strength to defend myself against the propaganda they would inject in me there.

"Some of the camps treated the girls very badly, especially the ones coming from good families, who were made to work harder than the rest because the Nazis wanted to show them that you are no better than they are. For instance, one friend told me that when the girls first arrived, they were lined up in a long row and were told that those who had high school diplomas should step forward. When these had come out of the ranks, they were told:

" 'So you are educated women! Well, your first duty will be to clean the toilets.' Only about 5 per cent of the girls in the work camps had high school diplomas.

"It happened that the camp I went to was an especially good one. The leader said, 'We will have comradeship here, and no one will be better than the others, but I want you to have good customs and good manners.' I was the only one out of the forty-five girls in this group who had a high school diploma and the leader told me she was afraid of having a girl like me among the others, because they might treat me badly. And she tried in every way to protect me.

"Now all girls in Germany who can think are so glad that both the war and the reign of the Nazis is over. Today, these are not good times but, for people of intelligence, they are better than the others."

"Why were you so much opposed to the others?" I asked. "And why is it so much better now?"

"Because I hated the way of uniforming all people! I wanted to be a person myself, and not just one of the crowd, compelled to do this and that, to be looked on only as a woman who has to get children! I hate the people who close the limits of the country, and will not let you know what happens outside of it, and when we are only told lies about other people! I hate to see wrong done, and you do not dare to oppose it!

"I hate that one man should have all power, and can do whatever he wants! I hated that one party has all right, and the other does not have any right!

"You say we young people have known nothing but Hitler, and that is true. But, knowing him, we have learned to understand and to hate things like this far better than you in the Western world, who have only read of them in books!

"I have heard Americans say pityingly that Germans are politically ignorant, and this makes me very angry. It is as though one would say to a man who has almost died of yellow fever that, of course, he is ignorant of disease. We who have once lost freedom love it far more than you who have always had it! Furthermore, I think we recognize even better than you the symptoms of those forces which hate freedom, and would like to take it away!

"And I think that we who have lost freedom will fight harder to keep it now, and also with more skill, than someone who has always had it, and so cannot know what a precious thing it is to lose!"

This was the story of a girl so young that she remembers only the reign of Hitler. She is not all of the youth of Germany, but I wish she were.

CHAPTER VIII

THE RUSSIANS IN GERMANY

IN JULY 1945, two months after the fighting had ended, the Americans, British, and French were allowed to enter Berlin and presently took part in the big Allied victory celebration. Soviet Russia was represented in the reviewing stand by Marshal Zhukov, covered with medals which extended from both shoulders down to his umbilicus. America was represented by Lieutenant General George Patton, surely no shrinking violet, except in contrast to Zhukov, since his medals were represented only by narrow ribbons.

As the parade began to pass, Zhukov stepped forward to take the salutes. General Patton, who had broken out of Normandy and jumped the Rhine, and who had been standing beside Zhukov, also moved forward to return the salutes, but what then happened is as follows:

Marshal Zhukov turned, said, "No, General," and putting his palm against Patton's broad shoulder, exerted pressure on it. It would be exaggerating to say that Marshal Zhukov shoved General Patton back to a subordinate position, one pace behind him and one to the left. That is, however, exactly where he placed him. In so doing the marshal had the book on his side, for General Patton had, at that writing, only three stars, and was indubitably in a position where Zhukov could pull rank.

This little incident of the rearward propulsion of George Patton pretty well sums up those early days in Berlin. And if the Russians did not always have rank, they certainly had seniority and made the most of it. They were there first and had two months to take their pick of what they wanted, and to organize what was left in their own way.

They thoroughly organized Berlin's city administration, putting it in the hands of their hand-picked Germans. They decided what political parties should be allowed to organize, and what Germans might organize them. They licensed newspapers which presumably represented all of these parties, thus putting under Soviet censorship not only the German Communist press but the official press of all the other parties as well.

Then, as a condition for admitting the other Allies to Berlin, they extracted an agreement that, after they arrived, this status quo could be changed only by unanimous agreement, which meant that any changes would have to be improvements from the Russian standpoint or else must be bought by concessions in other fields.

In those early days the Germans lived in considerable terror of the NKVD, which was continuing the same system of secret arrests and quiet kidnappings which they had known under the Nazis. Germans who showed a disposition to co-operate too closely with the Western Allies were obvious victims.

The head of the Berlin NKVD was Major General Alexis Sidnev, who never went out except in a beautifully polished bullet-proof German Mercedes, with motorcycle escort. By contrast his opposite number, the American chief of military intelligence, on the American side went everywhere unguarded, in a jeep which he drove himself.

However, it did not take the representatives of the democracies long to get the hang of the NKVD's methods, or to develop a certain crude skill of their own. One night, three well-known German judges, equivalent in rank to an American superior court judge, and known to be non-Communist, mysteriously disappeared from their homes in a non-Soviet sector. There had been many other such disappearances, but when representatives of the Western Allies, in their routine meetings with Major General Sidnev, complained that Germans were saying the NKVD was responsible, Sidnev would always deny it blandly, and if pressed, would invariably say, "Whom do you believe, me or the Germans?"

There had been no good answer. Now one of the intelligence heads decided that something should be done. Presently rumors began to circulate that in a certain address in the area occupied by his government, lived two merry German bachelors, one an atomic physicist and the other a specialist in rocket propulsion.

It worked. Soon Russian plainsclothesmen were prowling the neighborhood and finally one night a dozen of them, riding in a closed truck, moved in for the kill.

Next morning General Sidnev received a formal call from one of his Allied colleagues, who again complained that Germans in his sector were fearful of kidnappings by the NKVD.

As usual Sidnev shrugged his shoulders. As usual he said, "Whom are you going to believe—the Germans or me?"

"Well, General, under ordinary circumstances it always gives me the greatest of pleasure to believe you. But it happens right now I'm holding twelve of your men in my jail."

There followed a very long pause. Then General Sidnev said, "All right. How can I get them back? What do you want?"

"Nothing. I'll make you a present of them, old boy. They'll be released late this afternoon. But I wanted you to understand that we are getting concerned about these kidnappings, and hope that none of your people start disappearing."

We must, as the fellow-travelers used to say, learn to understand the Russians. In Berlin the Western Allies are slowly learning, with the result that while Germans still disappear in the Russian sector of Berlin, this has largely stopped in the British, French and American sectors.*

With its arrival in Berlin, the Red Army went through a revolution in thinking. First, there was considerable pilfering of the

---

* But, alas, only temporarily. As recently as March 1947 the New York *Times* chronicled another wave of "disappearances" of German men actively identified with non-communist German parties who were known to be friendly with Americans.—WLW.

homes of working-class Germans, the Soviet soldiers thinking they were homes of the bourgeoisie. And when it finally percolated through their minds that this was not so, the Russian AWOL rate began to soar. The trouble was, of course, that there was no place to go. But anyway they tried.

Shortly after we got into Berlin, a stream of Soviet officers, including a number of full colonels, began coming to our headquarters, asking if they could enlist in our army and thus obtain American citizenship. We politely explained that we had no provisions for accepting enlistments from the Soviet army, and they would go sadly away.

I asked the American official who told me this if they came in a body.

"No," he said, "always separately. Nobody bothered to count them, but we had many colonels, as many as four Soviet majors come in one day, and lower officers without number. In the cases of those of the rank of sergeant and under, we put them under arrest as deserters and turn them over to their own people. Simply as a courtesy. What happens to them after that? We don't know, and it isn't our business."

"The first week we were here, one of my lieutenants happened to be standing by his jeep on the street corner when a Russian captain came up and asked if he could join our army. When my man told him it couldn't be done, he said, well, then at least he wanted to buy his jeep and offered him 30,000 Reichsmarks for it—that's $3000. He had the money, too—pulled it out of his pocket.

"When my man told him it was no go, he walked off shaking his head, very discouraged at the whole deal.

"Pretty soon, however, word got around among the Russians that we weren't taking any Soviet enlistments, and presently the stream tapered off."

Meanwhile the difference in living standards was making trouble for the Russians back home, and to counteract it the Soviet government began a radio campaign to their own people, the climax of which was a little jingle which translates into English approximately as follows:

A little pig once traveled abroad.
There he became very lazy and fat,
He acquired luxurious possessions and returned home.

Now nothing is to his taste.
Always it was better back there!
He doesn't like this!
He doesn't like that!

The Moral is clear: a pig is ever a pig,
And such pigs will meet the fate of a pig!

Turn now to politics. The Russians early moved to get control of German labor unions, and presently held union "elections" as follows. In their sector they assembled several hundred Germans who presumably represented 20,000 workers. Mixed with them were many Russians in uniform.

A stooge would then arise and nominate a candidate as follows: "Here is Willy Schmidt—a good boy, a good Communist [or maybe he's served in concentration camp or been to workers school in Moscow], he's the people's friend and we should elect him president." Then they would go on down the list of offices to be filled, making one nomination for each. Then the chairman would say, "We have here presented six fine, public-spirited men to be your delegates. Is there anyone here who opposes their election?"

The Germans would look around the hall. This is the procedure with Moscow labor unions, as it was in Hitler's labor front, but it was not the practice before 1933 in Germany. "However, with all those Russian uniforms, no German dared open his trap," explained my observer, "so the six were unanimously elected."

When the Americans started talking for secret ballots and participation of all parties in these and other elections, the Russians were frankly shocked. This was no part of democracy as Moscow understood it.

However, the Americans point out that there is no trick of machine politics which the Berlin Communists don't know. They have a leader in every block, as did the Nazis before them, and if a woman whom they have spotted for a potential party member becomes ill, the leader sees to it that she gets quick medical attention and an increase in food rations. These tactics get results, just as they do in any machine-ruled American city.

But there is always that old familiar dilemma of democracy: if we win, we don't liquidate our opponents, whereas the other crowd does. The vast majority of Berlin Germans, and particularly intellectuals, look eagerly to the West. But many of them are afraid to have this known, not only because of the kidnappings, but because what would happen to them if there were a high-level fuss and the Russians kicked us out of Berlin? In America this fear seems childish; in Berlin it is ever-present.

Consequently, one of our high-ranking officers, whose duty it was to make friendly contacts with German intellectuals and who had many close German friends, always wore his civilian clothes when they invited him to their homes. They liked it better that way, explaining that, should we ever leave Berlin, the Russians would remember.

From the minute the Red Army entered Berlin, the Russians were squarely back of the German Communist party, reorganizing it, financing it, and giving its leaders every facility.

The American policy was the exact opposite—to do nothing, to stay entirely out of German politics. Before Hitler the strongest anti-Nazi party in Berlin was the Social Democratic party, which represented the great majority of German labor then, and has even more of it today. At the beginning they got no help from us. The Russians presented the Communists with an imposing five-story office building, equipped with twenty-one telephones; the Social Democrats had difficulty in renting a single bombed-out room. The Communists got all the motor cars and gasoline they needed, extra butter and food rations for all leaders of any importance and any Social Democrats who would desert to them. The Communists had all the printing presses they could use and an unlimited supply of paper. The Social Democrats had none of these things.

And then came the house on Gelfertstrasse. Although officially we stayed out, a number of Americans, interested in holding German labor for democracy, got in as private citizens, and most of them were just that. Leon Dennen, for instance, happened to be visiting Germany as a relief representative of the AFL, but the non-Communist wing of the CIO was in it too. Big, good-natured Bill Kemsley, a friend of Walter Reuther who had just won his UAW election against the Communists, was there, as well as Newman Jeffrey, and the hardest worker of them all was probably George Silver, a young American of Jewish origin who as a child had lived in the Eastern European ghettos and so knew the price of human misery.

All of these men know labor and labor's politics. They arrived at a time when German Social Democracy, traditionally the party of free German labor, was being pushed to the wall by the Communists for lack of the means to fight back.

These American civilians couldn't, of course, hope to equal the aid the Red Army was giving the German Communists. But our boys, if they could not have printing presses, might at least have a few typewriters. And when the Americans discovered that a carton of Chesterfields would buy a couple, cables went whizzing from their house on Gelfertstrasse to Detroit, with the result that in a few weeks, what with the air mails, German Social Democracy had at least a few mimeograph machines, enough paper on which to send out their notices and, best of all, the feeling that labor in the West had not abandoned them. Some day the whole story can be told of how the German Social Democratic party in Berlin was initially set up in business with the aid of fifteen cartons of airmailed cigarettes from Detroit.

Other things came later. The American group couldn't match

the heavy food rations or the motor cars supplied to the German Communist party by the Russians. But at least vitamin tablets could come by air mail from America—the house on Gelfertstrasse had whole dresser drawers tightly packed with them—plus a few food parcels, so that, if you wanted to fight for free German labor, your family need not starve as the penalty.

And you had a place to go—warm, well-lighted rooms where the young people could roll back the rugs and dance to the phonograph in the evening, and the feeling that, if the American government officially didn't care whether free German labor lived or died, there were Americans who did, and that free American labor was stretching out a helping hand to German labor, beckoning it to a free world after fourteen years of Hitler.

So much for the Russians in Berlin, and now for the Russian zone itself, in which Berlin is an island. Americans who have traveled there (they are not many and it is not permitted often) report that the Russians have done as good a job as we have in getting the country organized, and sometimes better. They have, in the larger German towns, more or less the same military government set-up that we have in ours, and their people seem well qualified and serious about their jobs.

The Russian WACs, who in the early days did much of the policing, have been demobilized and returned to Russia. The Russian girls who are waitresses in the Russian messes are DPs. There is no unofficial fraternizing or public parading with *Fräulein*, and while a certain amount of it goes on in private, it is severely punished.

In contrast to our zone, where the Americans occupy the best houses, the Russians lead a comparatively spartan life in theirs. The offices of the German *Bürgermeister* and town council in any German city in the Russian zone are a good deal more luxurious than are the offices of the Soviet *Kommandatur*, which are usually starkly furnished, the only decoration being the inevitable portrait of Stalin.

Typically the Russians live together in a guarded compound, just as they do at Karlshorst in Berlin, to which no one is admitted without a pass. However, they treat the German officials well, courteously return their salutes (which we do not), and entertain them with official banquets from time to time.

Where they lag, in comparison to us, is in the matter of permitting any political development which could lead to a free and democratic Germany. The propaganda of the Russian-sponsored *Einheits* party flares from every billboard, and, within the Russian zone, other parties are almost as impotent as they are in Russia or were under Hitler, although they are permitted to exist.

In 1946 the Russians held a great fair in Leipzig which included many exhibits of German industrial products. The crowd soon discovered, however, that most of these were samples and the rest were not on sale, but were earmarked for export to Russia as reparations.

Constantly the Russians at this fair told the Germans: "Again Germany is producing—at least in our zone. That is because we have a plan. In the British and American zones, there is no plan."

But as a German who visited that fair later told me, "That may be true, but in the British and American zones, although their courts are strict, at least an accused German may state his case and it is considered. In the Russian zone there are no courts; you simply disappear. We would rather have fair courts and not so good a plan."

Although the Russians deal sternly with war criminals and prominent Nazis, the small fry are unmolested, and many in the Russian zone have joined the Communist party. Now they argue loudly that Germany is hemmed in and encircled by capitalists (two years ago they were saying it was by Jews) and that her only hope of survival is to join with Russia, where the bread basket of the Ukraine will be available to feed German workers. It is Kaiser Wilhelm II's *Drang nach Osten*, or, as Hitler said, "Only give me the Ukraine, and what would I not do with it!"

These recent converts to Communism have only subordinated

their German nationalism, not abandoned it. Just as Hitler dreamed of revolutionizing and developing Russia's raw materials with skilled Nazi technicians, it is now skilled German Communist technicians who will do the same job, building a mighty striking force for World Revolution, and the only thing which has changed is the slogan on the banner.

However, the Russians are not entirely satisfied with many of their converts. A German who works in the Soviet-controlled city administration of Berlin tells me that, in the early days of occupation, the Russians were always bringing in nondescript Germans and insisting that they be put to work in key positions, on the grounds that they were loyal Communists or "democrats."

Now they often tell the Germans, "If they are bad workers, you can turn them out," which is a great improvement. Actually Germans now are beginning to suspect that in many instances German Communists claim to be backed by the Russians when actually they are only bluffing, and that many Russians have a low opinion of German Communists. A high Russian officer told my German friend that "There is a great difference between German and Russian Communists—the Germans are centuries behind us!"

Germany's problem both for the present and in the future is food and here the Russian zone is better off than those occupied by the Western powers, for the region is largely agricultural.

Germany's population before the war was 69 millions, and she needed to import much food. Today, in spite of her war losses, her population is 70 millions, owing to the fact that many Germans formerly living in East Prussia, Silesia or the Sudeten have been dumped into the new reduced Reich. Moreover, in the lands which have since been taken away from her and assigned to either Russia or Poland, Germany once raised 22 per cent of her food—and this includes 25 per cent of her potatoes, 23 per cent of her cereal grains and 12 per cent of her sugar beets. She must now feed more people with this much less land to till.

In times of near-starvation, when a diet is measured only by its ability to sustain life, it is counted in calories. However, if it is to grow healthy bodies, proteins are essential. American dietary experts estimate that each person needs at least seventy grams of protein a day, and that animal proteins are far more valuable than those which come from beans or grain.

Before the war, the average German was getting 92 grams of protein per day, of which 55 came from meat, eggs or milk. He is now getting only 25 grams of protein, of which only 4 come from animal products. While such a diet may keep old people alive, dieticians predict that the next generation of children cannot possibly develop healthy organs on it.

Probably less important than the land which Germany has lost is the machinery, which moved eastward in three waves. When the Russians first arrived, they took what they needed, crated and shipped it to Russia. But suddenly these shipments were stopped, as a result of the protests of German Communists, who argued that they could not be responsible for running the country unless something was left. This argument was also presented to the Russians by the former German Social Democratic leader Grotewohl, who, before he would promise to unite his followers with the Communists, made the Russians promise that, if he went through with it, they would leave something behind.

However, this did not apply to railways, which constituted the second wave of dismantling. For instance, all of Germany's principal towns used to be connected with double track lines. Typical of the Russian zone today is the one from Berlin to Leipzig, which is now single track, and from which the Russians have also removed even the block signals, so that now, when a train passes the spot from which one has been removed, it must slow down while the stationmaster holds out to the engineer a paper message on the end of a long stick, which tells him whether or not he can proceed. Germans, ruefully viewing all this, say that their railway system is now back to where it was in 1840.

The third wave of removals in the Russian zone came after

the Russians were disappointed in the results of their forced merger of the Social Democratic and Communist parties, and with the German elections which followed. And many observers also consider it a sign that the Russians have given up the idea of holding onto their zone as a separate unit, that they now expect to join it with a unified Germany, but intend to pluck it clean before they do.

But the Russians have their side to all this, and no one understands it better than the high level Americans who weekly sit down with them to thresh out reparations problems.

The original Russian reparations man was General Shabolim who, during the war, had charge of moving Russian plants behind the Urals, and now quite understandably wants German plants to replace the ones destroyed. He was later replaced by Koval, whom the Americans find to be "a very able, polished, intelligent man, who knows what his government wants and does a damned good job of getting it."

And if the Russians are strong on reparations, "we would have the same point of view in their position," says our General Draper, who deals with them. "The Germans left Russia an industrial desert. Russia's basic need for capital equipment has always been tremendous. They have a low living standard themselves, so they don't worry about one for the Germans."

Nor is an even deeper sympathetic understanding of the Russians lacking in the lower echelons of our American set-up in Berlin. Particularly I have in mind the specialist who now sits daily at the elbow of another American general who deals with the Russians, to advise this officer on a subject in which he is an authority, and I shall call this expert Jones, because that is not his name.

I met him across a luncheon table at the big cafeteria in the AMGUS building, and, as we were finishing our coffee, more or less to make conversation, I asked him how he, as an expert, thought we were making out. He looked at me darkly.

"In what way?"

"Just in general. In Berlin. In Germany. In Europe. How are we Americans doing?"

"Now, I wouldn't want to be quoted."

"Oh, no. Nothing like that. I just wondered how you felt about it—for general background."

"But now this isn't for publication—"

"Oh, not at all. Just like to get your slant."

"Well," he said, "as an American I'm heartbroken."

"About what?"

"Well," he said, "if I'm not to be quoted—and I can't be, because I'm in an official position and these are my private views—I must say that it is very clear now to Europe that America has failed. Europe expected much of us, but we have proved inadequate to the task. All Europe sees that America cannot organize the world. She had a great opportunity, but didn't take advantage of it. She could not, because she was not worthy. And, of course, as an American, this makes me very sad."

"Of course."

"But since America had failed, it is natural that all Europe should now look to the Soviet Union, and will do so increasingly in the future."

"Why?"

Jones gave me a sweet, sad smile. "Because," he said, "it is clear to Europe that Russia has the only true democracy, that only in Russia do you find true social security for the Common Man, only in Russia do you have real free speech, while in America we have none of these things."

I had been listening most intently. Now Jones stopped and gave me his long, sweet, sad, forgiving, understanding smile again. "Do you agree?" he asked.

I said not entirely, but that I felt it was a most interesting view.

And so I do. But I was thinking of the four Russian majors

who, separately but all in one day, dropped into our headquarters to find out if there was a chance that they could join us and become American citizens, and then went sadly away. Somehow I had more admiration for their forthright handling of their disillusionment than for Jones.

CHAPTER IX

TOO MANY PEOPLE?

WE WERE about a dozen American correspondents down from Berlin, touring the British zone. Our hosts had given us a heavy day and got us back to the press camp at Herford a little late for dinner. Herford is a fair-sized town in Westphalia, and the press camp had been its best hotel. The British had set up a bar there, but it served only British drinks, which are small and mostly variations of pink gin.

We had also slept there the night before. When we now walked into the lobby, we were surprised to see, already settled in armchairs around the big fireplace at the end of the lobby, about a dozen officers in Red Army uniform.

"Who are they?" I asked our British conducting officer.

"Russian correspondents. We are giving them the same kind of trip you chaps are on. They have been out about ten days."

"I suppose it's a deal; I mean you finally got them to agree to let twelve British correspondents into their zone, so now you've agreed to admit twelve of theirs?"

"Not quite that. From the very first we told them that they were welcome to come into our zone at any time, and go wherever they liked; we didn't care.

"But you're right about one thing: we did have a devil of a time getting them to admit any of our chaps to theirs. It took a lot of talk and then some trading, but finally they agreed. They told us they'd take a few on a conducted tour, told us how many they would allow and exactly where they would go each day.

"So that was settled, but it wasn't the end. They said they wanted to talk again to me, and their Number One man said:

"'You say you let Soviet correspondents come to British zone?'

"'That's right,' I told him. 'Any amount of 'em, any time they like.'

"'You say they go anywhere they wish?'

"'Absolutely. Wander all over the place.'

"'That not enough,' this Soviet chap said.

He really had me there. "'Well, old man,' I said, 'what else can we do?'

"He looked at me very sternly. 'We want conducted tour!' he said.

"So now they're getting it. We submitted them a schedule of the towns we thought they might like to see. They didn't seem to care so long as they were conducted."

"Well, is there any reason why they should all stay in that end of the room, and we in this?"

"Not at all. Come along and I'll introduce you. They're nice chaps."

"Can I offer to buy them a drink at the bar?"

"Why not? Very sound idea. Come along."

In any Russian group there is always a leader, and this one seemed to be Colonel Nitikin, correspondent of the *Tägliche Rundschau*, the official Soviet-controlled German paper in Berlin. In turn, he introduced me to the correspondent for Tass, the *Red Star*, *Pravda*, *Izvestia*, and many other Soviet papers whose names have slipped me. They too seemed to have had a hard day, but they rose and were as polite as anyone can reasonably be whose feet are hurting.

Then I mentioned my proposed round of drinks. Several of them looked at Colonel Nitikin, but he said nothing: perhaps he had not understood. So we compared notes on what both parties had seen during the day. The colonel's English was not bad, but certainly not fluent. I talked with the others in German. Presently the colonel said to me:

"You are the first American I have ever met."

It turned out also that he had met no Englishman, and when I complimented him on his command of our speech he seemed pleased. Then I again mentioned my round of drinks.

Instead of answering, the colonel now waved his right arm. A little German waiter appeared, to whom he whispered briefly; the waiter nodded and left. By this time the other American correspondents had drifted over, had been introduced, and were mixed with the Russians. Presently the little waiter returned, lugging two enormous suitcases, one of which contained bottles of Soviet vodka and the other of which was filled with carefully-packed glasses. These he distributed to all of us.

It seemed that once more I was back in the clutches of Soviet hospitality, where the foreigner can buy nothing for himself or others, but where his smallest whim is law.

As the waiter went around with the vodka bottle, we all settled our chairs into a large semicircle around the fireplace. I remarked on how good it was to get genuine Russian vodka again, and how much better it was than *Schnaps*.

"But where have you tasted Russian vodka?" asked Colonel Nitikin.

"In Russia," I said.

"You have been in Russia?" he said, surprised. "When were you there?"

"During the war," I said.

"What year during the war were you there?" he asked.

"In 1944," I said.

Then I waited to see if he would ask, "What did you say your name was again?" Since he did not, I said how much I had enjoyed the country and its people, and how nice it was to have real vodka again.

The American and Russian reporters were all busy trying to talk to their neighbors in our big semicircle.

Mine was a handsome, somewhat chunky, blond and blue-eyed major in his early thirties, and we had no trouble because his German was good. He was one of the editors of the Berlin edition of the Soviet army newspaper *Red Star*. He seemed to be a straight-shooting, friendly, extremely intelligent soldier. I liked him, and I think he liked me. The vodka was good, but the glasses were small, so we had a couple more. We talked about our trip and he thought that the British were a little too excited about how underfed the Germans were. There was something to it, of course, but other people had been hungrier.

I agreed. Then I said that we had not yet seen the coal mines, but they were alike all over the world. And if you wanted coal—which was what the whole country needed—you had to give the miners a heavy diet. It wasn't a matter of patriotism or politics. In any country, if you didn't put in the food, you didn't get out the coal.

He agreed I was absolutely right. After a minute he leaned over.

"There is something I really want to know," he said, very earnestly. "Here we are, two great democracies. The others do not matter. They count for nothing." With a sweep of his hand, he pushed the British, the French, and the rest of the world out of the picture. I said nothing, but nodded so that he would go on.

"But what is this trouble about?" His tone was a little plaintive, a little angry, and very earnest. "We know that you do not want any of the things that we want!"

"That's right, we don't."

"And you must know that we don't want any of the things that you want."

"We know that too."

"Then, what is it about?" he said, puzzled and angry. "All these disputes, these arguments between us—we, the two great democracies, who need nothing that the other wants—why— why should this be?"

I could do one of two things. I could, of course, have gone diplomatic on him. But because he was being honest with me, I decided to play it straight with him. So I said:

"My friend, you seem to me to be a man of good heart, so I will not be polite, but will tell you what I truly think."

He leaned forward. "That's what I want," he said. "Tell me why you really think it is."

"You have said that neither country wants anything which the other needs, and that is true. You have also said that we are the two great democracies. It is true that no one else is stronger than we are. But, my friend, you are right that there is trouble, and you are right that you and I both fear there may be still more trouble, and I think that all of these troubles come from only one thing, and it is this: that when you use the word democracy, and when we use it, we mean two opposite things."

He had been leaning forward, listening intently to my every German word, and now he in turn had the chance to go diplomatic, to talk like Molotov or the Dean of Canterbury or Edgar Snow—to say smoothly that, of course, each country had that form of democracy which suited it best.

I liked him already, but I liked him still more because he didn't smoothly evade. Instead, he glanced around the circle. No one seemed to be listening closely to what anybody else was saying, yet our chairs were fairly close together. Then he glanced over his shoulder through the arch into the other room, which was empty. Now he picked up his vodka glass, motioning me to pick up mine.

"Let's go in there," he said.

We sat down on the big sofa, putting our vodka glasses on the coffee table. He offered me a cigarette. I took it and then I lighted his with my lighter.

"Now the first thing I want you to understand," he said, "is that I am not a member of the Party. Before the war I was a metallurgist. But this thing about democracy; first it must be understood from the historical standpoint.

"Now when democracy first began, in the sixteen, seventeen or eighteen hundreds, in England and in France, voting was the concern in each country of only a few hundreds of thousands of people. That was all right. Then it would work. But today we have to deal with hundreds of millions of people. That's too many people," he said, "and it won't work."

"We don't have hundreds of millions," I said, "but we have a hundred and forty million. With us, it works. Not always well, but it works."

He now seemed to be thinking of something else and did not answer at once. Then he said:

"Now, another thing, it is *not* true that we do not have freedom of criticism in Russia. We do have! [I had not mentioned this.] Just take my case. In time of peace I am a metallurgist. I know this subject well. If my government does something in the field of metallurgy which I think is wrong, I do not hesitate to criticize! I tell them frankly it is being badly done, and they listen. This is because I know metallurgy. Of course, other fields I do not know—politics, literature, many others. In these I do not criticize, and should not. I leave it to the ones who know."

"Well, in my country," I said, "it works like this. Suppose I'm only a ditch-digger. Suppose I'm not a very bright ditch-digger. Suppose I know nothing whatever about foreign affairs, but I think I do. I can stand up and say anything I like about those who are handling my country's foreign policy, and nothing happens to me. Furthermore, when the election comes, I can go down to the polls and vote against those people, and my vote counts for as much as the vote of any other man."

"But we let all those people vote in my country," he said. "Their votes are counted."

"I've been to your country," I said. "They vote, and their votes are counted. But I noticed one great difference. In our election the majority wins, but no matter how popular the issue, there is always a large minority—30 or 40 per cent, sometimes more. But, in your country I notice that in every election 99½ per cent of the votes, and sometimes more, are for the government, while only one-half of one per cent is against it. And we cannot understand how that can be."

He didn't answer immediately and I noticed the corners of his mouth were moving in a curious way. He leaned forward to look into the other room. The others were sitting just as we had left them. I now realized that he was grinning. Russians often smile, but foreigners seldom see them grin. He put his hand on my shoulder.

"My friend," he said, and he leaned close to my ear, "I do not understand it either."

I laughed and clapped him on the back. I said that now there were between the two of us no more misunderstandings, nor any reason to talk further. He, still grinning, said now we could go back into the other room, which we did.

The rest of the evening was non-political. There was more vodka, and somehow we got started singing. Toward the end I talked the Russians into giving us "Lubeme Gorod," which was to the Red Army in this war what "Lili Marlene" was to the Germans, and, in the last war, what "Madelon" and "Tipperary" were to the French and British, but which, curiously enough, is completely unknown in America.

With the Russians was one woman, of about 45, who had a plain, but kindly, flat Slavic face, and who wore a very plain gray dress, crudely cut out of a coarse material. In America, one might have taken it for the uniform of a matron in some women's penal institution. But she also wore the ribbons of several military decorations, and these gave her far more dignity than jewelry. She was the only one who spoke good English and seemed to be the interpreter, but we had little need of her, since all of both Russians and Americans spoke at least a little German.

It was a very pleasant evening. Of course, we told the Russians that as soon as we and they were back to Berlin, they must come over to dinner at our press camp. They seemed pleased to be invited.

However, none of them said anything to us about visiting them in theirs. We got no very clear idea as to whether or not they had one, but we gathered that, while they were certainly not inhospitable, any invitation to a foreigner to eat in a Russian mess was a serious matter, not to be extended on the spur of the moment, but only for an official reason of which the higher authorities approved.

And although we had all had a nice evening, we doubted that we would ever see any of them again. But that did not spoil it.

When it came time to go, Colonel Nitikin came with me to the door. We had been singing "Lubeme Gorod" for about the fifth time. As I walked on down the steps toward our car, he continued to sing it, his hearty Russian voice echoing down the darkened streets of that little German town.

CHAPTER X

"MEET THE ENEMY"

WE DID see Colonel Nitikin again, but I must first introduce the Baroness von B. One of the surprises which greet every newly-arrived American in Berlin is the breath-taking beauty of the German girls who work in the American press camp office. This is housed in a private mansion a few hundred yards from the club where the correspondents eat. The dozen German girls who handle the clerical work (and some of the administrative details as well, when a lieutenant or master sergeant takes the after-noon off to play tennis) at first glance seem as uniformly beautiful as Powers models, as pleasantly well-bred as the grad-uating class of Miss Spence's School, and as intelligent as the Vassar College chapter of Phi Beta Kappa.

There are two very understandably human reasons for this. The first one is that, outside of the Allied armies, all of Berlin is hungry to the point of malnutrition, and since Germans who work for our army are provided with one square American meal a day, we can have our pick of the entire population. The second reason is that the personnel officer who originally picked them, and has since returned to the States, seems to have been in every way a normal young man of combat age with the result that, instead of surrounding himself with bearded pro-fessors from the University of Berlin, he instinctively chose these girls between the ages of eighteen and twenty-five who could do the work as well and would, meanwhile, be easier on the eyes.

The one who took down the details of my credentials when I first arrived was a neat, pleasant-mannered, slender child of about nineteen whom the master sergeants called Annie. When she finished making out the form she asked me where I had learned my German.

When I explained that I had learned it here in Berlin in 1939 when I had been a correspondent, she eagerly asked me if I knew a mutual friend, naming a well-known correspondent.

Of course I did, for this correspondent had been in 1939 not only one of the journalists who knew Germany best but also, in the American colony, one of the leading anti-Nazis, second only to Bill Shirer.

So when I said of course I did, the girl introduced herself as Anna von B., said that in 1939 her mother had been one of this correspondent's very best friends, and possibly I had heard the correspondent mention the Baronin von B.?

Dimly I thought I had. I did remember that some of this well-known correspondent's best anti-Nazi contacts, who gave much information about the palace intrigues of the Hitler régime, had been members of the old German aristocracy who were, with few exceptions, strongly anti-Nazi. This aristocracy had close ties with the army, which in turn was full of more or less hostile but fairly accurate gossip about the power intrigues within the Nazi party.

I now thought I dimly remembered the correspondent's having mentioned a baroness and, when the girl said her mother would be so delighted to hear this, I said I hoped that while I was in Berlin one evening she and her mother could have dinner with me at the press club.

Only a very new arrival in Berlin would have said this. The girl's face immediately fell. She said her mother would be so anxious to meet me and to have any news of her old friend, but that my invitation could not be arranged, she was afraid.

I soon found out why. A wise but irksome regulation prevented any American newspaper man from inviting any German to a meal at the press club. The conquerors may not sit down to dinner with the vanquished, which creates an even deeper social barrier than that which divided the British from the Hindus in Kipling's day.

Politics did not enter into it. Even if the German had spent years in a concentration camp or was perhaps a German Jew who had survived the war in hiding, he was, for the purposes of the order, a German.

I hasten to add that the order does not apply to German dogs. There are many fine ones in this country, but now, what with food shortage, few Germans can afford to keep them. So they are given or sold to Americans, and several correspondents have so acquired them. Each night the owners of these dogs would go back to the kitchen to receive from the German kitchen employees a large can of table scraps.

No waste was involved here, for the regulation also severely punished anyone who gave garbage from an American mess to non-canine Germans. For a while there was confusion in interpreting the order, and one mess presented its garbage to a grateful German hospital, which processed it to remove the oils and fats which they then gave to their hungry patients. This, however, was soon clarified, and the garbage is now being either destroyed or fed to dogs.

You don't like this regulation? I think it is wise for several reasons. For, although I think we should send more food to Germany, we are already sending a great deal, and this is being equally distributed to all Germans in the usual rationed channels. In a country where food is so precious it should continue to go in this way, rather than to individual Germans who are in a position to do favors for individual Americans, and thus get themselves invited to dinner. Furthermore, if Germans were allowed to have the garbage from American camps, enterprising American mess sergeants would presently start selling it to them for high prices, and would order more food than was necessary in order to increase the amount of salable garbage.

The difficulty for American reporters is that anyone who is trying to do a serious job in Germany must endeavor to know and understand its people, and this cannot be done by studying the official health and mortality statistics, or by reading the German press which is in itself censored by the conqueror. One must also be on friendly terms with at least some Germans, which becomes difficult and artificial if you cannot eat with them.

Then, why not take them out to a German restaurant? The food, of course, is poor at best, but it is what they are used to, and you would learn something by sharing their misery. You cannot, because every item on the menu requires German food stamps, and these are not issued to Americans who, being bountifully supplied by their own messes, are not supposed also to eat the meager crusts designed for the conquered.

There are some relaxations to the rigor of all this. While the reporter may not take German guests upstairs to eat with him in the second floor of the press club, they are allowed as far as the first floor, which has many attractions for them. It is a spacious house with large rooms, and in the central one there is a four-piece German orchestra which plays every night for dancing. They have learned a few American tunes, such as "White Christmas." In addition, they play "I Lost My Heart in Heidelberg" and other traditional German numbers, but may not play anything which could be called a German war song.

When I was in Germany at the beginning of the war, they were all singing "Wir Fahren Gegen England." One evening I had as my guest an English captain who was anxious to hear it. The German orchestra was equally eager to perform, but the leader regretfully explained that it was not allowed. The ban, however, does not apply to "Lili Marlene," which is officially considered as a former German war song later liberated by our troops during the North African campaign and, since it is now American property, it may be played without fear of stirring militarism in the German soul.

In the back room is the bar which has an even greater attraction for Germans, not because of its liquor, but because there is usually set out either a bowl of peanuts (so rich in scarce oils) or perhaps American doughnuts, issued free to all messes by the American Red Cross to sustain the morale of the occupation army, heavily dusted with American sugar and, when you bite inside, yellow with American eggs.

Germany, in the old days, was noted for its rich pastry. These doughnuts are good, but nothing much. At home you might lay one down after a single bite but today, in occupied Germany, two of them are to a German a deliciously rich meal long to be remembered.

Furthermore, the rooms are heated, which no private home in Germany is, even in the dead of winter. So no wonder that the German girls who work at the press camp eagerly put on their best dresses to come to dance for an evening at the press club when one of the young American press officers condescends to ask them.

Occasionally (usually on Saturday nights) some roistering visitor from another mess would bring in a hard-eyed tart he had picked up on the Kurfürstendamm, but the great majority of the German girls who were asked were not only beautiful but obviously well-bred girls from the middle and upper classes. I noticed one curious thing about them.

The occasional Kurfürstendamm tart who got in with the Saturday night crowd would ravenously, but surreptitiously, gobble all the peanuts and doughnuts within reach. The others, however, even if these things were piled in heaping bowls before them, and although they were probably even hungrier than the Kurfürstendamm girls, would only take one when urged, and then would eat it slowly and with an air of great casualness. However, not one crumb was left on their plates.

If you don't admire this, you can call it stiff-necked German pride. If, as I do, you rather like it, you might say it was only decent self-respect. In actual practice, it is never pleasant to watch members of an "inferior" race scrambling or groveling for crumbs from the table of the conquerors, and I liked these girls because they so carefully did not, keeping it instead on a strictly social plane, as though they were there only because they found Americans to be pleasant people, and our food the least of our attractions—a remarkable feat of self-control in this ravenously hungry land.

A few evenings later one of the young American lieutenants brought Anna von B. to the press club dance. She told me that her mother had been delighted to hear that I, a friend of her old friend, was in Berlin, and hoped very much to meet me. Just now, however, her mother was out on their estate (or rather what was left of it) which was out in the Russian zone, not too far from Berlin, but presently she would be in town.

While Anna's young lieutenant danced with someone else, I sat with her at a little table near the bar and, over a glass of Coca-Cola, of which she said she had become very fond, I found out a good deal about them.

Her family had always been anti-Nazi and her mother had spent eight months in a Gestapo prison, on the suspicion that she had given to foreigners information unfavorable to the Nazi party. This was during the war. However, when it began her father and brother had felt it their duty to fight in defense of Germany, no matter who was its leader, as the men of her family had always been in all of Germany's wars.

They had both been killed and, when the collapse came, Anna and her mother had been left alone in the big house out in the country when the Russians arrived.

Six Russian officers were now billeted with them. But if, at this point, you expect an atrocity story, you will be disappointed. Of course, it is never pleasant to have six soldiers of any foreign army living in your house, but that seemed to be about the end of it. She and her mother had been terribly afraid at first. But when they got to know the six officers, they turned out to be rather like other people. Some of the six they had liked very much; others they didn't particularly care for.

I gather that the Russians, after their first shock of surprise at the idea of living in the same house with a Prussian baroness and her daughter, had come to the same conclusion. They had learned something of each other's ways and now sometimes they had jokes together.

Anna said the six Russians were careful of the house and the only time they gave any trouble was when occasionally they would have vodka parties in the dining room on Saturday night, and presently would almost insist that she and her mother join them for a friendly glass. But this certainly would have happened if six homesick American boys had been quartered there. I could not see that it had taken any more of Baroness von B.'s quick wit and tactful firmness to handle these Russians than she would have needed to handle as many Americans.

As for food, Anna said that of course the Russians always lived off the country, in contrast to us Americans who always bring in our own, but I gathered that even so they did not live very well and that the diet was mostly potatoes, like that of the surrounding Germans. In fact, rather than requisition the remaining livestock of the peasants, Anna said that every now and then her Russians would take a car and drive to Stettin, where they would load it up with provisions from the Soviet supply dump there, as a relief from the monotony of potatoes and cabbage.

Yet life was very uncertain, as it is for all Germans and particularly so for them, with all the men in their family dead. So her mother had been greatly delighted when Anna was able to get a clerical job in the American press camp, which she got mainly because of the fact that in her girls' school she had studied English, as well as music and French. This English, when it had left the girls' finishing school, had obviously been correct, if a little stilted, but certainly adequate to get her around any drawing room. It was now heavily studded with hair-raising bits of GI slang, Iowa vowels and Brooklyn diphthongs, which she had picked up in all innocence from the master sergeants who were her bosses in the office.

I asked her if she also went out with German boys of her age, and what they were like.

Sometimes, she said, but the trouble was they were so serious. She understood why. It was because they had all spent so many years in an army which was now defeated. Of course, the world was now hard for all Germans, for her as well as the boys. But they could talk only of these things, of their disappointment, and of their worries as to what they would now do in the world.

There would come a time for this, but now she was 19, which she felt had always been an age for lightheartedness. There had been very little of this for her during the war in Germany, so now she liked the Americans, all of whom were so easy and so gay, and, if they had any worries, never talked of them.

Of course, there were many things one could not forget, and now she began to talk of her dead father. He had been such a fine man—so well educated, so kind, and so brave! Ever since she had been a child she had loved France; not because she had been there, but only from what he had told her of it—the softness of the people and the country, the beauty of their little villages, the mellow wisdom of their Latin outlook on life, the warm sun and the flowers; so different from the cold, stern north! This was why, even as a child, she had studied French, so that even now she spoke it better than English, because she had always hoped that one day she could go there and see it with her father. Now that he was gone she would like to leave Germany forever and live always in this land which he had loved so much. Did I not think she still might do this?

Of course, one day she would like to get a look at America, but she felt that in France people would be just as gentle and understanding as he had been, and sometimes Americans were not very understanding because, no matter what the sergeants in the office said, she could not be now ashamed that she was German.

There were bad Germans, of course, as her own mother who had spent eight months in a Gestapo prison could well tell them. But there were fine and brave Germans as well. And she could *not* be ashamed of her father and her brother! They were *not* a couple of dirty pro-Hitler "Krauts"! They had fought, not for him but for their country, which any decent man in any land would do! She would *not* think of this as shameful, but be *proud*, as she always had, of the brave things they had done before they died, proud to be the sister and the daughter of brave and honorable men; no matter what they now tried to tell her, she would be *proud* as long as she could remember them!

She was by now crying, but this did not greatly matter because, being a well-brought-up child, there was no mascara to smear on her cheeks. The well-drilled and ever-smiling German orchestra was rather stiffly playing "Begin the Beguine."

CHAPTER XI

OUR ENEMIES MEET OUR ALLIES

THIS is the story of a party which failed but before you can understand how, you must know how it was that I came to get Colonel Nitikin and his dowdy interpreter mixed in with Baroness von B. and her beautiful daughter. It came about in this wise: on Wednesday Anna sent word to me by a press relations officer that her mother was coming in from their country place to spend the following weekend in town in her daughter's little apartment, and that they both hoped that the officer and I could come over for cake and coffee Saturday evening because her mother would like to have any news that I might have of her old friend.

So far it was all according to the books. It was, after all, her country (although we had conquered it). It was, therefore, proper that she should first invite us, that the meeting should take place on her home ground.

The press relations officer's angle was, why shouldn't we both go, because it ought to be interesting. Annie was a bright kid, and probably the old lady had plenty on the ball. And after having eaten some of their cake, whatever that turned out to be, then we could bring them back here to the press club, where Annie could dance with the lieutenants, and the old lady could have a chance to get around some doughnuts.

It happened that the following afternoon General McNarney met the Allied press in the spacious conference room at AMGUS building.

I arrived late, after most of the places had already been taken by American, British and French reporters, and was startled to see that the Soviet press was represented by Colonel Nitikin, with whom we had sung "Lubeme Gorod" at Herford in the British zone, and that with him was the same plain, dowdy, earnest woman interpreter in the same drab gray dress. So, after McNarney was through, I hurried over to ask them what about that dinner at our press club, to pay them back for the vodka they had given us in Herford? And why shouldn't it be some night this week?

For half a minute the two of them talked it over in Russian. Then the Colonel said, cordially but very gravely, that possibly this could be arranged, but the only free time he would have would be Saturday.

Saturday was fine, I said, forgetting for the moment all about the von B.s' invitation.

And at what o'clock on Saturday evening, Colonel Nitikin asked?

I told him we usually ate around seven, and gravely he made a note of this. Also a careful note of the street address and of the press club telephone number because, as he gravely explained, should he find that they would be unable to come, he would telephone me before six o'clock this evening. Then, very formally, he thanked me, and very formally the two of them withdrew.

At this point I suddenly remembered the von B.s. But what could be done? Perhaps the conquerors need not be over-scrupulous about keeping engagements with the vanquished, and yet so much careful planning had gone into their little invitation that I couldn't be so rude.

But why not combine them? The von B.s, being our enemies, of course could not come to dinner. But after eating with Colonel Nitikin, perhaps I could slip away to the von B.s' for just long enough to have some of their proffered cake and coffee. Then, bringing them back to the press camp in a jeep, we could merge them with the Russians who surely would not object to spending part of an evening with a German woman who had spent eight months in prison for anti-Nazi activities. It seemed the best solution.

On Saturday, and on the stroke of seven, Colonel Nitikin and his interpreter, who had declined my offer to send for them in a jeep, arrived in a somewhat dilapidated commandeered German car. Half a dozen of the correspondents who had been with us at Herford met them at the door, and then introduced them to the others. They acknowledged all of this courteously.

The American correspondents are proud of their press camp, which sets a high standard even in Berlin, a city where the Americans, British and French vie with each other in the matter of luxurious billets. We knew we had no reason to be ashamed of it before the Russian correspondents who, so far as anybody knows, have no press camp at all, and live, with all other Russian officials, crowded into their spartan-like and carefully guarded compound at Karlshorst,* and to which no outsiders are ever invited except an occasional German Communist politician, although the Russians occasionally accept invitations from the other Allies, as was the case this evening.

Gravely and without comment, Colonel Nitikin and his interpreter inspected our spacious living room, the rather good pictures on the wall, the obviously expensive rugs, the long bar and the German orchestra players, who had already arrived in their neatly brushed dinner-coats, to provide the American press with dinner music and later with dance tunes. At all of this the Russians looked carefully and said nothing. The cor-

---

* If the Russians' quarters at Karlshorst are dingy and crowded, there is no reason to be sorry for them. Before they would admit the other Allies to Berlin, they divided that city into its present sectors, keeping for themselves the part which contains the city administration buildings, what was left of the German government buildings, the University of Berlin, and all of the more important electrical, industrial and radio installations, leaving for the decadent Western democracies Berlin's better suburbs, which allow for luxurious living but which, from the standpoint of governing the town, are of no importance.

"In other words," as a high American officer told me, "they kept themselves exactly what I would have picked for us if I had had first choice."— WLW.

respondents were already gathering at the bar for a martini before dinner. The Russians, however, surprised us by politely and very firmly declining. They would take nothing, not even a glass of the vodka which I had gone to some trouble to provide.

A little nonplused, we all went upstairs for dinner. A table had been set apart for those of us who had been in Herford and it was also provided with two bottles of French claret, which again both the Russians politely declined. It crossed my mind that possibly they had received permission to come only on this condition. The meal was an ordinary press club dinner —a glass of tomato juice, followed by pork chops, fried potatoes and spinach, with coffee on the side, and ending with a small dish of canned peaches.

By American standards, it was nothing to apologize for. However Russians, although they may starve themselves between banquets, always lay out an elaborate and sumptuous table for foreign guests. By such standards, ours was falling down badly. But if they also thought this, they gave no sign of it.

Conversation was even worse. No topic seemed to last longer than a few sentences, although several good starts were made.

Something had happened since Herford. Perhaps it was because we were back in Berlin, with its atmosphere of tension and suspicion. It occurred to me that the Russians had not come with any idea of enjoying themselves, but only because they did not want to be on record as having refused.

While they were finishing dessert, the press relations officer and I excused ourselves and, leaving the Russians to the others, went out to collect the von B.s who were the other half of this so far not too successful Saturday night party.

We found them in a tiny apartment, consisting of two furnished rooms on the second floor of a middle-class German residence. And now for the mother. She was my age, which is to say the middle forties, still pretty, and with Anna's light brown hair and clear skin—in general, a plumper version of her daughter. But it was curious to find, in Prussia, an exact duplicate of the bubbling vivacity of a Virginia belle.

Visiting Northerners, from General Sherman's army on down to our times, have often thought that this constant stream of small talk was a token of a vacant mind. They are wrong. This pleasant chatter is like the graceful sparring of a good boxer. Behind it there is usually a good mind, frequently a firm purpose, and occasionally a Sunday punch.

In the case of Baroness von B., the purpose was all too clear to everyone, nor could I see that it was sinister. Dr. Goebbels has the advantage of me in having read more than the reviews of *Gone With the Wind*, but clearly here was a Prussian version of Scarlett O'Hara, her whole world in ruins, and now fighting somehow to survive, using charm, wit, firmness and gaiety in turn, whenever they were needed. And I'm sure that the six young Russian officers quartered on her saw this as clearly and probably respected it quite as much as we, at the same time thanking God that none of our womenfolk would ever find themselves in her position, and also wondering if they would do as well.

There was no need for her either to conceal or to stress her purpose with us. She knew we were well aware of it. It was, in a quaking and uncertain world in which all Germans—even the most democratic ones—feared that their country was about to be swallowed up by Asia, that we were valued ties with the civilized and humane West, linked to a world of which Germany had been a part in centuries past.

It was not only that the press relations officer was Anna's employer in a job which provided a still-growing girl with at least one nourishing meal a day in the face of semi-starvation, or that I happened to know an old, trusted and now powerful friend who might bring further help. It was that we were ties with Europe.

I had forgotten their cake, which we now accepted along with two cups of imitation coffee. On the credit side, the cake was delicious-looking—large, snowy white, of about the texture of angel food, thickly covered with a fluffy white frosting. I had always heard of voluptuous German pastry, but so far had had none, because the cooks in our mess, while they had all ingredients, were not pastry cooks. Into this cake obviously had gone many hours of work and careful planning. I stabbed a large piece of it on my fork.

Now for the debit side: it was the most insipid garbage which I had ever put into my mouth. It had been obviously concocted without either butter, sugar or eggs, as though for an elaborate joke on April Fool's Day, using water, gelatin and flour.

Hastily we explained the confusion in dates, insisted that we would like nothing better than to spend the entire evening consuming the whole of this cake, but would they not now please come with us to the press club so that we could combine this party with our other guests? Very willingly, they put on their coats over their summer formal dinner dresses, and climbed into our jeep.

It was a warm evening in late May. The big glass double doors at the press club, giving out onto the spacious veranda just at one side of the little dance orchestra, had been thrown open. And we found our Russian guests and several attending correspondents waiting for us around a coffee table.

"And now," I said when they were seated, "what will you have to drink?" The press relations officer had his usual. The Russians again politely shook their heads but I finally prevailed on the interpreter to try a Coca-Cola after I explained that it was a popular non-alcoholic American drink. Anna, of course, took Coca-Cola; the Army had introduced it to her long ago.

"And for me," said her mother, "nothing to drink except what I have been longing for so much for all these years, just a cup of *real* coffee!"

And now how could I tell her? Her request was most reasonable. Coffee all over Europe is served just after dinner and not with it. The meal upstairs was just being concluded, and here we were all seated at a coffee table. Why not?

Because, according to the carefully worked-out rules of the club, only alcoholic drinks, peanuts, Coca-Cola and doughnuts may be served to Germans—coffee being reserved for the conquerors and their Allies. The Russians were just finishing theirs. Baroness von B., of course, had spent those eight months in a Gestapo prison. But even if, in addition, she had been Jewish, it would have made no difference; a rule was a rule. And so, pretending not to have heard her request, I brought for her, instead, a brandy.

Why had I not realized that this party would never work? Let us start with the Baroness. She already had six Russians quartered in her home, and inviting her, a German, to spend a presumably pleasant evening with two more, must have seemed like a bad practical joke, even if it was not so intended—much as I had felt about her cake. However she felt about this, she did not show it. And perhaps that was the trouble. For, instead, she worked too hard and too successfully to entertain us, and somehow was too great a contrast to the silent and polite Russians, gravely and courteously performing their task of accepting the hospitality of the American press.

It must have been even harder for the Russians. They had, of course, been told of her eight months in prison, but concentration camps were hardly a novelty in their country. And as they now quietly watched her, a gay creature from another world, so well dressed in the Western fashion, chattering so much and so lightly, it may well have occurred to them that eight months was not enough to bring so frivolous a woman to some sense of the hard realities of life.

There was also the fact that Soviet regulations forbid them ever to meet Germans except on an official plane. Here their rules are on the whole more sensible than ours. A Russian commandant may entertain the local German town councilors at a banquet and eat with them, which ours may not. Russian officers always punctiliously shake hands with German officials and return their salutes, which ours are not allowed to do. But here it stops. Anything outside of official business is severely punished as fraternizing with the enemy, and conduct degrading to the Red Army. Even a Soviet officer caught associating with German girls is reduced to the ranks and sent home.

So, listening to this beautifully-dressed German woman's patter, the Russians gazed on through the glass doors to watch tall, well-fed-looking young American officers dancing with still other pretty German girls who, if they also had been in concentration camps, certainly showed no marks of it.

The press officer, also seeing that things were not going well, turned to the Russian woman and asked her what decorations were represented by the military ribbon on her worn gray uniform.

She glanced down at them and smiled a little.

"They are decorations of no importance," she said. "I only wear them when I go out on the streets here, so that your American soldiers will not think I am a German woman and whistle and call after me."

Baroness von B., who had stopped talking to lean forward and look at the decorations, now settled back in her chair and looked away. It was several minutes before she said anything.

And now the press officer had a real inspiration. Rising and stepping over to the orchestra, he asked them if they knew any Russian songs. It turned out that they knew "The Volga Boatmen." Since this is almost the only Russian song which any foreign orchestra knows, it must have been hackneyed to our guests. And yet they seemed to like it, or at least our gesture in playing it for them. And when they were through, the Russian woman told me it brought back her youth in the village, and memories of the old country dances when she was a girl.

When the press officer asked her if she would not please show us how they were done, at first she refused. But when all of us, including the von B.s, joined in coaxing her, at last she consented. We got her out into the middle of the dance floor, the orchestra struck up an old folk tune and, as the other dancers stood aside to watch, she gave us what was clearly the outlines of an ancient peasant dance, one hand on her hip, the other curved overhead, a dance which sometimes seemed to be the ghost of a Virginia Reel and at others of a very primitive jig—her flat, kindly, earnest, weather-scarred peasant face lighting up with old memories as she danced—and somehow the strong, primitive spirit of Old Russia came into that room as we watched. When it was finished and she came back to our table through the applause, I asked her if she would think it rude if I wanted to know something about her life.

She said there was little to tell except hard work for her government and her country, that she and her eight-year-old daughter lived alone in a little room in the Russian sector. Except for work it was, she said, a quiet life, but she was happy.

"And your husband is with you?"

"No."

"He is dead?"

"No," said the plain woman firmly and wearily, "no, he is not dead."

"Then where is he?"

"I do not know," she said. "I think by now he is back in his village." And then, with rising bitterness, "I only know that I hope that never again in all of both our lives will we ever see him!"

What tragedy lay behind her bitterness I knew I should not ask. Perhaps it had been a long and unhappy marriage, fortunately ended by the war. Again, perhaps, as so often happens, it had been ended by the war itself. He had been thrown with some younger, prettier woman in the army, and she, now forsaken and cherishing their child, had brought the little girl to Berlin so that she might have this glimpse of Europe instead of always the grim, workaday world of Soviet Russia, to which even what is left of shattered Berlin is by comparison a miracle of comfort and luxury. What a wonderful thing for a little Russian child, and how many sacrifices this earnest worn woman must be making to have given it to her!

"Are there many Russian children now in Berlin?"

"A few, and more are coming. Even now we have a school for them."

"I have a little girl who is nine," I said. "How does yours like her new school?"

One of the young press officers had just asked Anna to dance and, smiling, she had risen and was following him to the floor. The Russian woman was watching her.

"She does not go to the school," said the Russian woman, still watching Anna. The two of them were dancing near the door. The lieutenant was trying to show her a new step and Anna, very young, very healthy, very supple and slim in her simple little dance dress, was following the new step well.

"I will teach her everything at home," continued the Russian woman, still watching Anna. "I teach her English and French and German. Also history."

"Then you don't like the Russian school?"

"It is a very good school," said the Russian woman, her eyes intently, I would even say enviously, on Anna who was swaying so lightly in the doorway. Somehow I had the fantastic illusion that there were tears in the Russian woman's tired blue eyes.

"But if the school is good, why don't you send your child? Surely she is old enough."

"Because," said the Russian woman quietly, still watching Anna, "she is paralyzed and cannot walk. Maybe there can be braces later, but now she can only drag herself around the room on her hands. It was spinal meningitis, which she got in the first year of the war when I was called up and not there to care for her. But it does not matter so much about the school. Because she learns well, and already she knows more than those of her age who are in it."

There are times when you can think of nothing adequate to say, and it is then best not to try. So I said nothing, but we both watched Anna, who was following the young officer's lead so gracefully. During the war the Germans, even pro-democratic ones like Anna's family, were better off than any other people in Europe. In addition to being beautiful, she was intelligent and had been very well raised. Somehow you knew that, no matter how dark things looked for the moment, in a few years her life would straighten out.

"She has lost both her father and her only brother in the war," I said to the Russian woman. After a minute she said:

"Have you ever been to Nürnberg?" The papers that week were full of the trials.

"No."

The Russian woman's blue eyes became very intense and she clenched her work-hardened peasant fists, which were on the table. "Oh, I would *so* much like to be there!" she said almost piteously. "If only for an hour! Just to look into the faces of those men who have brought so much sadness to the world! Just to stand there long enough so that I could meet the eyes of each of them, and see their faces now—for this I would give anything!" Her voice, and her worn, tired, flat peasant face, were deeply earnest. Baroness von B., who was chatting with an officer, had not heard. If she had, I am sure she would have sincerely and gaily agreed.

It was just at this point that Colonel Nitikin, who was sitting half-turned away from us, glanced at his watch. I glanced at mine. He stood up. It was just ten o'clock, and I noticed that the colonel had timed it as punctiliously as we had measured the time which we had devoted to toying with the Baroness von B.'s April Fool's cake; he could not have left a minute sooner without seeming rude. Of course, we protested that it was too early. The Russian woman, who had also risen, shook her head to me.

"But not for my little girl," she said. "She will never go to sleep until I return."

The dance floor was now crowded with the regular Saturday night dance. A few correspondents of course, a few American girls from AMGUS, but many French, British and Americans from other messes bringing girls of various nationalities in and out of uniform, for it was well known in Berlin that the American press club had the best Saturday night dancing set-up in the town.

I escorted the two Russians through the crowd toward the door, wondering what they thought of it all. We brushed past the little German orchestra, now playing "Roll Out the Barrel," plump on American food which was far more important to them than the few marks they got for playing at our dances. Perhaps over in the other zone they would have been put to work clearing bomb rubble, and would not be quite so plump. Somehow tonight we did not seem to me to be very serious about building either our own kind of a Germany, or any other.

As we passed the library door, Colonel Nitikin stopped. On the big table was a high pile of paper-bound books, of the kind distributed to the overseas forces. They were in good order because the correspondents rarely looked at them. Everybody had read the few good ones years ago, and the rest were only detective stories.

"Mr. White," said the Colonel, "might we ask just one more favor, after all of your other wonderful hospitality?"

I suspected that the colonel was being faintly ironic. I think he also meant me to suspect this.

"But of course," I said. "What is it?"

"If we could only take back a few of those books in English—"

"Anything you like—"

"And perhaps you could suggest to me which are the best."

This was not easy and it meant plowing through piles of trashy, whodunit fiction. I finally gave them *Arrowsmith*, by Sinclair Lewis, *Hunger Fighters*, by Paul de Kruif, and *The Late George Apley*, explaining that while this might not be easy for them to understand, it was by one of our greatest writers and was a satirical, and yet often sympathetic, study of a way of thinking and of life which in America had almost passed, showing both its weakness and its strength.

They listened very intently to everything I said about each of the books. I felt that now for the first time they were really interested.

We had wrapped up a doughnut in a paper napkin as a present for the little girl, because the Baroness had said that when she was a child she was always disappointed if, when her mother went out to a party, she did not bring back some little present or favor, and the Russian woman, smiling at her for the first time, had said that children were alike the world over.

At the car I bade them goodnight. Again they thanked me and I told them they must return soon and please to bring with them some of the other Russians from Herford. Of course they said they would, but of course both they and I knew that they would not.

Then they drove off toward their world, and I walked back toward mine, feeling that at least I had tried.

I am sure they felt the same way about it.

Part II

WILSON'S PEACE AND OURS

CHAPTER XII

NINETEEN-NINETEEN

I FIRST saw the Germans early in January 1919. I had seen their dead a few weeks before—shapeless skeletons in field-gray uniforms, soaking in puddles which filled the bottoms of shell holes just above Château-Thierry and in the Argonne Forest, where I had gone on a little pilgrimage with my father, retracing the fighting path of our Kansas and Oklahoma National Guard Division, the Thirty-fifth, to find the grave of a high school friend who had been killed there.

The American dead had by this time been neatly collected, but our Graves Registration Service had not yet begun the task of burying our enemies who lay as they had fallen, crouched over machine guns or sprawling in shell holes. The battlefield on which they lay was also rich with souvenirs.

I had, of course, seen German prisoners working on the ballast of the French railways. They would stand aside to stare blankly into our train windows.

I was only eighteen and I can remember the thrill when, driving north out of Luxemburg, we passed what had been a frontier barrier and reached enemy soil. The war, after all, was still on, for this was only an armistice. I remember our road winding up the Moselle and Rhine valleys, terraced vineyards rising from the water up to the bastions of the little crumbling medieval castles which crowned every hill, lovely even in winter.

The Rhine valley was then split into three Allied occupation zones. The British held Cologne; the French held Mayence and Strasbourg, and we were headed for American occupation headquarters at Coblenz. It was a clean, picturesque little provincial capital which has been badly mutilated by bombs in this war but was untouched in that, except for the fact that then as now, food was terribly short, particularly fats and soap.

Our American Army had only recently arrived for, after the Armistice was signed on November 11, it had taken six tedious weeks, without enemy opposition, to move this Third Army across Northern France and Luxemburg and get it settled into the Rhine. There were at the time hotheads who said that, instead of signing an armistice, we should have fought on to Berlin—some five hundred miles away; there were few of them among the soldiers of the Third Army, who were glad it was over, and now only wanted to know when we, who had just come up from the Paris Peace Conference, thought they could go home.

If, during those weeks I spent with our Army on the Rhine, I talked for more than a minute with any German, I cannot now remember it. In the early days of that occupation there were strict rules against fraternization, as there were during the early days of this. It took them about the same length of time to break down, first into open disobedience and then repeal. While I was there our boys were seeing a good deal of the German girls, but it was managed quietly. Later, of course, they married them and brought them home in boatloads, as they surely will in this.

In that occupation American troops, from privates to generals, were billeted with German families and presently came to know them well. In this one it is a strict rule that all Germans must be moved out. There were other differences. Then, as now, the American Army was souvenir crazy, but a 1919 souvenir consisted of a Luger, a German trench helmet picked up on the battlefield or, better still, the kind of spiked parade helmet made of black patent leather which the German troops wore behind the lines. There was then no talk of diamonds, Leicas, or wrist watches. Any American soldier who "liberated" anything like this from a German civilian would have been regarded by that bashful Army of 1919 as a thief.

There were occasionally atrocities, and one of them occurred while we were in Coblenz. One night, half a dozen American doughboys were in a German beer cellar. Across, at another table, sat an elderly "Hun" whom they didn't like because he had his head clipped close, Prussian style, as they had seen in cartoons. They thought it would be fun to give him a shampoo, getting him down, pouring beer onto his clipped head, and then rubbing it in with their knuckles.

This was, in 1919, considered shocking conduct. They were all court-martialed and sentenced to disciplinary barracks.

I don't argue that it was a knightly Army. The age of chivalry was dead. But it was still a friendly, kindly Army even in victory, with something left of the spirit of Grant when he returned General Lee's sword and said that the Confederate officers could tell the soldiers they could keep their horses, which they would need for the spring plowing.

Of course, they faced another enemy. That Army of the 'sixties had fought for human equality and liberated four million slaves, but not even Harriet Beecher Stowe had ever accused Simon Legree of crowding Negroes into a concrete room and then turning a valve which scalded them in live steam.

Yet even in 1919 the idea of restraint in victory was still strong. I remember one day early in that Rhineland journey we were walking, through a winter drizzle, down one of the narrow, cobbled streets of Cologne, not far from the old cathedral, and, as we walked over the cobblestones still wet from a winter drizzle, I was blithely whistling the "Marseillaise." An old German whom we passed, recognizing it and seeing my uniform, half turned to give me a mildly resentful look from under his umbrella, whereupon my father gently reproved me, pointing out that these people were defeated and powerless, and that it was very bad manners on my part to rub it in ostentatiously, and also discreditable to my country in that we were being judged by our behavior here.

Later that winter, wearing the old type American uniform with its high choker collar, I stood behind a rather ornate pillar in the grand hall of the Quai d'Orsay which housed the French Foreign Office on the banks of the Seine in Paris. Outside a light mist rose from the river and there was a gray winter drizzle over the city. Inside, the huge gold-encrusted First Empire room sparkled with enormous crystal chandeliers which lighted the equally dazzling uniforms of Commanders of the Allied and Associated Powers as well as the soot-black cutaway coats of their leading statesmen.

But I had already seen these as they filed into the room and took their chairs around the dais and now I was looking at and intently listening to the man in the black frock coat who was speaking from that dais.

His narrow face ended in a long jaw, a sensitive yet most determined face. It had the yellowish pallor of one who has long been cloistered in a study. He spoke, or rather read from a manuscript, with the soft, precise voice of the man of letters. Yet there was firmness in it, and today even a note of triumph; for the man was Woodrow Wilson, and he was reading aloud for the first time the text of the Covenant of that League of Nations which, together with the Treaty of Versailles which these statesmen were drafting, was to keep the general peace of the world for the next twenty years.

My duties at this great ceremony were appropriately simple. As our President read the Covenant, his words were taken down by a battery of stenographers, as there were no advance copies for the press. When one of the girls finished a page she handed it to me and I would slip out a rear door and into an army Cadillac and in a few minutes, driving through that chill winter mist, would arrive at the Eiffel Tower from where that page was sent to America by wireless telegraph, which was still one of the world's experimental wonders. Then I would go back to the Quai d'Orsay and wait behind my pillar while the pale man read, until another page was typed. Two other Cadillacs and messengers were working in relays with me. When he had entirely finished this assembly broke up and I tiptoed out and rubbed elbows with the now half-forgotten great of that dead world as, chatting with each other, they moved toward the pair of high gold-ornamented doors which had been thrown open.

Rather than to list them it would be simpler to say that every world leader of that decade was there except Lenin. I remember starting guiltily when Clemenceau peered in my direction and then moved toward me. But no, he only wanted a word with Maréchal Foch, who was just over my shoulder.

Clemenceau was very old—old enough to have taken part, as a man of thirty, in the Paris Commune of 1871 which Lenin had studied so intently. So old that his head nodded rhythmically from palsy while his hands, which he held up in front of him, just below the level of his chest, trembled in unison as he now talked with Foch.

Clemenceau, who had risen from the Commune to lead France to victory almost half a century later, was Woodrow Wilson's principal antagonist during that six months' peace conference which I attended in Paris. In some ways he occupied, in that situation, the place which Stalin holds in this (though the France of 1919 was no less solidly democratic than America).

The differences between Clemenceau and Stalin are as significant as the similarities. It is of no moment that they look alike; Clemenceau's political nickname was "Le Tigre" while Stalin's Kremlin intimates refer to him privately as "The Cat." It is significant, however, that both were endowed with that kind of biting sense of ironic humor which makes it difficult for its possessor to treat with an idealist as an equal.

When someone at Yalta mentioned the Vatican, Stalin said: "The Pope? The Pope? How many divisions has he?" and when Wilson proclaimed his Fourteen Points as a guide to the coming peace, Clemenceau growled, "The good God Himself gave us only Ten Commandments."

France in 1918 felt, with some justice, that she had borne the brunt of that world struggle, emerging with her industrial areas devastated, and with two million dead out of her population of 38 million. In the Second World War the Soviet Union has lost about 9 million killed out of a population of 175 million, and half of her industry has been destroyed.

In 1919 France (like Russia today) regarded plans for world organization as the valueless products of Anglo-Saxon sentimentality, and instead put her faith in her Army, which (like the Red Army today) was the largest military force remaining on the European continent, plus a diplomatic barrier consisting of a system of satellite states in Eastern Europe—Poland and the nations of the Little Entente—which would be her secure allies in any future struggle.

Here the parallel ends, for France in 1919 had abandoned all dreams of extending her domain. If one skips back another century, there is a better parallel. Following her revolution in 1789, for more than two decades the armies of France carried the banner of liberalism against a feudal Europe. And although under Napoleon this liberalism was thinly diluted, his name and the French tricolor were rallying points for well-organized political factions all over Europe—in Italy, in Germany, in Spain —even in England, Napoleon's most relentless opponent.

But by 1919 France, with her falling birth rate, had no men to spare who would die to spread a doctrine. Her leaders knew she was now on the defensive and that her only hope was to hold what she had against the teeming Teutonic people to the north and east. These were now prostrate, and it was the hope of French conservatives like Poincaré to keep them so. It was the passionate resolve of France to keep these German armies forever on the other bank of the Rhine, but to hold this Rhine frontier, Poincaré and Foch argued, France needed diplomatic pivots in Middle Europe and the Balkans among the small Slav states to whose interest also it would be to keep the Germans down.

Wilson's opposing thesis (one which could be comfortably held by a nation five thousand miles from Europe) was that the old balance-of-power system could be replaced by a world organization in which not only France but all the world could be secure through a system of justice under law. Now Wilson has often been called an idealist and Clemenceau a realist. But the latter, although wise in the ways of European power politics, was also a veteran radical who understood that there could be a deep realism in idealism. Because concepts of the world state had failed before, he knew that it need not always be so.

But was this the time when it could succeed? Once the temporary, warborn glow of unity among Allies had faded, would England and America still stand with France to ensure world peace? New forces, he knew, would inevitably arise. Would this concept of world law take root in the peoples of the world in time to harness these to the cause of peace? With all these uncertainties, could he bet the security of France on a dream?

In the end he did, and yet he hedged the bets rather heavily. Often he followed Wilson, or rather yielded to him, on many of the territorial settlements which Wilson insisted were necessary for world peace, but which Clemenceau's political opponent Raymond Poincaré and other French chauvinists insisted were against the interests of France. And finally, so that he could face these critics, Clemenceau extracted from Wilson and Lloyd George the promise of an alliance which would bind the Anglo-Saxon powers to come to the aid of France against Germany—a bulwark which Clemenceau felt would stand even should the League dissolve.

Now for a time he felt safe and so did France. But when America rejected not only this alliance but even the League which her President had proposed, it seemed to the French that Poincaré had been right all along. So Clemenceau fell from power, Poincaré succeeded, and after that there was no idealistic nonsense about soft treatment for Germany, but only hate born of a not-unjustified fear.

The French and other critics of Wilson have charged that in redrawing the boundaries of Europe to conform to the wishes of its people, he Balkanized that continent, leaving it a crazy-quilt of economically unsound and militarily unstable little states which could end only in war.

It is easy to criticize the incompleted framework of Wilson's structure by ignoring its over-all design. His conception was of a Europe and indeed a world composed, not of tiny warlike nation-states, but one in which the fierce fires of petty nationalism would presently subside, or rather blend, into a feeling of world-unity or global patriotism based on justice under law—a world in which both national armies and national tariff barriers would dwindle because they would have become obsolete.

But Wilson saw that minor injustices in boundaries should be corrected so that world justice would rest on firm foundations. Poincaré, Foch, and to a certain extent Clemenceau could see the map of Europe only in terms of French safety, its boundaries so drawn that, in terms of rivers, coal, mountains, oil, and iron deposits, the future allies of France would be strong and her enemies weak.

It was Wilson's 1919 task to persuade Clemenceau and Foch (Poincaré was beyond redemption) that the true security of France lay not in this venerable balance-of-power system, but in a league of democratic nations which would enforce justice and preserve the peace.

In 1919 the French fears of Germany were justified by the fact that France had only 38 million people, with a falling birth rate, facing 60 million Germans. By contrast today it would seem that Russia's 175 million people, with a rapidly rising birth rate, had comparatively little to fear from 70 million Germans with a declining birth rate.

But the task in 1919 of organizing a world was far simpler than it is today because the big three of that time—France, England, and America—were all free democracies. And there was among them no dispute as to the meaning of this word.

Looking back twenty-eight years to that golden age, I think it may prove to have been the high tide of freedom for this century. The Hohenzollern and Hapsburg dynasties had crumbled in defeat. In their places were a German republic and a half-dozen liberated nations, all of whom paid considerably more than lip-service to democratic forms. The Romanov autocracy was in the ruins of civil war from which the Bolshevik autocracy had not yet emerged victorious. Parliamentary government in Japan seemed to be gaining; there was much hope for a democratic China under the guiding spirit of Dr. Sun Yat-sen.

The three victors of that war wished to spread democracy, not through a sentimental zeal to impose the blessings of liberty on others, but because they felt that democracies were essentially peace-loving, and seldom if ever engaged in aggressive war. To this rule there are embarrassing exceptions: America has within the past hundred years attacked with little provocation Mexico in 1848 and Spain fifty years later. It is true, however, that it is impossible for a democracy secretly to prepare an attack, for public opinion must be convinced of its necessity and this cannot be done in weeks or months.

Democracies are proverbially slow to defend themselves. It is impossible for them to pick the time and execute that carefully planned surprise attack of the Pearl Harbor type which may end the wars of the future a few months after they are begun. Woodrow Wilson's reasoning that the only world which is safe for democracy is one which is preponderantly democratic is even more valid today than it was in 1917.

CHAPTER XIII

MOVING TOWARD PEACE: THEN AND NOW

VON CLAUSEWITZ has pointed out that war is an extension of foreign policy. Unlike a football game, war's object is not victory for the sake of winning, but to gain specific ends which could not be got peacefully: the generals simply take over where the diplomats leave off. In a general conflict each nation, of course, has objectives of its own; among Allies they may be as similar as those of America and England in the war just past, or as divergent as those of England and the Soviet Union.

In the First World War Woodrow Wilson was keenly aware of this basic interlocking of diplomacy and warfare. Before the war's end he clearly defined America's objectives in the Fourteen Points, which may be compared to the Atlantic Charter of World War II, although the latter was much more nebulous.

Let us review Wilson's strategy which took Germany out of the war. His Fourteen Point speech was made as Congress opened in January 1918. It was a momentous month, marking the low point in Allied fortunes. Lenin and Trotzky's Red Guards had just broken up the initial meeting of the Constituent Assembly in Russia. This body had been fairly elected under free speech after the Czar's abdication, but two thirds of its delegates were non-Bolshevik: it had to go, and with it went any hope that Russia would reorganize an eastern front.

In the west, American troops had not yet arrived and Ludendorff was massing men and supplies for a supreme effort, a great drive which split the French and British armies at their juncture near Amiens and almost—but not quite—drove the British back onto the Calais beaches.

The Fourteen Points made a profound impression within Germany. It clearly offered a decent peace, but in January 1918, the militarists could still promise their people victory.

A similar low point in World War II coincided with the issuance of the Atlantic Charter. Hitler reigned supreme on the European continent, invasion of England still seemed a possibility, submarines were taking terrific toll of British shipping, and in Africa Britain's armies seemed overwhelmed.

At this juncture Churchill and Roosevelt drafted the Anglo-American war aims which were in spirit a paraphrase of Wilson's Fourteen Points, providing for "no aggrandizement, territorial or otherwise," "no territorial changes that do not accord with the freely expressed wishes of the peoples concerned," "the sovereign rights and self-government restored to those who have been forcibly deprived of them," so that "men in all the lands may live out their lives in freedom from fear and want."

The climax of World War I came in July 1918, following Wilson's Fourteen Points. The German advance was at its peak, but had exhausted its power. American regular Army and Marine divisions were fighting at Château-Thierry and at this juncture Wilson delivered, at Mount Vernon on July 4, his "Four Point" speech in which, instead of closing the door to peace, he opened it, for the "Four Points" continued, even extended, the principles of the previous Fourteen. German liberals could read that, while America sought the destruction of "every arbitrary power" that could "disturb the peace of the world," Wilson nevertheless promised that in the peace, every political, economic and territorial question would be settled "upon the basis of the free acceptance of that settlement by the people immediately concerned, and not upon the basis of any material interest or advantage of any other nation or people which may desire a different settlement for the sake of its own exterior influence or mastery."

This made a profound impression on the Germans. In the

armistice negotiations which followed, Wilson kept his own counsel and pursued an independent policy, not consulting his Allies and sometimes not even his cabinet. His policy was not, at the time, universally popular. Both Foch and Pershing, of course, were for unconditional surrender. Even ex-President Taft complained that Wilson, acting without the British and French, "recognizes no obligations of partnership." The British were quick to point out that the other Allies did not consider themselves bound by the Fourteen Points on which the Germans were offering to make peace.

Wilson, however, told his trusted secretary, Joseph Tumulty, that a march to Berlin would cost a million unnecessary casualties. And while America's differences with her Allies were not then the chasm in viewpoint which today separates us from the Kremlin, Wilson nevertheless, in the fall of 1918, did not want to see the German people utterly crushed, wanted an armistice soon because, as he told Colonel House, "too much success or security on the part of the Allies" might endanger "a genuine peace settlement."

He therefore moved without sentimentality to bring Allied objectives into line with our own, at a time when the German Army was still a fighting force which could not be defeated without American help. Colonel E. M. House, the Harry Hopkins of that realistic day, was sent to Europe in October 1918 for the purpose of sounding out Lloyd George, Clemenceau and Italian Premier Orlando, who were assembled in Paris for that purpose.

Their main objection to Wilson's Fourteen Points was that these conflicted drastically with various treaties under which the European Allies had pledged themselves to divide the spoils of victory in the best nineteenth century imperialist traditions.

Colonel House heard them out quietly. Then he said that, since the Germans agreed to Wilson's program but the European Allies did not, our President might have to ask Congress whether the United States, having attained its war objectives, cared to go on fighting for those of its Allies.*

The three men were stunned as, under similar circumstances, a Soviet delegation might have been in World War II. Finally Clemenceau asked if this meant that America would make a separate peace. Colonel House confessed that "it might." After that there was no more talk of our European Allies rejecting Wilson's Fourteen Points *in toto*.

Furthermore, after the last gun was fired on November 11, 1918, there was no frantic haste to get the doughboys back home, until it was clear that peace terms had crystallized. Wilson made, of course, some important compromises. He did not dictate the peace at gun's point. In both England and France men like Lord Robert Cecil and Briand gave the Liberal idea strong support. But until the treaty was signed an American Army remained on the Rhine, slowly demobilizing but proportionate in size to those of the other Allies, with the result that agreements made with us were carried out, with no quibbling as to whether the word "democracy" or any other word actually meant what it said.

Of course, the minute the fighting ceased, the doughboy of 1918 was just as clamorous to leave Europe as the GI of 1945. I remember clearly a scene early in the following spring in the immense Palais de Glace, a Third Empire relic which the American YMCA had taken over as an entertainment center for our troops. The American Eighty-ninth Division was putting on a musical comedy there when some incident in its second act touched off the homesickness of that khaki-clad audience and they stopped the show for ten minutes with thunderous cries of "When do we go home?"

The "brass" of that day was busily explaining to them that the war was not over, but the doughboy knew that what was

* *Woodrow Wilson and the People*, by H. C. F. Bell, New York: Doubleday and Company. To his sound and balanced scholarship I wish here to acknowledge a considerable debt throughout this chapter.—WLW.

technically only an armistice actually was a peace. So when at long last he was demobilized, he did not have the heart-sick feeling of many GIs who, now looking back at Europe, feel that what they were told was a peace too often resembles an unsteady armistice.

Let us now compare the diplomatic dénouement of World War II with its predecessor, with first a brief glance back at its beginnings. Viewed from the democratic standpoint, Europe's freedoms were menaced by the German and Russian dictatorships which in the 'thirties were clearly moving toward a conflict, and which, although tagged "rightist" and "leftist," actually contained in their structures more similarities than differences. Both systems were the antithesis of free government.

At Munich it was the policy of Chamberlain and Daladier to "isolate" the coming struggle as a war between Hitler and Stalin in Central Europe, in which the Western democracies would remain neutral and, after the two rivals had fought to exhaustion, would retain the balance of power.

In retrospect this analysis seems to have been a bad one, because from what we now know of Russia's under-industrialization, it seems probable that two years fighting an un-aided Russia would have put Hitler astride the Urals and in possession of all European Russia, from which vantage point, and in control of all the grain and oil of Central Europe as well, he would have been a far greater menace to the Western democracies than is the Soviet Union today.

In any case, however, public opinion both in England and France would not permit such a policy, and in the spring of 1939, when Hitler entered Prague, the press of the democracies, including our own, clamored that it be reversed.

Chamberlain complied, and in so doing committed an even greater blunder when he guaranteed the security of Poland (and later of Rumania) without first having made sure that the Soviet Union also joined in this guarantee.

For once Chamberlain made this unilateral pledge, he found

that in effect he had guaranteed Russia's western frontier as well, without having obtained any assurances of aid from the Kremlin, thus leaving Stalin free to follow the Anglo-French strategy of Munich; to remain neutral in an exhausting struggle between Hitler and the Western democracies, following which Russia would emerge stronger in the balance of power.

Although it is now clear that neither the Western democracies nor the Soviet Union could have subdued Hitler without the aid of the other, Stalin now repeated Chamberlain's mistake. In explaining the Hitler-Stalin pact to the Supreme Soviet on August 31, 1939, Molotov insisted that it "brilliantly confirms Stalin's prevision." While it is most improbable that Stalin foresaw that the democratic forces on the continent would be crushed after a few months of fighting, it was nevertheless true, as Molotov boasted, that "the USSR is pursuing its own policy, based on the interest of the peoples of the USSR and only their interests. If these gentlemen," he added jocularly, "have such an uncontrollable desire to fight, let them do their own fighting without the Soviet Union. We would see what kind of fighting stuff they are made of!"

At best, however, it was an uneasy alliance, for within three months Hitler, in a top secret speech to his commanders, was pointing out that "Russia has far-reaching goals, above all strengthening her position in the Baltic. . . . We can oppose Russia only when we are free in the west. Further, Russia is striving toward the Persian Gulf. That is also the goal of our foreign policy. Russia will do that which she considers to benefit her. At the present moment she has retired from internationalism. In case she renounces this, she will proceed to Pan-Slavism. It is difficult to see into the future. . . . For the next one or two years, the present situation will remain."

It lasted until June 22, 1941, when the Hitler attack on Russia was launched, and again as in World War I, the military climax did not come until a considerable American army had crossed the Atlantic. But by January 1943 it was obvious that

Germany's greatest effort was in vain. As Ludendorff was thrown back across the Marne in July 1918, so von Paulus failed to cross the Volga, his army was trapped in Stalingrad and, as in July 1918, far-seeing Germans realized the war could at best be only a draw. In 1918 the climax was marked by Wilson's renewed peace offer to the German people. On January 14, 1943, Roosevelt and Churchill met at Casablanca, Stalin having refused for the fifth time to attend such a meeting. Instead of opening the door to peace, they closed it, with the announcement that they would accept from Germany nothing but "unconditional surrender." This was a direct reversal of Wilson's 1918 strategy, by which, with the proffer of a fair peace, he had brought about a weakening of the German fighting morale and a revolution with the overthrow of the Hohenzollern dynasty. The unconditional surrender formula closed the way to peace not only to Hitler but also to any German faction which might assassinate or overthrow him. If there were any doubts on this point, Churchill cleared them up in his speech to Parliament when he said: "No such arguments will be admitted by us as were used by Germany after the last war, saying that they surrendered in consequence of President Wilson's Fourteen Points. 'Unconditional surrender' means the victors have a free hand."

Its effects were immediate and far-reaching. It was first of all of immense propaganda value to the Nazi party within Germany. Every Gauleiter could point out to discontented Germans that the Western democracies had rejected all traffic with German "traitors," that the German people's only hope to survive was to fight on under Hitler's leadership.

Second, in relation to the Russians it was a blunder comparable to Chamberlain's 1939 guarantee of Polish security, without first having bound Russia with a similar pledge. As in 1939, Russia could now profit by an Allied pledge but pursue her own policy, which very sensibly she proceeded to do.

Within a month Radio Moscow was broadcasting to the Germans a speech by Stalin in which he said: "Occasionally the foreign press engages in prattle to the effect that the Red Army's aim is to exterminate the German people and destroy the German state. This is of course a stupid lie and a witless slander against the Red Army. . . . It would be ridiculous to identify Hitler's clique with the German people and the German state. History shows that Hitlers come and go, but the German state and the German people remain."

Stalin was, of course, already bitter about the delayed second front, which had been promised him first for 1942 and still later, at Casablanca, definitely for 1943. To an English-speaking visitor who saw him in that month, the above speech sounded like that of "a man who, if the Germans would agree to leave Russian soil, was preparing to get out of the war, blaming it on the Allies."

Lacking a second front, there was at least Lend-Lease, and here Russian demands were being given priority even over our own or British needs, and the Russians in Moscow, according to Lieutenant General John R. Deane, head of our military mission there, "resented any enquiry as to whether they needed it or not. In March 1943, President Roosevelt ordered our staff to comply without question. It was the beginning of a policy of appeasement . . . from which we are still suffering. They demanded and got a vast amount of material of use only after the war." *

In May 1943 Churchill with eighty assistants arrived in Washington to convince the Americans of the feasability of a second front that year, since the Axis had just surrendered in Africa. The British favored a blow at the "soft underbelly" of Europe, with landings on the Adriatic or in Greece, followed by a drive toward the Danube valley into rich territories now ruled by the Red Army. It would have cut off the German war machine from invaluable supplies of food and oil. It would, according to the carefully worked-out British plan, put Anglo-American forces in Berlin sometime in 1945. As an afterthought,

* *The Strange Alliance*, by John R. Deane. New York: The Viking Press.

it would also have permitted free elections, under Anglo-American supervision, in countries now controlled by Marshal Tito and other Soviet puppets.

The American Joint Chiefs of Staff felt that this British plan was too slow, too costly in vital shipping, and furthermore felt that the only way to fulfill Stalin's expectations was by an invasion through France. Since there were then few American troops in England, we proposed that the British make this initial French thrust in 1943, with American troops replacing their losses as fast as ours were available.

It was understandable that Churchill should reject this, arguing that England alone could not stand such losses, and that an invasion through France was impractical until 1944.

The minutes of this meeting were sent by courier to Stalin, and produced a stiff answer which arrived by cable on June 14. He pointed out that he had been promised a real invasion for 1943, had made his dispositions accordingly, and neither the African victory nor the proposed "soft underbelly" invasion would relieve pressure on the Red Army. While he conceded that our bombing of Germany had in spots been from 40 to 50 per cent effective, German industry was nevertheless only 7 per cent destroyed. Any 1944 invasion, he added sternly, would be too late, and since the proposed 1943 program was unacceptable, the Soviet government, he added ominously, "must deal with the situation as best it can."

What could this mean?

On July 1 the first report came to Washington that Soviet and Nazi diplomats in Sweden were discussing possible terms of peace—and why not? For the Russians were not bound to demand "unconditional surrender" even of Hitler, and they felt a second front long overdue. Six days later British Intelligence in Stockholm reported the talks to London, and Churchill was again urging on Washington that "soft underbelly" campaign which, he felt, would relieve pressure on the Red Army now and save the Balkans later.

Also in July Moscow's "Free German Committee" was organized with prisoners in Russia, and their manifesto to the German Army was beamed by Radio Moscow toward Berlin, calling on the brave German Army to overthrow Hitler and make peace with Russia. It was the old 1918 technique which had overthrown Wilhelm II, but would the Germans believe Stalin as they had trusted Wilson?

Meanwhile Stockholm reports said that the diplomatic talks were continuing. The Russian food and industrial situation was critical, the people war-weary and ripe for peace, but Hitler was still refusing demands for a Carpathian frontier and freedom for the Russians to foster Soviet influence and protectorate governments in the Balkans and Eastern Europe.

Perhaps the Big Three together could settle Allied difficulties. Gathering at Quebec on August 24, Churchill and Roosevelt once more hoped in vain for Stalin. Again Churchill urged the Balkan invasion—again he was turned down—but at least, pending final decision, the Anglo-American Allies could take the toe of Italy, where the Foggia airfield might later be used as an airbase in a Balkan thrust. All agreed that a serious invasion of Europe via Italy was impractical because of the terrain.

In October the Big Three foreign ministers were having a fruitless conversation in Moscow. Cordell Hull, who took the Atlantic Charter seriously (he had served in Woodrow Wilson's wartime Congress), was for rejecting Russia's political objectives. The British, however, would not back him up, pointing out that if the Anglo-American powers rejected Russia's demands for her swag under the Molotov-Ribbentrop pact (Bessarabia, East Poland, and the Baltic States) Russia would in the end demand even more.

But what with these uncertainties, Stalin again (on November 6) turned publicly toward the Germans. "It is not our aim," he told the Wehrmacht, "to destroy all organized military force in Germany, for every literate person knows that it is not only impossible . . . but also inadvisable from the point of view of the victor."

It was an appropriate curtain-raiser for Teheran, which began less than a month later. The really important memoirs of diplomats and generals who attended that conference have not yet been printed. However, a high-level American account agrees with a similar British account in all important details, and the substance of both is as follows: After the polite and unimportant preliminaries, the Big Three meeting was dominated by the now open secret that Stalin could get from Hitler immediate peace terms which would give the Soviet Union a sphere of influence up to the borders of Germany, with annexation of the Baltic States, East Poland and Bessarabia. Stalin's position now frankly was that Russian losses had been tremendous, his people were tired of the war, and while he preferred to go on and destroy Hitler, he expected concessions from the Western democracies equal to those which Hitler was now willing to give him.

Note here that Stalin used against the Anglo-American powers exactly the tactic which Colonel House, on behalf of Wilson, used against the European Allies at the 1918 meeting with Orlando, Clemenceau, and Lloyd George. The difference was that Wilson had refused to make peace with the Hohenzollerns, while Stalin's scruples against signing another friendship pact with Hitler were, in December of 1943, not unsurmountable. There was the further difference that Stalin's and Wilson's political objectives were poles apart.

To Stalin's proposals the Anglo-American leaders had opposite reactions. Churchill, discussing them later with Roosevelt, was strongly in favor of turning them down. He argued that, while no doubt the Hitler offer of a separate peace to Russia was genuine, Stalin, having had previous experience with treaties with Hitler, must know that it would last only so long as it served Hitler's purpose, and that therefore Stalin's implied threat to withdraw from the war was only a bluff.

Even if it were not, the British view was that if Russia did make a separate peace, the Anglo-American military situation would not be intolerable and perhaps would even be better, because Hitler could not hope to get supplies from an exhausted and war-torn Russia. The Anglo-American Allies had cleared North Africa and their line just above Naples, embracing the Foggia airbase, could now be securely held. So why not turn to finish off the Japanese war, meanwhile blockading Germany and pounding her cities to dust from the air? Two years of this treatment, Churchill was sure, would finish off Hitler and free Europe with far less loss of life than an invasion.

But Roosevelt was against it; the risks of a showdown then with Stalin were, he felt, too great.

Back in the Big Three meeting Churchill again proposed the "soft underbelly" Balkan invasion, but this was again turned down, it being clear to General John Deane that "Stalin wanted the Anglo-American forces in Western, not Southern Europe." Churchill now said that if "spheres of influence" were to develop in the coming peace he must have a Mediterranean one for Britain which would embrace Yugoslavia and Greece. To this Roosevelt and Stalin offered no objection.

And what was now left of the Atlantic Charter? Something, perhaps, and clearly Roosevelt hoped for more. In the matter of free governments for Europe, he told Congress on January 6, after Teheran, that we were to "use our influence" in the hope that "no temporary or provisional influence" would "block the eventual exercise of the people's right freely to choose." As for the actual text of the Charter, it was "good to have principles at which we can aim." And if this was not, as Senator Vandenberg called it on January 10, an "almost jocular and even cynical dismissal" of the Charter as a "mere collection of fragmentary notes," it was surely a retreat.

But "situations," as the President also told Congress (without explaining what they were), "are not as easy or as simple to deal with as some spokesmen believe" and no one, outside the im-

mediate entourage of the Big Three, knew of the possible im-
minence, in late 1943, of another Stalin-Hitler pact.

What the President himself thought at that time of Teheran
is embodied in a *Saturday Evening Post* article * written by Forrest Davis, who interviewed him shortly after his return, and
whose text was corrected before publication by the President
himself. Here we find that "the core of his [Teheran] policy has
been the reassurance of Stalin." But "suppose that Stalin, in spite
of all concessions, should prove unappeasable . . . what assur-
ance does the Roosevelt approach hold that he may not capture
all of Poland, the Balkans, Finland, and even Germany from
within, once his armies occupy those countries and he can
recognize his own Moscow-dominated undergrounds?" A Europe
so dominated "might suit this country's vital interests less than
the torn and distracted Europe of 1939."

The answer? Well, the President was not unmindful of this
grave danger but was "betting that the Soviet Union needs
peace and is willing to pay for it by collaborating with the
West." There was also Mr. Roosevelt's "celebrated charm."
The President realized he was "gambling for stakes as enormous
as any statesman has ever played for." Certainly he did not
then think he had lost, for "You know," he told Frances
Perkins shortly after Teheran, "I really think the Russians will
go along with me about having no spheres of influence. . . . I
think that is going to be the solution." †

And now for Yalta. There was in February 1945 no fear
that Stalin would quit the war, which was practically won.
But the Anglo-American powers were now confronted with his
faits accomplis in Europe. Between Teheran and Yalta, Com-
munist-dominated or puppet régimes were in the process of being
established for Czechoslovakia, Poland, Bulgaria, Albania, Yugoslavia, Rumania, and Hungary.

* "What Really Happened at Teheran," by Forrest Davis. *The Saturday
Evening Post*, May 13 and May 20, 1944.
† *The Roosevelt I Knew*, by Frances Perkins. New York: The Viking
Press.

"No single event of the war irritated me more," writes General Deane, who watched it, "than seeing the President of the United States lifted from a wheel chair to an automobile, to ship, to shore, in order to go halfway round the world as the only possible means of meeting Joe Stalin. . . . Perhaps we were friends, but it was difficult to believe it."

At Yalta, Stalin was further reassured by getting three votes in the United Nations Assembly and a veto provision in its Charter. In exchange for an agreement to break his non-aggression pact with the Japanese three months after the German surrender, he was promised roughly the rights and frontiers in Asia enjoyed by Czar Nicholas II before 1905.

As to his frontiers in Europe, the gains promised him in 1939 by Hitler (the Baltics, East Poland, and Bessarabia) were in effect now ratified by the democracies in what amounted to an amendment to the Atlantic Charter, whereby the Big Three bound themselves to restore self-government only to those peoples deprived of it "by aggressor nations," the Soviet Union being by definition a "peace-loving state."

And as for "spheres"? If we had surrendered here we did not yet believe it, for on his return from Yalta James Byrnes could boast that "In Greece, Poland, and Yugoslavia, we saw what looked like spheres of influence were being set up. . . . The United States assumes her share in decisions of this character. . . . The Three Great Powers . . . will act jointly to set up provisional governments and supervise free elections." But in the next two months before Roosevelt's death much of this illusion was to pass. The Committee of Big Three ambassadors meeting in Moscow which was to achieve this for Poland was getting nowhere in spite of Roosevelt's cables to Stalin, and in other Balkan countries our armistice commissioners were being treated by the Russians as something between tolerated spies and privileged prisoners in countries which they had expected to help govern.

Of all this the general public then knew little and had

digested less. The war-born hysterical wave of love and trust of Russia was, in the press, at its peak. It was different in the White House. The President's severest critics never called him naïve, and in those days, just before he left for Warm Springs, he was deeply perturbed.

The important memoirs of this pivotal period in American foreign policy have not yet been printed. When they are, they will present a picture of a mood in the White House which differed sharply from the public opinion of that excited hour. They will reveal a President already sick in body but mentally as alert and vigorous as ever, looking toward the future, already drafting the speech with which he expected to open the San Francisco conference. But they will also reveal a President profoundly troubled over the recent course in Europe, one who not only realized but could say heatedly to an old and trusted friend that Stalin had not kept a single one of the solemn and clear-cut promises made to him at Yalta, a President who could say that he was still sure his broad objective (peace through Big Three unity) had been right, but it now looked as though his means (the unflagging reassurance of Stalin) might have been wrong. He still believed Stalin was sincere, but now wondered if Stalin had as much power at home as all had assumed he had.

Yet he was not depressed, and, looking back at April 1945, we can ask, why should he have been? Because even if his heavy Teheran bet on "reassurance" seemed to have failed, there still remained both the time and means to hedge it, and thereby salvage much. Was he not commander of the world's largest fleet, its mightiest air force, and its third largest and most thoroughly mechanized army, already plunging across Germany toward the Elbe? So long as this army and air force, intact and alert as a mighty weight in the balance scales for a just peace, remained in Europe to make sure that those solemn Yalta pledges were fulfilled without quibbles, why should the President, early in April of 1945, have feared for his place in history?

Yet history also should deal gently with the inexperienced man who, on April 12, suddenly fell heir to all of this fast-moving confusion. The new President was surely no blind worshiper of Stalin, for, the day after Hitler's 1941 attack on the Soviet Union he had remarked that America should back whichever seemed to be losing.

"If we see Germany is winning, we ought to help Russia, and if we see Russia is winning, we ought to help Germany, . . . although I wouldn't want to see Hitler victorious under any circumstances." *

However, since that date both the Missouri senator and American public opinion had, with increasing momentum, and somewhat blindly, followed Roosevelt down the long road of "reassurance."

Had President Roosevelt himself halted at that crucial hour, the country would have understood and accepted, knowing that their leader, having tried his utmost, saw at last that he had reached the end of this road. But, in this new situation, could any leader suddenly call a halt without being bitterly accused of reversing the Roosevelt policy before giving it a fair trial?

Whether or not the policy subsequently followed would have been Roosevelt's, for the next few months it followed the path of least resistance and exactly fitted the public mood. The American people, weary of war, clamored to have the boys back from Europe. Demobilization based on the "point system" was immediately begun, with the result that what had been the world's finest army and air force was thrown into chaos, and our generals were complaining that not a single armored division or air squadron in Europe was capable of taking the field.

A few saw the danger. "If there is disintegration of our forces," warned General Eisenhower, "American influence will be weakened in Europe."

This again is in sharp contrast to 1918 when, as President

* Senator Harry S. Truman quoted in the New York *Times*, June 23, 1941.—WLW.

Wilson sailed for Paris to begin peace negotiations, the American Third Army, fully equipped and in complete battle array, was marching into Germany, not leaving it, and this Army was a factor in that peace.

The Truman policy was at the time popular partly because most people assumed it was an extension of the Roosevelt policy, but mostly because the American people, tired of war, wanted desperately to believe that Russian objectives also were ours, and that there was a sound basis for that peace for which all yearned. With love and trust of Russia on so firm a foundation of wishful thinking, anyone counseling firmness or caution ran the risk of being denounced as a hysterical warmonger.

CHAPTER XIV

RUSSIA IN THE LAST WAR

LET us now look back almost three decades at Russia in the last war. I well remember the wave of joy which swept American liberals at the news that the bumbling Romanov tyranny had been overthrown. Many felt the whole war worth its price in blood if its only gain were the disappearance of this ancient despotism.

By the time I arrived in Paris, Kerensky had been overthrown, Russia was in civil war and one still saw, on the streets of Paris, an occasional forlorn officer in his gray-green Czarist uniform with the tiny oval Romanov eagle emblem in his military cap, with the glittering epaulets over that blouse which looks to Western eyes like a shirt worn with its tail out and which the Red Army retains. The Russians in Paris that spring were torn into as many political factions as those which distracted their country, each beseeching Allied recognition and aid in the bloody civil war. There was still a little bedraggled hope. Kerensky's diplomats continued to occupy Russia's embassies in Allied capitals, although they were without funds, and the non-Bolshevik exiles had not yet gone to work as doormen, taxi drivers, and dress designers.

Although Wilson's task at the Peace Conference was vastly simplified by the fall of the Romanov Empire in Russia, there remained the expansionist aims of the other Allies, and it is interesting to compare these imperialisms of World War I, which Wilson fought so staunchly and on the whole so successfully, with those of today. In 1918 Wilson found these claims embedded in a series of secret treaties between the Allies—all made before

America entered the war—which it was his task to nullify. Of course, the Allies protested. In a joint memorandum Lloyd George and Clemenceau protested that "surely the victors . . . are entitled to some more substantial reward than theoretical map-makers, working in a void, may on abstract principles be disposed to give them." But under Wilson's principle of self-determination, helpless nations and provinces were not the spoils of war, to be dismembered or moved at random on the map. Mankind should retain dignity and basic rights even in defeat. Even the vanquished could choose their language and flag. It was the duty of a just conqueror to see that these basic rights were respected.

Most shocking of all the secret treaties was the one which had been signed by Poincaré for France with Pokrovsky, the Foreign Minister of Czar Nicholas II, just a few weeks before the Romanov dynasty fell in the spring of 1917. In courtly language Pokrovsky announced the willingness of his Imperial Majesty the Czar of all the Russias to allow France to fix the western frontiers of Germany where she pleased, but added that "we expect that the Allies will give us equal liberty in delimiting our frontiers with Germany and Austro-Hungary." In plain terms this meant that the Czar's minister invited France, if she liked, to push her frontiers to the Rhine or the Ruhr, provided France would not object if the Romanov eagles perched on the Oder. To this France agreed. Previously the Allies had conceded Constantinople to the Czar, along with control of its straits. Both treaties, however, were kept secret.

After the fall of the Czar and the rise of the short-lived liberal Kerensky régime in Russia, news of these deals began to seep out. On April 10, Kerensky published his peace aims for the new Russia which were, according to Ray Stannard Baker, President Wilson's biographer, "almost exactly like Wilson's," and urged the Russian people to go on with the war. But the Bolsheviks, his principal opponents, were attacking him savagely, not only demanding a peace with "self-determination of peoples, no annexations and no indemnities," but charging that Kerensky wanted Russia in the war only for imperialist reasons. The Allies finally published the secret treaty clause giving Russia Constantinople, hoping it would strengthen Russia's fighting spirit. Its effect was exactly the reverse. These secret treaties now became one of Lenin's principal propaganda weapons against Kerensky.

Lincoln Steffens, then in Moscow, in his *Autobiography* described one of the early Workers' and Peasants' Soviets in Petrograd at which "the first law passed by that representative stinking mass . . . was against capital punishment and the second was against war and empire; the Russian people should never conquer and govern any other people." John Reed, another American observer of Lenin's revolution, in *Ten Days That Shook the World* wrote of a simple Russian soldier who rose before such a crowd to demand why the army was fighting: "Is it for Constantinople or a free Russia?" Kerensky sent by Lincoln Steffens a message to Wilson, pointing out that ever since the Russian workers, peasants and soldiers learned "that there were secret treaties showing that we, the Allies, were all out for conquest, they won't fight," and pleading with Wilson to call a public conference and "abrogate the treaties." Then, said Kerensky's message, "I might get our people to go on with the war."

This was the mood of the Russian masses in that brief period between the Romanov and the Bolshevik dictatorships when they enjoyed free speech. They did not want Constantinople or a free hand in Poland or the Balkans. They did not want to plant the Romanov eagles, the Hammer and Sickle, or any other Slav banner on the banks of the German River Oder.

When the Bolsheviks finally overthrew Kerensky in November 1917 and seized the archives of the Czar's Foreign Office, one of their first acts was to publish, in *Izvestia*, on November 17, 1917, the secret treaties which, it should be remembered, gave the Czar almost the same territory which Stalin now claims.

But *Izvestia,* in publishing them, declared angrily that "the people should have the documentary truth about those plots which were hatched in secret by financiers and industrialists, together with their parliamentary and diplomatic agents." They used these secret treaties as justification for withdrawing the Russian people from what they charged was an imperialist war of conquest.

Moscow was not officially represented in Paris in the spring of 1919, and yet Lenin's shadow fell on our little bourgeois peace during the General Strike on May 1, 1919, called not for wages or hours, but to show working class solidarity with Lenin's and Trotzky's revolution. It was a brief but great drama which is now forgotten because, fortunately, I think, for the world, it lacked a second act. But the opening scene was beautifully staged. Remember that only recently had Lenin and Trotzky overthrown the beginnings of democratic government in Russia. Kerensky had fled (he was now in Paris seeking aid) and the Hammer and Sickle flapping over the yellow palaces of the Czars along the Neva was both new and disturbing to the statesmen at Paris. World opinion, and particularly liberal opinion, had not yet crystallized on this new government of workers, soldiers, and peasants. No one knew exactly what it wanted or where it would go. Yet it was already a source of great interest to the world, deeply stirring new hopes and old fears. In this situation French labor proclaimed on the first of May a twenty-four-hour general strike.

Paris, remember, was at that moment host to the conquerors and victorious statesmen of the world, who were housed in her magnificent luxury hotels. President Wilson and the leaders of the American delegation were at the Crillon, at one side of the Place de la Concorde. The British were further down the rue de Rivoli at the Continental. Our hotel, the Vouillemont, faced it across the narrow rue Boissy d'Anglais which emptied into the Place de la Concorde, and the Vouillemont was, for the Americans, second in importance only to the Crillon. On May 1

the statesmen of the world were to get a smashing demonstration of the organized power of French labor, for, after dawn,
not a wheel turned in the great city. The subways, taxis and
busses were motionless.

The night before there had been many rumors. Americans,
for instance, were ordered under no circumstances to venture
out into the streets. This was a purely domestic affair of the
French in which we should not get involved. In addition, a
curious rumor was circulating among French workers. The
uniformed Americans stationed in Paris had been given a dis-
tinctive shoulder insignia for their uniforms—a white fleur-de-lis
embroidered on a patch of black velvet. Someone had picked
this design from the coat of arms of the city of Paris, innocently thinking it would be apt for Americans stationed there.
French labor, however, was darkly suspicious, for it associated
the fleur-de-lis with the Bourbon dynasty. Rumor circulated
that French royalists were planning a *coup d'état,* and that these
American troops, already wearing the Bourbon lilies, were stationed here to help them quell the people of Paris. It had,
of course, been officially and repeatedly denied. Yet because
it still circulated, our orders to stay off the streets on May 1
were stern.

We foreigners the night before went to bed uneasy. There
had been men recently back from Petrograd with exciting stories
of mutinous soldiers who had refused to fire on the workers,
of the mobs which had pushed past sympathetic guards into
the palaces of the Czars and the assembly chambers of the
Duma. Paris was the city of mobs—half a dozen times since
1789 they had roared out into the boulevards and changed the
government of all France. Tomorrow's demonstration was to
show the sympathy of the toiling masses of France with their
fellow workers in Petrograd. Would the elected government of
France need troops? If so, could they be depended on?

I slept lightly, and about three o'clock was awakened by what
I first thought was a dream—the sound of many horses' hooves

clattering on the cobblestones below my window in the narrow rue Boissy d'Anglas. I leaned out and saw, in the flickering gas-light, a cavalry squadron. It was presently followed by hob-nails clicking in unison as an infantry regiment passed.

Old Clemenceau, the tiger of the 1871 Commune, being wise in the way of mobs, was taking no chances with this one. But, to avoid antagonizing it, his troops were being slipped into Paris in the deep night—three divisions of them—peasant boys from the provinces. If it became necessary to fire on the mob tomor-row, the elected rulers of France, possibly remembering the recent fate of Kerensky after the mutiny of the Petrograd garrison, wanted to be sure their orders would be obeyed.

Next morning before breakfast I went down to look at the regiment which was standing around its stacked arms along the rue Boissy d'Anglas. They were village boys from Brittany, sun-bronzed, sandy-haired, blue-eyed, for the most part fairly tall and light-boned—almost a different race from the dark Parisians. They also came from the old province of La Vendée, where their grandfathers once before battled the Jacobins of Paris.

The dining room was that morning (and all day) deserted of waiters so we filed by, cafeteria style, for our coffee and rolls. Afterward we went back upstairs (the elevator, of course, was deserted) to make our own beds. It was the same in the Crillon and all over town. The French workers were teaching a lesson to the assembled victors of the bourgeois world.

Then I sneaked across to the Crillon and went up to its roof which gave Americans front seats for the day's drama. Just below us was the Place de la Concorde, with the old Sun King's statues representing the great provincial cities of France, that of recovered Strasbourg now stripped of its mourning purple and piled high with flowers. Across the Seine rose the dome of the Invalides and the Chamber of Deputies.

It was a drama in miniature. The crowd had come up from the Place de la Revolution (the old Place Bastille) and was now trying to force its way out into the open expanse of the Place de la Concorde toward the Chamber of Deputies. Whether or not this body was then in excited session I do not remember. Faintly we could hear the roar of the mob as it pushed against the tight line of the *Garde Républicaine*. The *Garde* was mounted; we could see their horses occasionally rear up as they pressed against the mob. Sometimes the *Garde* would be pushed back—a great bulge would develop in their thinning line. It looked as though it would snap and the black mass would vomit forth into the huge empty square. But then the *Garde* would rally, and push back the mob, roaring angrily. Once the mob did make a gap, and we could see tiny figures streaming through the breach, making for the bridge over the Seine to the Chamber of Deputies. But reinforcements for the *Garde* came galloping across the square, the gap was closed and the stragglers rounded up.

Once the mob succeeded in surrounding a guardsman who had pressed too deeply into its black mass. They got hold of his reins, then someone dragged him from his horse and he disappeared while they trampled him to death; from the Crillon roof we could see only his lunging horse. But presently we saw his empty battered helmet rising on a pole, its brass and horse-tail crest glittering and bobbing with the surge of the crowd, just as heads with half-closed eyes had swayed and wobbled on pikes over crowds on these same cobblestones in 1793.

It was all very French.

We learned later that one of the rioters had been killed, and next day the Government gave the unions permission to hold an enormous public funeral, honoring him as a martyr of the working class, and this ended it. That night the divisions from Brittany and La Vendée marched out of Paris as quietly as they had entered it. The middle classes learned (if they needed the lesson) that civilization will stop if the workers withhold their brawn. The unions learned (but perhaps they already knew it) that French democracy would not hesitate to use its strength to defend itself against the dictatorship of any minority.

And now another memory touching Russia out of this dead past—an evening with Kerensky at the Paris house of Charles R. Crane. Our host was a most distinguished, intelligent, urbane liberal millionaire. His millions came from the plumbing fixture business; the origins of his liberalism I never knew. But he had early been a friend, and probably also a financial backer of Wilson, for he had served as his Minister to China. He was a plump, meticulously dressed little man in his early fifties, with piercing blue eyes and a crisply-trimmed white goatee which gave him a Continental air. He had leased in Paris a magnificent house, lavish with crimson carpets, flowing with velvet curtains, and dripping with chandeliers in the best Empire style. He did not self-consciously hold a salon here during that peace, but he knew good food, he knew good wine, and he knew whom he wanted to talk to: the leading American and foreign liberals of that day. Of course, he was keenly interested in Russia.

I went to Crane's house several times with my father who, when he was invited, was at a loss to know how to dispose of me, so Crane would indulgently tell him to bring me along. Once we met the Grand Duke Alexander who, after Nicholas II was shot with his family in that Ekaterinburg cellar by the Bolsheviks, aspired to play the rôle of the liberal Duke of Orléans. The Grand Duke was a huge, thick-fingered, Slavic bear of a man, who wore the broad crimson ribbon of some order across his starched shirt front. After the triumph of the White armies he hoped to establish in Russia, so he explained, a constitutional monarchy of the type headed by his not too distant cousin George V. The American liberals questioned him politely, and I think concluded that his enthusiasm for constitutional democracy was shallow, and largely a product of the seeming expediencies of that confused hour.

Other Marco Polos returning from Moscow to Paris that spring were Bill Bullitt, later to be Roosevelt's first ambassador there, and Lincoln Steffens, who told American newspapermen at the Crillon dinner table, "I have seen the future and it works!" His burning faith in it lasted his lifetime, while Bullitt lived to see Russia crystallize into another nationalistic dictatorship.

But most unforgettable was Kerensky. It must have been early in the spring, for I remember him sitting in front of the huge marble Empire mantel in Crane's drawing room with the flickering light from its fire playing around the heavy Slavic bones of his face. He had not yet told his story so often that it was threadbare. Exactly what he said I do not remember; it came to us translated out of Russian and broken French. But he had been the leading actor of a great tragedy who now was reliving his part before us—explaining why he could not have done other than he did—bringing up the events and the other actors of a dozen minor crises of which we knew nothing —explaining, justifying, pleading, it seemed, that we understand the forces which, from both sides, had converged to crush the slender hopes for a free, liberal, democratic Russia. Eloquence and tolerance had not been enough, and now the fire picked out for us dramatic highlights of agony in the face of this man who could not, even then, quite admit that he had failed.

CHAPTER XV

THIS PEACE AND THAT

Russia did not, however, hold the spotlight in Paris that spring of 1919. She was only a noise offstage, and Wilson's real problem was to handle the imperialism of the other Allies.

France, as we have seen, a nation of 38 millions facing a Germany half again her size, wanted that Germany weak. She first proposed outright annexation of the Rhineland but even Lloyd George agreed with Wilson that "we must not make another Alsace-Lorraine." Then France wanted to establish an independent Rhineland republic. When Wilson opposed this, she demanded that Allied armies should hold the Rhine for thirty years. The compromise was fifteen years. (The French armies actually withdrew after ten.)

On Germany's eastern border, Wilson favored, purely on grounds of self-determination, an independent Polish state. France wanted a Poland which could serve as a counter-weight against a weakened Germany, and also favored giving to Poland the German city of Danzig, thus pitting Poland perpetually against Germany and making her the natural ally of France. But Lloyd George again agreed with Wilson that this would create in Europe a trouble spot for future wars because there were more than 2,000,000 Germans in the territory which Clemenceau proposed to take from Germany, and only about 600,000 Poles. It was, Lloyd George felt in 1919, "a most dangerous proposal." (The prophetic little Welshman was still alive when, exactly twenty years later, the Second World War started over this Danzig question.) However, in 1919, Clemenceau did not entirely get his way. Wilson and Lloyd George forced on him a compromise under which Danzig became a Free City. Nor did Poland get all of Upper Silesia, as Clemenceau wished. Instead a plebiscite was held here so that the people, and not the great powers, would decide under which flag they wished to live. When the western communes of that province voted to go to Germany, they were allowed to join.

Today, not only Danzig but the equally ancient German towns of Koenigsberg and Stettin, not only all of Pomerania but East and West Prussia as well have been taken by Russia either for herself or for her puppet state of Poland. Although the seizure would never have been countenanced in Wilson's day, the Kremlin's reasons would have seemed sensible to Cardinal Richelieu and Prince Metternich. For Poland, having been robbed by Russia in the East, is now loaded with western lands which have for a thousand years been German. Even if a truly democratic Germany should rise from the ruins of Hitler's Reich, that Germany must always hate Poland, so Poland (willing or unwilling) must always be Russia's ally.

The weakness of America's present position is that, having feebly acquiesced in the Russian annexation of Poland's eastern provinces, we then protest loudly when Russia rewards her puppet with purely German lands. To any Pole our policy seems compounded of short-sighted "realism," open pro-Germanism and fear of Russia, and is without consistency, equity or dignity.

It was Wilson's hope to remove from Europe those hates which break out into wars. Against Wilson's theory was opposed the old theory of the balance-of-power system, which assumes that there must always be war, which may, however, be postponed by skillfully balancing hate against hate. And if a strong permanent hate does not exist, but is needed to even the scales, then that hate must be manufactured, as the Kremlin is now doing, following the precedent of Clemenceau who, by creating Danzig, lit the twenty-year-long fuse which began World War II.

I have often wondered why the Sudeten Germans, who almost disrupted the peace of the world in 1938, did not present their case at Versailles. The second-best hotels of Paris in 1919 were thronged with sad-eyed delegations from the Dodecanese Islands, from the suffering and oppressed Armenians, from the Ukrainians, Georgians and various other little nations now within the Soviet Union, and from various Arab states. The Jews had a lobby in behalf of Palestine. Almost every conceivable minority with a grievance on the face of this globe managed to get hold of at least one hotel room and a mimeograph in that spring of 1919—except the Sudetens.

The reason probably was that the Sudetens, if indeed they had a grievance, decided it would, in 1919, be prudent to keep quiet. Living along the fringes of Old Bohemia when it was part of the Hapsburg Empire, the Sudetens had for a century been militantly Germanic, and their grievance against the Hapsburgs was that this dynasty, although German in race and speech, pandered disgracefully to the Slavic and Hungarian elements in the Empire, granting them preferences and high offices at the expense of the noble Teutons. During the war, however, the Czechs were recognized by us as fighting Allies and, after it, were to be rewarded with their independence and substantial postwar aid. The Sudetens were thus in a dilemma. Had they sent a delegation to Paris protesting that they were German and invoking Wilson's principle of self-determination, the President probably would have backed them, with the result that they would have been separated from the victorious Czechs and segregated with the defeated Germans, who were about to be saddled with war guilt and a heavy indemnity. So the Sudetens did not rediscover their ancient Teutonic virtues until Hitler smashed the Versailles Treaty and it was no longer imprudent to be German.

Ever since watching the making of that peace I have viewed the little minorities of Europe, people of mixed loyalties on the borders of greater neighbors, with a mixture of cynicism and sympathy. There was, for instance, the matter of Alsace-Lorraine. The language, architecture, physical appearance—even the cooking—of this area is as German as Bavaria. But before the rise of nationalism in Europe they became subjects of the French Bourbons, took part in the French revolution and came to consider themselves French. Bismarck restored them to the German Empire in 1871. Clemenceau restored them to the Third French Republic in 1918 and there was much official rejoicing in which probably a majority of the Alsatians joined.

Early in the spring of 1919 the French government took a trainload of French and British newspapermen on a propaganda trip to that region for the purpose of allowing their Anglo-Saxon Allies to see the ecstatic delight of the Alsatians on being reunited to France; my father managed to get me in on the trip. The French put on for us a great pageant. Strasbourg is an ancient Rhine town, and the old stone façades and gabled roofs with their stork nests in its main *Platz*, could have been steel engravings out of a book of German fairy tales. The liberating French had changed most of the German names to French ones—Hohenzollernstrasse, if there was one, would become rue de la République. Possibly the Germans had made similar changes after 1871.

The French had arranged a packed day for our party, but at noon I struck out on my own for a few hours because I wanted to see Strasbourg. We had just come from France, where the people were heavily rationed and pinch-faced from four hungry years of war. Here I was amazed to see the food shops blazing with oranges, bursting with chocolate, great tubs of butter, huge shelves of flaky pastry and other delicacies undreamed of in wartime France. I discovered that the French government had shipped trainloads of these goodies out of its own half-starved country into this Rhine valley region just behind its liberating troops, as a gentle reminder to the Alsatians of the delights of French citizenship.

For lunch I dropped into a modest *Gasthaus* and was starting my meal of succulent horsemeat stew when an Alsatian boy about my age sat down beside me and ordered the same. I was a little startled because he was obviously just demobilized from the German Army, and my neck bristled at his field-gray uniform and the pewter buttons stamped with the old Kaiser's eagles. It was a little too soon for me to sit down comfortably with the enemy—if, indeed, he was an enemy. I noticed that he was also eyeing my uniform.

Presently we began to talk, and I made some remark about his pleasure as an Alsatian in being French again. He appeared to have no enthusiasm for this topic. But when we began to talk of the war, he thawed. He spoke little French and I had only a smattering of German, but he explained that most of his time had been spent in the German submarine service. The Germans, I later learned, had not trusted their Alsatian conscripts to fight on the Western front, but had used them either in their navy or against the Russians. The French were equally prudent in this war in dealing with this people of mixed blood and loyalties.

And now he really warmed up, with pride in his old ship, in the bravery of his crew, and in the skill of their commander. He told of their skill in torpedoing Allied ships, and the tricks they had used in escaping American and British destroyers. It was the pride of any boy of any country in his old outfit, and what they did in the war. But he told it a little defiantly, as though he were hurt that this story had not been universally popular, as though now, for some strange reason he was supposed to be ashamed of his old outfit, and he was determined not to be. And he seemed a little disdainful because, although he and I were both eighteen, it developed that I had only been in the infantry and had not got overseas for any fighting. It would not greatly have mattered to him how or on what side I had fought, provided I had fought. It was, for me, a mellowing experience.

That night old General Gouraud, the French military governor of liberated Alsace, gave us the best meal I have ever eaten, or ever again hope to sit down to, and I say this as one who has been a humble guest of Molotov at Spiridonovka, where the Bolsheviks preserve, as carefully as they do the corpse of Lenin, the majestic cookery of the Czars. But that night in 1919, as guests of the Third French Republic, we were eating as only the fat old Bourbon monarchs ate, by comparison with which Commissar Molotov's rugged Romanov food was like an avalanche of delicatessen from Lindy's Broadway restaurant. As a special fillip, this 1919 banquet was served in a spacious château which had once belonged to the Hohenzollern family, and we ate it off their crested china, and drank the many wines out of a procession of goblets of the clearest, thinnest crystal, each of which bore in gold the Hohenzollern eagle. This I particularly liked: remember, I was eighteen.

After this symphony in food we went out into a great hall for coffee, and sat around at gilded baroque tables with marble tops while the waiters brought around champagne. Nobody had so far made a speech asking the reporters either to write something or not to write it. At the other end of the room, curtains were now drawn and we were led out onto a balcony overlooking a large court. On the engraved menus which we had been given, this event was shown following immediately after the cigars, and was entitled "A demonstration of loyalty on the part of the populace of Strasbourg on the occasion of their reunion with France." As we stepped on the balcony we heard a muffled roar and looked out into a sea of waving flambeaux, by the light of which we could see the upturned faces beneath. Old General Gouraud (he died only last year) was smiling happily from our balcony.

Looking more closely down into this spontaneous demonstration of joy on the part of the liberated Alsatians for the benefit of their Anglo-Saxon allies, I noticed that all but six of those upturned faces belonged to uniformed soldiers of the local French garrison who were dutifully waving the kerosene torches, and that the muffled roar in the background came from twelve kettle-drums in the semi-darkness of the other side of the court, also being thumped by stoical French *poilus*.

Peering back at this event over the twenty-eight intervening years, perhaps even now seeing it through a golden mist of the great wines of France, I truly believe that a majority of the Alsatians would have been glad to be French again, even without the aid of the oranges and chocolate, and that it was only sensible of them to lie warm beneath their German featherbeds instead of getting up well after midnight to expose their patriotic motions to the somewhat alcoholic admiration of their Anglo-Saxon allies on that balcony above.

The other side of this story I learned the next morning when I opened our hotel room door as we were about to go down to breakfast, to find thrust under it a leaflet in fairly good English, with only a few misspellings, addressed to the English and American correspondents, admonishing us not to be misled by the propaganda of the French, and assuring us that the great majority of the people of Alsace, while glad to be delivered from German rule, had no desire to be governed from Paris, but wished instead to be an autonomous republic as we would quickly discover if a plebiscite were held in this land following the high principles of "that great leader, Mr. Woodrow Wilson of America."

This trip gave me an early insight into the psychology of those little peoples which lie along the boundaries of Europe's greater powers, which pass with the fortunes of war from one flag to another, and which furnish to both sides their quotas of incorruptible patriots and plausible spies. With the Alsatians should go the Luxembourgeois (call them Luxemburgers if your sympathies are German), the Belgians, so evenly divided between French-speaking Walloons and Teutonic-speaking Flemings, the Sudetenlanders, the Tyrolians, the Lithuanians, Latvians, and Estonians, the Schleswig-Holsteiners, the Silesians on Poland's western border who are partly German, and the provinces of Wilna and Lvov on her eastern border which have now been taken by the Soviet Union because they included Ukrainian and Byelo-Russian minorities.

Soviet Russia presents a special problem in regard to minorities. For instance, the minor nationalities of her Baltic provinces, although they had languages distinct from Russian, were almost as contented subjects of the Czar as the Welsh have been of the British crown.

With the coming of the Bolsheviks, however, all of them broke away, proclaimed their independence and furnished supplies for the White armies fighting Lenin and Trotzky. Wilson, however, was slow to recognize the Baltic States and Finland. Russia was still in the turmoil of civil war. Who knew what might emerge? Perhaps a democratic Russia, within which the Baltic States would be content. While he would do nothing to force them back under Bolshevik rule, still he did not want to see Russia dismembered in her helplessness. So for some time we did not recognize their independence. For these same reasons Wilson forced the Japanese to withdraw their armies from Siberia.

Today Soviet Russia, which tacitly claims practically all the old domain of the Romanovs, has settled the Baltic problem by quietly annexing the three states by "plebiscite" in 1940, a few months after Molotov had loudly declared that such an annexation was unthinkable. Although America has not yet officially recognized this seizure, there is clearly nothing we can do about it.

In the present situation there are many other echoes of 1919's disputes. Wilson, Lloyd George, Clemenceau and Orlando spent weary weeks over the Italian-Yugoslav boundary, which has similarly occupied Byrnes, Bevin, and Molotov. But Wilson was resisting the then extortionate claims of our then Allies, the Italians (they wanted not only Trieste but even Fiume), against the newly-born Yugoslav state.

My hotel in Paris also housed a delegation from the Dodecanese Islands. These people are Greek by race and language, but unfortunately occupy in the Aegean Sea a strategic position. They had belonged to the defeated Turks. But under the secret treaty by which France and England had bought Italy into the First World War, they were to go to the House of Savoy, although their people wanted to rejoin Greece. Wilson finally yielded and they went to Italy; it was one of many little compromises he was forced to make in gaining greater ends. At the end of this present war Russia claimed them as a trading point but finally yielded to Bevin and Byrnes so at last they revert to Greece.

Colonies, which are a minor matter in this our 1947 settlement, were a major one in 1919, for the victors had to liquidate the spoils of the considerable German and Turkish Empires. Wilson's formula here was simple and also in the finest liberal traditions: these subject peoples were not to be the spoils of war, but each colony would be guided to freedom under the League of Nations. In 1946 Secretary Byrnes proposed an almost identical solution for Italian Tripolitania to which only Russia objected. Also involved in the 1919 colonial settlement was a British secret treaty with Japan who had been assured on February 16, 1917, that she could keep the German naval base in China at Shantung, as well as all German Pacific islands north of the Equator, those south of it going to Australia and New Zealand.

In the matter of these islands and Germany's other colonies, Wilson was only partly successful. Japan and the various British dominions which had conquered them clamored for full sovereignty. In the compromise, they were allowed to "administer" them under mandate to a League sovereign at least in theory. (Had America thrown her weight into that League it might have become sovereign in fact.)

In this war, by insisting on virtual sovereignty for these same islands rather than intrusting them to the United Nations, America has made a wide departure from Wilson's principles. Significantly the American claim was instantly accepted by the Russians, who welcomed such a precedent to strengthen Soviet claims for sovereignty or control over the far more wealthy, populous and strategically important lands occupied by the Red Army.

In one respect—publicity for the peace negotiations in process —Secretary of State Byrnes succeeded in Paris in 1946 where Woodrow Wilson failed in 1919. Wilson's Fourteen Points had pledged to the world "open covenants of peace openly arrived at." But when he got to Paris he could not persuade the others, and the important deals were made between the Big Three of that day in secrecy as deep as that which later was to shroud Casablanca, Teheran, Yalta, and Potsdam.

But Woodrow Wilson was not always on the side of the angels. In 1919 the Japanese led a long but losing fight to get into the League Covenant some kind of racial equality clause —if not a guarantee, at least a polite phrase indicating that equality was desirable. They were willing to trade anything for this, were bitterly disappointed when they lost, and who can say that this bitterness did not lay the foundations of "Greater East Asia"? They had, in their long struggle, the support of the Chinese, the Italians and the Czechs. Lloyd George was probably sympathetic but did nothing because of violent opposition from the British dominions, particularly South Africa and Australia, which had Negro and Japanese minorities. Wilson, knowing that if the League were to be ratified he would need the votes of Southern and Pacific Coast senators, did nothing to help this racial equality clause.

But his greatest error was in not paying still more attention to the political situation back home. Maybe he did not because he could not. Perhaps the mind of one man is too small to encompass both the shifting complexities of European power politics and those of the American Senate. Even so, Wilson was by temperament impatient with those who disagreed. He did not suffer fools gladly, nor could he easily co-operate with equals. Although two leading Republicans, ex-President William H. Taft and ex-Secretary of War Elihu Root, agreed with his League concept, he did not ask their help in Paris. Instead he took with him a delegation of political nonentities, in contrast to the Roosevelt-Truman policy of taking the opposition into camp by appointing to the delegation powerful and representative Republicans, thus removing the peace from partisan controversy.

It was a tragedy for both Wilson and the world that he made in 1919 what America could only see as a strictly Wilsonian peace. This not only forced it on the Republicans as a partisan issue (the political pendulum was swinging in their direction anyway) but alienated within his own party powerful leaders who felt they had not been consulted.

It is fashionable today to say that the American people, in these intervening years, have reversed their previous isolationism. But how isolationist were they in November of 1919 when, even in the Republican-controlled American Senate, Wilson's League, in spite of his grave political blunders, commanded a majority vote, but failed only to get the necessary two thirds which our Constitution requires?

But back to the Versailles Treaty: in 1919 there were German war criminals even as now. Lloyd George had in fact won an election on the slogan "Hang the Kaiser," but the idea that the victors should prosecute, judge, blindfold the war criminals, and also spring the gallows trap revolted the squeamish liberals of that distant day. Certainly Wilson never joined this hue and cry for *ex parte* justice. There was in 1919 some talk of calling in neutral jurists, but the task of bringing German war criminals to trial was finally left by the Treaty to the Germans themselves, who promptly and enthusiastically acquitted most of them.

I think properly so. Because the First World War may well be the last great conflict to be fought more or less within the bounds of the ancient rules of "civilized warfare." While it was in progress there were of course rumors, on the Allied side, of the spiritual shortcomings of the wicked Hun, who bayoneted babies, raped nuns, crucified prisoners and then washed himself with soap concocted from their boiled corpses. But when war hysteria died away it was established that almost without exception such stories had been manufactured and spread for propaganda purposes. Indeed it may be said that in this war the Nazis methodically and on a mass scale perpetrated every atrocity of which, in the last war, the German people were unjustly accused.

We can be sure that no future investigation, reviewing the evidence on Belsen, Auschwitz or Lublin, will ever exonerate the Nazi party leaders of the mass slaughter of helpless Jews and war prisoners. With this a neutral court, or even a court of German judges, chosen by a free Germany, would certainly agree. But whether or not a dispassionate neutral court of Swiss and Swedish jurists would have convicted men like Keitel or Jodl of participation in these crimes is questionable.

It may be true, of course, that had we lost the war, Roosevelt, Willkie, Churchill, de Gaulle, and Stalin would have been hanged by the victors. Perhaps the old concepts of Anglo-Saxon common law from which America drew her codes are outmoded. Maybe the totalitarian concept of justice will prevail, and in the future, victors will judge and hang vanquished with a conscience as clear as that with which Marshal Tito disposed of our former gallant ally General Mihailovich. Or as Stalin has, from time to time, removed various political rivals in the Soviet Union. I know, however, that these innovations in our Anglo-Saxon conceptions of justice would have been deeply shocking to Woodrow Wilson. If there was hanging to be done, he would have insisted that the trials be conducted, if not by a German court then by a neutral one, but certainly not by the victors. We have moved far and fast since his day.

There is also some evidence that President Roosevelt did not have too strong a stomach for hysterical self-righteousness, particularly in its more pompously legalistic manifestations. As our armies fanned out into Germany and it became clear that German leaders would be captured, he remarked to Secretary Perkins that "Of course there's got to be severe treatment, but I wouldn't make too much of it. It's pretty obnoxious. Just a few drumhead courts-martial in the field and have it over quick." *

The 1919 American position in regard to an indemnity from Germany was originally the same as it is in this peace settlement. Wilson claimed no indemnity for America and opposed such claims by other nations. However, since the war had been fought on French soil, he agreed that it would be only just if Germany paid for a fair share of the civilian property destroyed there. From this position he was quickly forced deeper by the clamors of the Allies. In the end Germany was saddled with a preposterous sum in "reparations," not because British and French statesmen thought she could pay it but because, in their campaign speeches, they had promised that Germany would pay all the war costs. "We shall squeeze Germany until the pips squeak!" Lloyd George had boasted in the khaki election.

Roosevelt hoped that our present peace settlement would avoid this error of leaving over the German people so great a debt that it crushed all hope. "By compelling reparations in kind," he said in his March 1, 1945, speech, "we shall avoid the mistake made after the last war, of demanding reparations in the form of money which Germany could never pay."

Wilson's original position against a crushing indemnity was borne out by history, as Roosevelt had seen. The fact that Germany after the last war actually paid little of this theoretical debt, and that what she paid was more than balanced by later repudiated loans from American bankers, is beside the point. For the ensuing German generation was never free from the threat of reparations. Why should they work to rebuild the country when the victors, greedily inspecting a disarmed and helpless Germany, would view any sign of revival as a signal to demand more?

Wilson originally saw the First World War only as one of

* *The Roosevelt I Knew*, by Frances Perkins. New York: The Viking Press.

the perennial recurrent explosions of the European balance-of-power system, and put the blame for its start, not on Germany or any single nation, but on the system itself. After the heat of wartime emotions faded historians agreed, but this was not, of course, the view of the war-weary, propaganda-drugged masses of the victorious countries in 1919 who insisted that a defeated enemy should pay for all. Consequently the victors at Versailles ballooned Wilson's original reparations into a crushing indemnity, and, to justify this, wrote into the treaty an admission by Germany of her responsibility for starting the war which the protesting German delegates at Versailles were forced to sign.

I did not see the ceremony on May 7 at which the text was first presented to the German delegation in the Grand Château at Versailles. It was held in the great Hall of Mirrors, which I tiptoed through a few days before, when they were shining the chandeliers, the same hall where in 1871 Bismarck had proclaimed the German Empire and dictated his terms to a broken France. The French, by picking the same room in 1919, displayed a sense of historical drama equaled only by Hitler's when, in the summer of 1940, he forced Marshal Pétain's representatives to sign the armistice in the same railway car at Compiègne in which Marshal Foch had forced the German High Command of 1918 to accept his terms.

I could not be in the room, but a boy of 18 could wander outside the palace of the Sun King, listening to the horses' hooves of the French ceremonial guard, with burnished cuirasses and plumed brass helmets, clattering on the ancient cobblestones; could watch the great of that day arriving before the palace gates in their motor cars (and these included Herbert Swope and Bernard Baruch, side by side and resplendent in top hats); could even go to the hotel, a few hundred yards away, where the German delegates were housed and, peering with the crowd through its high iron railings, watch them, pale and bitter in defeat, emerge for the ceremony.

The clauses at which these somber German diplomats and Social Democrats protested most bitterly were the war-guilt and indemnity provisions which Wilson had been unable to soften. Few men on the Allied side could in 1919 foresee that the victors of Versailles had, in these provisions, written into their treaty clauses which made inevitable the death of German democracy. One of those few was Frank L. Simonds, America's leading foreign affairs commentator, who saw the mistakes of Versailles with a cold clarity which was frightening for his day. Writing of this war-guilt clause six years later, when the name of Hitler was still unknown outside a small group of fanatics in the floundering German Republic, he pointed out that "peoples may believe they have been deceived, misled, mistaken. . . . But no people can believe in the moral turpitude of their race. . . . In the eyes of every German, resistance to the Treaty of Versailles was resistance to a verdict which not only condemned his race on the ground of moral turpitude, but thereby supplied the pretext for the physical destruction of his country as well."

Simonds, who had watched the rise of German democracy in the spring and summer of 1919, felt that "no objective examination of Weimar and the Constitution there made can fail to establish the conclusion that democracy in Germany was at this moment authentic," but "by the most cruel and fatal of all conceivable circumstances, the Allied peoples, who had fought to make a world safe for democracy, were now demanding" that this new Republic sign a treaty which "would make democracy impossible for all Germans." Its signature was, Simonds pointed out, "the death warrant of the German Republic."

Simonds wrote this in 1926 *—seven years before Hitler was to execute that death warrant. Since the Germans were "condemned as a pariah people; subjected to treatment which wounded every sensibility and aroused every surviving circumstance of national pride," they were "thrown back upon them-

* *How Europe Made Peace Without America*, by Frank L. Simonds. New York: Doubleday and Company.

selves and within themselves." Thenceforth "the wretched ministers of the German Republic existed between the bayonets of the armies of Foch and the passions of their own people. To resist Allied demands was to invite Allied sanctions, new invasions, and fresh hardships; to comply with Allied demands was to insure the utter discrediting of the democratic régime. . . . Not only had the government no power to compel disarmament, it had no public sentiment behind it. In every undertaking, it became in the eyes of its fellow-countrymen the instrument of foreign oppression," and therefore, at each election, from that of the Weimar assembly onward, "control slipped steadily through Republican hands."

In 1926 even so astute an observer as Frank Simonds could not predict that Germany would presently be in the hands of a little Austrian anti-Semite with a mustache. Yet even then Simonds could see the vacuum which would conjure up this little man from nothing, could write that "if there were in all German public life a man of Bismarckian stature, it is unbelievable that the Republic could survive these humiliations."

It is not likely that the present peace will furnish a sounder basis for a democratic Germany, since its burdens promise to weigh much more heavily than did those of Versailles.

The present postwar situation differs from the last largely in the fact that in 1919 the victors, although they differed somewhat among themselves as to boundary lines, were basically united as to the kind of Europe they wanted to create, and occasionally divided only as to the means. The peace in 1919 was made by three powerful democracies, whose peoples hoped to shape a world which would grow around this concept. Had the Romanov dynasty survived there might have been the even greater problem of curbing Czarist Russia's imperialist aims, which would have been basically the same as those of Soviet Russia today. However, Wilson might have curbed these exactly as he did those of the other Allies: by stating clearly America's war aims and then, when they were accepted by the Germans, threatening to withdraw from the war unless his Allies agreed.

In 1943 our leadership took the opposite course, serving notice on all Germans that there was no hope now, for any of them, but to fight to the bitter end. Even then some of them did not quite believe us, and in July of 1944 made an attempt, which almost succeeded, to kill Hitler and pave the way for peace. But it failed, so the bloody struggle went on.

In war diplomats and generals weigh the lives of soldiers against the value of military or political ends which the nation seeks. History will ask of America's leadership in this war what we got by spending those additional American lives, which the "unconditional surrender" formula cost us, that we could not have achieved by following Woodrow Wilson's tactics. Temporarily we gained "unity" among the Allies, but only at the cost of postponing major peace problems until after the war, when Russia would be occupying most of the disputed points, and our bargaining position would clearly be weaker.

Wars, unlike, say, high-school basketball games, are fought, not just for the sake of victory, but for definite post-war objectives. It is true that America did not enter this one for colonies or spheres of influence. But she properly felt that she would not be safe if democracy in Europe were stamped out by a totalitarian dictatorship heated with expansionist dreams of world domination. Our problem in this war was, of course, that democracy in Europe was imperiled by two such expansionist dictatorships, and if one were overwhelmed, it would be vitally important to make sure that the other did not move into the power-vacuum thus created. It is here that America has failed. Most of our statesmen and all of our generals seem to have viewed the war as a super-basketball game. Those of the old world believe in victories for a purpose, and not for their own sake.

It is small wonder that sardonic Europeans see us as a quixotic, irresponsible people who intervene to tip the scales in Europe's wars, talking loudly of our wish for a democratic world, but then walk out without finishing the job. After the last world war we repudiated the League which our President had with great skill and pains erected as the keystone of world peace, and retired into an isolation as blatantly nationalistic as any of the European nationalisms which Wilson fought in Paris.

We enter this one with lofty words about freeing Europe from the slavery of Hitler's dictatorship, and leave that continent in the power of another dictatorship as deeply entrenched as Hitler was at his zenith. We have that world organization of which our people dreamed, and only now do they realize that into the heart of its text is written what may be its death warrant in the shape of the veto.

Why did we fail? Our objective of restoring freedom to Europe was devoutly desired by the masses on that continent. The striking power of our land, sea, and air forces made us the greatest military power on earth. We failed because our physical power was not co-ordinated, either in time or in place, with our objectives. We poured Lend-Lease aid into Russia without bothering to ask them for firm commitments. Later, when their own soil was free of invaders and our aid was no longer vital, they very sensibly refused to make the commitments which we so tardily asked, and declined to fulfill others which we were powerless to enforce.

If we are to be effective in this modern world, our military minds must be in close harmony with our diplomats, as those of England and the Soviet Union have always been. If we are to preserve what is left of democracy on the globe, our generals and statesmen must be brought to understand that a free election in Warsaw or Athens may be for us a stronger bulwark than a coral atoll in the Pacific.

Looking backward, I believe that our mistakes may be summarized as follows:

1. As a price of Lend-Lease to Russia we failed to get from Moscow a pledge joining us in renouncing all territorial claims. We should also have insisted that all reconquered territories be

held by American, British and Russian occupation armies of equal size, that no governments be recognized except following free elections supervised by the three powers.

2. Our unconditional surrender formula in retrospect seems only to have prolonged the war, cost millions of unnecessary lives, and put the Russians in the heart of Europe.

3. Churchill's proposed Balkan invasion might have prolonged the war by a few months but still more probably it would have saved the peace, and would have made unnecessary the present tragi-comic spectacle of our rush to the aid of Greece and Turkey, noisily locking the barn door long after the horse has been stolen.

4. Immediately after V-E Day we began a stampede to tear our armies to pieces and get them back from Europe. This débâcle was well under way by the time President Truman arrived in Potsdam. Consequently he lacked any bargaining power either to make new settlements with the Russians, or to force them to live up to the commitments which they had given at Yalta.

For our present situation we have to blame not the diabolical cunning of the Kremlin, but largely our own lack of foresight, first during the war and then in the immediate post-war period. Russian foreign policy has been neither brilliant nor conspicuously deceitful, but usually realistic and always without sentimentality. In attaining its ends it has only co-ordinated its economic and military power toward the objectives of its foreign policy, which would probably be those of the Romanovs, had that dynasty survived the last war to participate in this. The realistic means it has used to these ends are not new; they have been successfully practiced by Cardinal Richelieu, by Metternich and Talleyrand, by Cavour, Lord Palmerston, and Bismarck, and in our own times by Woodrow Wilson. For even Utopia must be founded on realism, rather than well-meaning sentimentality.

Over the intervening twenty-eight years I still hear Wilson's precise, somewhat flat, utterly uninspiring voice as it rose over a respectful silence in that great, gilded room on the banks of the Seine in 1919, and he grows greatly in stature. He was no glib opportunist but a profound student of history who saw clearly into the future, further than his country at that time cared to look. So long as men dream of world peace based on human freedom, I do not think that Woodrow Wilson's name will die.

The peace of the world today depends partly on the Russians, about whom we now can do very little, but also on the Germans, about whom something can be done. I have gone to some pains to depict the Germans as I found them, which was neither all black nor all white, but an unblended intermingling, much as one would expect in a people of great talent whose history includes Beethoven and Marx, Heine and Hitler.

At the war's end, indeed as early as 1944, Hitler and his gang were utterly discredited with the German masses, and, had the Allies wished it, they would have been wiped out by a German government which would have sued for peace. For there was no depth to the shallow Nazi philosophy, which was based only on continued successes brought about by the "intuition" of an adventurer. Once his chain of success was broken at Stalingrad, even the Nazis saw their idol's feet of clay, and after that there was only bitterness and despair.

What will they think of Hitler ten years hence? That page of history we victors are writing today.

If we permit a free and democratic Germany to emerge from the present chaos, in which this industrious and talented people may work and enjoy the fruits of their labors on an equal basis with other nations, as Woodrow Wilson hoped to do in 1919, they will then look back on Hitler as a madman who dominated a nightmare, who squandered the blood and wealth of Germany in a senseless war.

But if we repeat the mistakes of the 'twenties, if we allow the Germans to putrefy in poverty and idleness, then we would do well to break what is left of their strength, to cut even their present meager diet, to soften the bones and dwarf the brains of their children.

Because by 1957 they would inevitably look back at the Third Reich as at the Golden Days. Hitler would become for them a prophet who, because he tried only to lead Germany up to the light, was overwhelmed by her enemies. Goering's testimony at the Nürnberg trial would be their Holy Writ, just as was Napoleon's St. Helena testament for France in the last century, and in this despairing Germany a score of disciples would arise, to cry honor to Hitler's name over the parched stubble of Mr. Morganthau's goat-pasture.

If we do repeat this mistake, of course, we can also repeat piously that Germans are an incurably militaristic and aggressive race, which carries sadism in its genes: but will this be enough?

It is for us to say what Germans will think of Hitler in 1957. History's page is blank before us, the pen is in our hands.